Praise for *Lunch in Paris*

'From cassoulets to croquembouches, via her "tap dancing frog," Elizabeth Bard writes about food and Paris with passion and wit. A must-read for Francophiles and food lovers'

Karen Wheeler, author of *Tout Sweet* and *Toute Allure*

'Romance on the front burner... it's Eat, Stay, Love *with a side of spiced apricots*'

Adriana Trigiani, author of *Very Valentine*

'Delicious, romantic, and sexy, just as the title indicates. I devoured this book with all the gusto I would bring to a plate of steak tartare with *pommes frites*'

Giulia Melucci, author of *I Loved, I Lost, I Made Spaghetti*

'As charming and coquettish as Paris itself, Lunch in Paris reawakens our tired hearts and palates with a deliciously passionate journey through the city of lights'

Nani Power, author of *Crawling at Night* and *Feed the Hungry*

'A love story is always delightful, and one with recipes is also useful in the long run, part and parcel of a real French relationship'

Diane Johnson, author of *Le Divorce* and *L'Affaire*

a delicious love story, with recipes

LUNCH

in

PARIS

ELIZABETH BARD

summersdale

LUNCH IN PARIS

This edition published in 2011 by Summersdale Publishers Ltd.

First published in the USA in 2010 by Little, Brown and Company, a division of Hachette Group, Inc.

Copyright © Elizabeth Bard 2010

Summersdale Publishers Ltd
46 West Street
Chichester
West Sussex
PO19 1RP
UK

www.summersdale.com

Printed and bound in Britain

ISBN: 978-1-84953-154-2

Substantial discounts on bulk quantities of Summersdale books are available to corporations, professional associations and other organisations. For details telephone Summersdale Publishers on (+44-1243-771107), fax (+44-1243-786300) or email (nicky@summersdale.com).

ABOUT THE AUTHOR

Elizabeth Bard is an American journalist and author based in France. Her first book, *Lunch in Paris: A Delicious Love Story, with Recipes* has been a *New York Times* and international best-seller, a Barnes & Noble 'Discover Great New Writers' pick, and the recipient of the 2010 Gourmand World Cookbook Award for Best First Cookbook (USA). Bard's writing on food, art, travel and digital culture has appeared in *The New York Times*, the *International Herald Tribune*, *Wired*, *Harper's Bazaar* and *The Huffington Post*. You can follow Elizabeth's continuing culinary adventures on **www.elizabethbard.com**.

ACKNOWLEDGMENTS

Serendipity brought me to my agent, Wendy Sherman, an expert guide and buoyant presence from the first day. To my editor, Judith Clain, and the dream team at Little, Brown — I can't imagine finer or more caring partners in this process.

A good book can always be better, and this one is, thanks to careful reading, editing, tasting (and the occasional cooking lesson) from friends near and far: Sarah Kaplan, Betsy Levine, Amanda Gordon, Afra Afsharipour, Diego Valdarama, Mayur Subbarao, Elizabeth Calleo, Kelda Knight, and Katherine Prewitt. A special thank-you to Courtney Rubin, friend and mentor, without whom I might be a writer, but certainly not a professional.

Final thanks go to Mom and Paul, charter members of the Benevolent Parent Society, who believed in this and so much more.

And of course, to Gwendal. *Tout simplement, l'homme de ma vie.*

CONTENTS

AUTHOR'S NOTE

Certain names have been changed to protect people's privacy
(poor Gwendal, he didn't get that lucky).

LUNCH
in
PARIS

CHAPTER I

COFFEE, TEA, OR ME

I slept with my French husband halfway through our first date. I say halfway because we had finished lunch but not yet ordered coffee. It turned out to be a decisive moment, more important for my future happiness than where I went to college or years with a good shrink. The question was posed lightly: It looked like rain. We could sit it out in a café or, since his apartment was not far, he could make tea.

I was not fully aware at the time that American girls in Paris are sluts by definition, willing to do sober what British girls will only do drunk. It seemed like a simple choice; I like tea.

Mind you, I am not that girl. (Or at least, I wasn't.) I'm not the girl who swings from the chandeliers and screws men because she can, fixing her lipstick in the rearview mirror of a cab hailed at dawn. I'm the girl you call Wednesday for Saturday. The girl who reads Milton for fun and knows a fish fork when she sees one. A flirt maybe, but in that harmless,

3

nineteenth-century, kiss-my-hand-and-ask-me-to-waltz kind of way. Mostly, I'm a thinker, a worrier. Since I'm also a New Yorker, you can take that last bit up a notch. It's not that there's no free spirit in me. But it's a free spirit with a five-year plan.

As the waiter added up our bill with a ballpoint pen on the paper tablecloth, I took another look at the handsome stranger sitting across from me. Gwendal. Gwen-DAL. Had I been pronouncing his name with the emphasis on the wrong syllable all afternoon? Oh well.

He was tall, with thick dark hair that just touched his collar. A wayward strand stuck straight up on the top of his head; it had probably been that way since he was five. His turtleneck sweater was the color of warm milk. On the empty chair beside him was a stiff navy blue cap, the kind worn by boys selling newspapers on the snowy streets of Chicago in 1932. Though it was only one in the afternoon, I could already see the rising shadow of his beard. I was trying not to stare, but his hazel-green eyes seemed to be exactly the same color as my own.

Like any first date, I knew only a few tantalizing details. The strange name came from Brittany, on the Channel coast of France. His family was in Saint-Malo, a provincial port city he'd fled as soon as possible. He spoke passable English, much better than my leftover college French, but with an Australian accent — something he picked up during his year of military service at the French embassy in Canberra. He seemed shy and serious, but broke easily into a wide grin — mostly when I said something was *fascinating*.

We had met in late September, at an academic conference in London called Digital Resources in the Humanities. (Can you think of a less promising place to meet the love of your life?) He was finishing up a PhD in Computer Science; I was starting a master's in Art History. When I spotted him in a seminar on a hypertext version of *Finnegans Wake*, I knew he had to be European. The Americans were too fresh-faced, the

English so pale and rumpled. I suppose he could have been German, on account of his height (and the hideous light blue windbreaker he was wearing), but something about the dark hair, the square jaw, and the little glasses said *café crème*.

On the last day of the conference, I ran into him on the stairs. We Americans have that wonderful puppy-dog way of going up to complete strangers with a big smile and a dumb question. I rarely fight it — in so many situations, it's a gift. I asked him what his research was about. He took it from there.

Artfully worded e-mails flew back and forth. I even tried writing one in French, begging Gwendal in advance to correct my grammar. He waited several months to tell me that *corrigez-moi* doesn't imply "check my spelling" so much as "tie me up and tickle me with a feather duster." There should really be a footnote in those high school textbooks.

By December, I'd invented a reason to come to Paris, something about temporary exhibitions.

And now we were here, having lunch.

Gwendal had been strategic in his choice of restaurant. The Bouillon Chartier is a brusque canteen in the 9th arrondissement. To an American, this was movie-set Paris. Tucked into a narrow arcade between a Chinese restaurant and a *pâtisserie*, Chartier has been open since 1896, and served the same purpose then as now — filling up the masses before a stroll down the see-and-be-seen Grands Boulevards.

The room was vast, noisy, and completely full. Gwendal's glasses fogged up as he pushed ahead of me through the heavy revolving door. The walls were the color of new butter, and the light from the globes of ten enormous chandeliers was much brighter than the pale gray Paris afternoon we left outside. There must have been two hundred people, all with knives and forks poised somewhere between their mouths and their neighbor's nose (emphasizing a point, I imagine). Groups of tables were separated by dark wooden partitions, like the waiting room of a train station, and above the heads of the diners were gleaming brass hat rails heaped with folded coats, shopping bags, and dangling scarves.

The waiters certainly looked like they had a train to catch. Dressed in white shirts and black vests, they wove in and out of traffic, often holding a dozen *escargots,* a *boeuf bourguignon,* and a *baba au rhum* in the crook of a single thumb. There were tiny numbered cubbies along the walls, where regular clients once stored their linen napkins. The tables were small enough that if you put your elbows on the edge you'd have a hard time not holding hands with the person across the way.

Though I'd never been in this room before, something about it felt wonderfully familiar. Europe had that effect on me, ever since I stepped off the plane for the first time in college. I felt more like myself here: as though my love of art and history was natural and my inability to name the latest rock band didn't matter. In Paris the past is always with you: you look at it, walk over it, sit on it. I had to stop myself from grabbing Gwendal's arm as we walked up the narrow passage to the entrance: *Pardon me, sir, I couldn't help but notice; the cobblestones outside your door are older than my country.* The idea thrilled me. I've always been a bit of an old-fashioned girl. I feel good in old places.

As we waited for one of the turbocharged waiters to take our order, I prodded Gwendal about his PhD research. From the little he had explained to me when we met, it was something about how to archive film and video on the Internet. In fact, he was already working full-time for France's National Radio and Television Archives while he finished his degree.

"Archiving is a question of collective memory," he said, toying with a slice of baguette from the basket on the table. "When you decide, as a culture, what you want to keep, you also have to decide what you are willing to forget."

Honestly, he could have been humming show tunes. It's not that I wasn't listening, but mostly I was watching his face. I love to watch people talk about subjects they are passionate about, especially if it's something I know nothing about. How many nights did I spend in New York, seduced by some guy's discourse on nanotechnology, Kierkegaard, or jumping trains, hobo-style, in the Dakotas. I know it's not everyone's idea of a great pickup technique, but smart has always been sexy to me.

"Wow, that's fascinating." There it was, that word again. Must put a lid on the over-enthused American bit. "Do you know what you're going to do after you finish?" I asked brightly. "With the Internet exploding, you must have a lot of offers." He narrowed his eyes and tilted his head just slightly, as if he couldn't decide if I was being sarcastic, maybe making fun of him.

"Yeah," he said with a laugh (did I detect a hint of bitterness?). "Lots of offers." Clearly he wasn't used to such optimistic assessments of his future.

I glanced down at the menu, relieved that although I hadn't taken a French class since my sophomore year in college, I still recognized most of the words. Chartier's menu is full of classics: steaks and chops, grilled sea bass with fennel seed, sweet chestnut purée, and wine-soaked prunes. What girl could resist the charm of a restaurant that allows you to order a bowl of *crème chantilly* — simple whipped cream — for dessert?

"You must have missed this when you were in Australia," I said.

"We had our little tricks," said Gwendal, with a conspiratorial smile. "They sent the Camembert and the foie gras to the embassy in the *valise diplomatique*. Since it is considered as French government property, the Australian customs can't search it. Top secret security cables and cheese."

"It must have been a big suitcase."

"It did get quite large around Christmas," he said.

I couldn't remember the last time I'd been this hungry.

The waiter slapped down my *pavé au poivre*. It was not a particularly impressive plate — a hunk of meat, fat fried potatoes piled carelessly to one side. But something happened as I sliced the first bite — no resistance, none at all. The knife slid through the meat; the thinnest layer of crusty brown opening to reveal a pulpy red heart. I watched as the pink juices puddled into the buttery pepper sauce.

Gwendal looked up. I must have uttered an audible gasp of pleasure. "I don't know why you can't get a steak like this in England," I said, careful, even in my haste to lift the first bite to my mouth, not to drip on my sweater. My fork and knife paused in midair as I let the salt, the fat, the blood settle on my tongue.

Not to minimize Gwendal's many charms, but he was halfway to home base as soon as I cut into that marvelous steak.

Gwendal's tiny student apartment was located in the gritty 10th arrondissement, on a street that the phone company called *la rue des squatters* because of all the illegal inhabitants in nearby buildings. This was not postcard Paris, at least not yet. We walked past the soot-stained, graffitied facade of the Gare de l'Est, then across the Canal Saint-Martin, up and over a high Japanese-style bridge. There was a wet mist dripping through the trees. I didn't even know there was a canal in Paris.

Up two flights of narrow spiral stairs, the apartment was New York size — pleasantly cramped, really one large room with a flimsy wall down the middle and a plastic accordion door that led directly from the refrigerator to the bed.

Gwendal took an old teapot off a heavily loaded bookshelf. The bruised metal surface and graceful spout had the look of a family heirloom. "It belonged to my grandfather," he said.

8

"He died in the war in Indochina, just after my mother was born." There was a tiny mother-of-pearl disk at the top, to keep you from burning your fingers when you opened it.

I laid my coat over the top of the futon and shook out my hair like a soggy kitten. Gwendal was already in the kitchen. "Kitchen" is a generous term — it was a rectangle of linoleum with a counter and fridge on one side and a sink and hot plate on the other. He took a bundle of fresh mint from a glass beside the sink and plugged in the electric kettle. It hissed and sputtered to life.

"This is the important step," he said, pouring boiling water over the mint leaves, wilting them like spinach. "It takes away the bitterness."

While Gwendal's head disappeared under the counter, searching for the sugar, I looked around the apartment. There were bottles of sand from his desert treks in Australia, a postcard of Marcello Mastroianni watching the girls go by. There were books everywhere — philosophy (what is it about Frenchmen and philosophy?), literature, a book on American musical comedies (hmm), and a book called *Hollywood, mode d'emploi*. There were three lava stones beside the stereo, one red, one black, and one like a yin-yang, where the red and black teardrops had melted together.

Gwendal opened a box of gunpowder green tea, scooped some into the teapot, and threw in a few cubes of sugar. He was telling me about a conference he'd just returned from in Orlando, Florida. "The receptionist was dressed as Donald Duck," he said, as he added the wilted mint. "I thought I was hallucinating. The only Internet access was in the video arcade and the only newspaper I could find was the *Disney Journal*. It was like a whole universe created for five-year-olds."

I told him about my first trip to Paris, with my lactose intolerant, almost-vegetarian best friend. We stayed in a seedy student hotel in the 5th. Our one big bed had a hole in the middle, and the water from the tap ran rusty brown. "A donkey chewed on my cashmere sweater in front of Notre Dame."

"What did you eat?" asked Gwendal, no doubt doing his best to imagine a Paris purged of milk and meat.

"A lot of mango sorbet."

All the while, there was a parallel conversation going on in my head. *We hardly know each other. Maybe we should wait.* I heard my grandmother's voice. *If you like him, send him home.* It sounded so stupid I might have actually shaken my head. I suddenly understood the frustration of every man I'd ever left at the curb after a furious make-out session in the back of a taxi. There is something about the frankness with which Europeans deal with sex, you can feel it in the way people study each other on the metro, the way couples kiss on the sidewalk — it's just so . . . *normal.* If I walked out now, he wasn't going to think I was a *nice* girl, *the marrying kind* (again, the phrase my grandmother would use). He was going to think I was a girl who couldn't take on what she really wanted. And he would be right. I looked out the window down into the small interior courtyard. The walk through unfamiliar streets had left me turned around. I had no real idea where I was. I felt like I'd been given some kind of diplomatic immunity. I didn't really understand the rules; how could I possibly follow them?

Tiny gold-rimmed glasses appeared from out of nowhere. Storage space in Paris, I was soon to learn, is a matter of great creativity. Things are tucked into the strangest nooks and crannies. He poured the tea from a foot or two above the glass, making sweet and smoky bubbles on the surface.

He had not, he mentioned innocently, reserved for dinner.

Several hours later the rain had stopped, and I found myself on a folding chair beside the kitchen table in one of Gwendal's T-shirts, hair mussed and absolutely ravenous.

There was nothing in the fridge but plain yogurt, a jar of raspberry jam, two carrots, half an onion, a package of something that resembled chopped-up bacon, and a saucepan covered with a dinner plate. It was one of those ninety-nine-cent saucepans, with the plastic handle and the brown and mustard-colored flowers painted tastefully on the side.

He inverted the pan, shook it from side to side, and out of the ninety-nine-cent pot came a dessert fit for Louis XIV, a perfectly molded apricot charlotte, each ladyfinger standing at attention, held together by a layer of cream and studded with slices of fruit. Did he always prepare this way for lady visitors? He seemed the very opposite of a cad. Surely, cooking for a woman you hardly knew, on the off chance that she might find herself naked and hungry in your apartment, was sweet rather than predatory.

Gwendal lifted a thick slice onto my plate. He couldn't possibly have known why I was smiling. When I was a kid, my mother and I had a tradition called "backwards breakfast." To keep me from playing sick during the winter, each year I got to choose my own snow day. She would take the day off from work and we would sleep late, eat ice cream for breakfast or pancakes for dinner — you get the idea. In my real life I've spent a lot of time keeping things in line; I'm a stickler for form. But today felt like a snow day... dessert before dinner, sex before coffee. Things were so marvelously, exhilaratingly out of order.

We devoured the entire charlotte in fifteen minutes. I was ready for more. When I looked in the fridge I saw nothing, just leftover odds and ends. Gwendal saw dinner. This was to be the way with so many exchanges in our relationship. Our blind spots were different. Where one saw a gaping void, the other saw possibilities.

He took out a carrot and the onion half. I'm not sure I'd ever seen anyone use half an onion. Or rather, I'd never seen anyone save half an onion he hadn't used. The real secret ingredient, however, was the package of *lardons fumés* — plump little Legos of pork — deep pink and marbled with fat. He dumped them into a pan with the chopped vegetables (he may have washed the pan from the charlotte), and the mixture began sizzling away. A box of tagliatelle, the pasta spooled like birds' nests, completed the meal.

Maybe it was the sex, or the bacon — or both — but it was without a doubt the best thing I'd ever tasted. "This is amazing," I said, twirling another noodle around my fork. "You have to give me the recipe."

"There is no recipe," he said, smiling. "I use whatever I have. It never tastes the same way twice."

I had no way of knowing, that first damp evening in Paris, how much this man, and his non-recipes, would change my life.

Recipes for Seduction

FRESH MINT TEA
Thé à la Menthe

2 teaspoons loose green tea
1 bunch of mint on the stem (at least 7 or 8 sprigs)
4–5 sugar cubes, or more to taste
2 cups boiling water plus more for rinsing the tea and
*   wilting the mint*
Pine nuts to serve
A few drops of orange flower water (optional)

Place the loose tea in the bottom of a teapot. Add a bit of boiling water and swish the pot around to rinse the tea. Drain out the water.

Wash the mint thoroughly. Holding it over the sink by the stems, pour some boiling water over the leaves. Place the mint in the teapot, along with 4 or 5 sugar cubes. Fill the pot with the 2 cups boiling water and let steep for 5 minutes. Taste to see if you want more sugar; it should be sweet but not overwhelmingly so.

Sprinkle a few pine nuts in the bottom of a skinny glass teacup. A large shot glass would also do nicely. Add a drop or two of orange flower water if you like — but only a drop; it's very strong.

Pouring from high above the glass is not, it turns out, simply a foolish trick to impress girls. It aerates the tea, cooling it down and releasing the sweetly spiked scent of the mint. Virtuosos line up several glasses edge to edge and pour without stopping.

This tea is the perfect finish after couscous or a *tagine*.

Yield: Serves 2

"STUDENT" CHARLOTTE
Charlotte aux Abricots

A real charlotte is a ritzy affair, made with *crème pâtissière* and ladyfingers soaked in alcohol. To this day, I prefer the student version, *fromage frais* or Greek yogurt and canned apricots straight from the supermarket. This is essentially an arts and crafts project — all assembly — but it does need to be done the night before you want to serve it, so the ladyfingers have time to soak up the juices. Ideal for breakfast, brunch, or a casual dinner with friends.

> 25–35 crisp Italian sponge finger biscuits (savoiardi)
> 3 cups fromage frais or Greek yogurt
> 825 g can apricots or pears in heavy syrup

Line the sides of a small saucepan or soufflé dish, approximately 15 cm in diameter, with plastic wrap.

Line the sides of your mold with sponge finger biscuits. They should stand shoulder to shoulder like toy soldiers. You can use a dab of yogurt to keep them in place if you like.

Arrange a layer of biscuits on the bottom of the pan (cut them to fit). Try to make them symmetrical, as this layer will become the top when you serve.

Add a layer of *fromage frais* (about ¾ cup) and a layer of sliced apricots. Top with a layer of biscuits, press gently, then pour over ¼ cup apricot syrup.

Continue with 2 or 3 more layers, ending with a layer of biscuits topped with ¼ cup syrup. Pour an extra ¼ cup syrup around the edge to make sure the outer biscuits are moist.

Cover with plastic wrap and press the top lightly with a plate or saucer to condense the mixture. Chill for at least 12 hours, preferably overnight.

To unmold, place the serving plate on top of the saucepan and flip, giving the pan a gentle shake. Carefully peel away the plastic lining if it sticks.

Yield: Serves 4–6, or 2 sex-crazed individuals eating breakfast at six p.m.

Tip: Depending on the absorbency of your ladyfingers, there may be a bit of extra juice at the bottom of the dish when you unmold the charlotte. Just blot it with a paper towel.

PASTA À LA GWENDAL

I feel a bit ridiculous writing this down, since more often than not it's made with whatever Gwendal finds in the back of the fridge. If you have the bacon and an onion, you're well on your way. This simple dinner embodies so much of what I love about French cooking — being inspired by the ingredients at hand, turning humble bits into a hearty meal. I always have a package of *lardons* in the fridge; an alternative is to keep a hunk of slab bacon or Italian pancetta in the freezer for a rainy day. This recipe is ideal for the winter months. In the summer, I often substitute cherry tomatoes for the carrots and add a splash of white wine.

> 3 tablespoons olive oil
> 250 g lardons fumés, *slab bacon, or pancetta, cut into* ½ *cm cubes*
> 2 onions, diced
> 2 cloves of garlic, sliced
> 4 carrots, thinly sliced
> 1 bulb fennel, coarsely chopped
> 2 courgettes, sliced into ½ cm rounds
> 3 sun-dried tomatoes, diced
> 500 g De Cecco or whole-wheat spaghetti
> Chopped parsley, freshly ground black pepper, to serve

Heat the oil in a large frying pan. Add the *lardons*, onions, and garlic. Sauté 2 to 3 minutes, until the *lardons* have rendered their fat and the onions are translucent. Add the remaining veggies, stirring to coat. Cook, stirring occasionally, until softened and sweet.

Cook the pasta in a large pot of salted water. Drain, reserving a small cup of cooking liquid. Add the pasta to the sauce, with a bit of liquid if you feel it looks dry. Stir in the chopped parsley and a good grinding of pepper. By all means, take the pot back to bed. Nothing like a first date you have to carb up for.

Yield: Serves 4, or 2 who've worked up an appetite

CHAPTER 2

AN AFFAIR TO REMEMBER

I am leading a double life. By day I read about Victorian insane asylums in the British Library; by night I decipher X-rated e-mails with a French–English dictionary. Every few weeks I bring my overnight bag to work on Friday, hop on the Eurostar, and by dinnertime I am in Paris.

It is only a fifteen-minute walk from the Gare du Nord back to Gwendal's flat, but that's all the time it takes to shed my London life. I feel lighter; I empty my pockets of business cards and deadlines and to-do lists. My purposeful steps slow in front of darkened store windows and blackboard menus begging to be considered for our next meal.

Any weekend in Paris begins with dinner, and Gwendal and I quickly find our local. The Bistro Sainte Marthe is not the kind of place you just happen into. It's like a scene out of a fifties detective novel: *at the end of a narrow one-way street, tucked in the corner of a small square, under the burgundy awning, behind the velvet curtain, ask for Jacques.* When these buildings went up at the turn of the twentieth century, they would have housed blue-collar Paris, maybe the families of the men who worked at the old print warehouses down by the canal. Now they are full of immigrant families; fluorescent light glows harshly from the windows, illegal electricity cables creep up the sides of the buildings like vines. There's a Chinese revivalist church across the square, and one or two brightly painted facades — evidence of artists in residence, in search of cheap real estate and "authenticity." A pack of boys kick a soccer ball, barely avoiding the terrace tables where women with increasingly expensive handbags come to dine. I'm the last person in the world anyone would call a hipster, but I recognize a hipster hangout when I see one. Just as well my pearls are in a drawer in London. It's like Avenue C meets Beirut.

Inside is one narrow room with blood-red walls and eight or nine tables nestled around the bar. The high ceiling is covered with mismatched chandeliers. While we are waiting to be seated, I tuck my cold nose into the warmth of Gwendal's neck. There's always a moment after we sit down at the cramped wooden table, face-to-face after weeks apart. An awkward silence or too much talking before we fall back into the easy intimacy sparked by a long look or his hand in my hair. When I was a teenager I would have called this "twinkle toes" — the long-awaited touch you can feel from the top of your head to the soles of your feet. Though everyone (my mother, my best friends, my boss) knows where I'm off to, these weekends in Paris feel like a preciously guarded secret. *An affair.* All I need now is a trench coat and a cigarette holder.

Thinking ahead is a reflex for me, so before I order dinner I'm already doing strategic planning for dessert. Even as Gwendal translates our choices, I'm distracted by the smell of melting chocolate. Plate after plate leaves the kitchen, held aloft by waiters as they inch past the bar. I strain my neck to see which way the chocolate wind is blowing. The plates land at a table in the corner, crowded with scruffy young men and the women who love them. My view is obscured by a haze of smoke.

When *le dessert* finally arrives, it looks like an innocent upsidedown chocolate cupcake, accompanied by a small cloud of freshly whipped cream. But when my spoon breaks the surface, the chocolate center flows like dark lava onto the whiteness of the plate. The last ounce of stress drains from my body. I feel my spine soften in the chair. The menu says *Moelleux au Chocolat "Kitu."*

"'*Kitu*' is a pun," says Gwendal, with his best Humphrey Bogart squint. "It means 'which kills.'"

I have discovered the French version of "Death by Chocolate."

I like to think I was born in the wrong century. I'm sure I would have done very well with a hoop skirt, a fan, and a drawing master. (My mother likes to remind me that, more likely, I would have been a very nearsighted scullery maid.) Paris is the perfect city for my kind of mental time travel. There are very few streets that don't bear some small imprint of a grander, more gracious time — the swooping curve of a wrought-iron balcony or a fading stencil above the window of a *boulangerie*.

I've been playing this particular game for as long as I can remember. Like many only children, I spent a fair amount of time entertaining myself. I never had an imaginary friend, but I did have an imaginary life, many of them, in fact. My favorite toy was my dress-up box, an old clothes hamper filled with tutus, floppy hats bedecked with polyester flowers, and my auntie Lynn's wedding dress, dyed a garish pink and trimmed with rug tassels for a Chiquita Banana Halloween costume. I played princess, bride, teacher, queen. There was a turquoise sequined tube top that probably made me look like a very convincing streetwalker.

My mother was a special education teacher, my father a salesman. Just after I was born they moved from Brooklyn to a Tudor in suburban New Jersey. I went to a redbrick sixties elementary school a few blocks away. My worst fear, even then, was to be ordinary.

From the time I was very young, extraordinary was somehow linked to long ago and far away. While my kindergarten friends dreamed of becoming ballerinas or astronauts, I wanted to be an archaeologist. I had a picture book of famous digs that my father and I read over and over again, until the cardboard cover was nearly in shreds. I imagined myself opening up King Tut's tomb, gently lifting a gold bracelet or a wine urn undisturbed for thousands of years. I liked the musty smell of old books, the satin sheen of Sargent's portraits, and the glimmer of amethyst crystals in the darkened gem hall of the Museum of Natural History. When the age for dress-up was over, I immersed myself in novels, diving into other people's imaginary worlds. The streets of Dickens's London were much easier for me to get my head around than fractions. In high school I acted in plays by Shakespeare, Oscar Wilde, and Molière; I felt more comfortable in a whalebone corset than in the ripped cutoff jeans I wore to class. By the time I graduated from college, where I'd switched from a very practical psychology major to an English Literature thesis on *Paradise Lost* and *Peter Pan*, I was truly out of sync. I saw no choice but to cultivate it. My friends made fun of me. Kurt Cobain is the one in the plaid shirt, right?

Gwendal saw Paris the same way I did, a different century around every corner. He was still a student and he didn't have much money, so we spent many of our first weekends together simply walking around. Although he'd lived in Paris for ten years, he'd never quite lost the provincial boy's fascination with the big city. He was still open to the magic of this place. I didn't know a lot of people who were open to magic at all.

Everyone talks about Paris in the springtime. Maybe it's because my own Paris romance started in December, but I prefer the City of Light in the winter.

Paris in the winter is damp and close, so unlike the blinding sunshine and razor-sharp air of New York. In fact, the weather in Paris is exactly the same as the weather in London — Paris just has nicer places to hide. There is always a brasserie awning to hover under or an ornate doorway to duck into. I love the way the rain melts the colors together, like a chalk drawing on the sidewalk. There is a moment, just after sunset, when the shops turn on their lights and steam starts to fog up the windows of the cafés. In French, this twilight time implies a hint of danger. It's called *entre chien et loup*, between the dog and the wolf.

It was just beginning to get dark as we walked through the small garden of the Palais Royal. We watched as carefully dressed children in toggled peacoats and striped woolen mittens finished the same game of improvised soccer we had seen in the Place Sainte Marthe.

Behind the Palais Royal the wide avenues around the Louvre gave way to narrow streets, small boutiques, and bistros. It started to drizzle. Gwendal turned a corner and, tucked in between two storefronts, barely wider than a set of double doors, I found myself staring down a corridor of fairy lights. A series of arches stretched into the distance, topped with panes of glass, like a greenhouse, that echoed the plip-plop of the rain. It was as if we'd stepped through the witch's wardrobe, the phantom tollbooth, what have you, into another era.

The Passage Vivienne was nineteenth-century Paris's answer to a shopping mall, a small interior street lined with boutiques and tearooms where ladies could browse at their leisure without wetting the bustles of their long dresses or the plumes of their new hats.

It was certainly a far cry from the shopping malls of my youth, with their piped-in Muzak and neon food courts.

Plaster reliefs of Greek goddesses in diaphanous tunics lined the walls. Three-pronged brass lamps hung from the ceiling on long chains.

About halfway down, there was an antique store selling nothing but old kitchenware — ridged ceramic bowls for hot chocolate, burnished copper molds in the shape of fish, and a pewter mold for madeleines, so worn around the edges it might have belonged to Proust himself. At the end of the gallery, underneath a clock held aloft by two busty angels, was a bookstore. There were gold stencils on the glass door. *Maison fondée en 1826.*

I pushed past a sagging stand of postcards: lovers in front of the Eiffel Tower, a child running with a baguette under his arm, a nude woman squatting over a bidet. A ruddy brass bell tinkled on a chain from the doorknob as we walked in. The smell of dust and beeswax came from the carefully polished shelves, the color of dark chocolate, which lined the walls. In one corner there was a spiral staircase, so small a fat cat would have trouble climbing it. I could almost feel the bustle of my dress sweeping the floor. Clearly this city was not going to do any good for my already tenuous hold on the twenty-first century.

After a half-hour wait over a dish of green olives and a glass of the house *apéritif,* the waitress came to take our order. We were having a late lunch at L'Hermès, a small restaurant in the 19th arrondissement, up the hill from Gwendal's apartment.

"*Eh, alors,*" began the waitress, describing the day's specials. "We have duck with braised cabbage and apples, cassoulet, and very special" — she nodded for emphasis — "*du porc noir de Bigorre.*"

"What is special about this pig?" asked Gwendal, launching her into the grandest of explanations.

"Well," she said, putting down her pad on the counter. "He has short black hair. He's about this big." She stretched her arms wide enough to take in the length of our table and the one next to us. "He is very particular, very difficult to raise *en captivité*. You see, he likes to eat in the forest, whatever he wants." And stopping to consider the charmed life of this truffle-hunting, free-roaming raven-haired beast, she finished with a flourish. "*Il est heureux, quoi*. He's happy!"

I could see it on his face, Gwendal was more than convinced. What could be more salubrious than a luncheon of happy pig? I ordered the cassoulet.

I found that getting to know Gwendal was a bit like befriending a very personable (and sexy) alien. He looked like the people I knew, and spoke (sort of) like the people I knew, but he was clearly wired differently. Of course I'd had to get to know previous boyfriends — but I'd never had to get to know someone in quite this way. The boys I'd been out with before went to the same schools, came from the same towns. I could assume what they'd be thinking about a whole lot of things. I could never assume what Gwendal would be thinking about anything. Although we were roughly the same age, we didn't have the same cultural references. I didn't know anything about Serge Gainsbourg, he had never seen *The Breakfast Club* or eaten a Twinkie. On our way to the restaurant, we passed the Stalingrad metro station. "Why is there a metro in Paris named after a city in Communist Russia?" I asked.

"The battle," he said, looking at me like maybe I was speaking Russian. "When Stalin defeated Hitler on the Eastern Front."

Duh. It was only the moment that turned the tide of the entire Second World War, saving France from permanent occupation and humiliation by Nazi Germany. There was no metro station named D-day.

It wasn't just what we knew, it was what we wanted. Everyone I knew back home had a similar checklist, and the first item (underlined, with an exclamation point) was *success*. Like most of my friends, at twenty-five, I considered myself to be in the slog-it-out stage — doing whatever we had to do to become the people we wanted to be. If that meant working hundred-hour weeks at banks, law firms, tech start-ups, or newsmagazines, so be it. We were on the straight and narrow path toward partnerships, IPOs, Pulitzers, whatever would prove to us — and the world — that we had arrived.

Gwendal didn't seem to have a checklist. In fact, it was easy to get him to talk about anything but. Like that pig foraging in the woods, Gwendal seemed to have only one consideration when making a decision: does this make me happy, does this give me pleasure? Frankly, it struck me as a little odd.

The *porc noir de Bigorre* turned out to be a simple grilled pork chop served with sautéed potatoes and brussels sprouts. Under the toasted breadcrumbs, my cassoulet was a small hill of white beans, cooked to unctuous perfection with a piece of *confit de canard*, a nice hunk of sausage, and a hint of tomato. Somehow, I felt no particular need to know the hair color of the animals that had sacrificed themselves for my meal.

We were both yawning a bit over our empty espresso cups as we pushed back our chairs from the table. Thankfully, these leisurely winter lunches were usually followed by a nap. Gwendal had introduced me to the concept of *le cinq à sept*. Literally, it means "the five to seven," that hard-to-account-for time after work when lovers meet for a quick tryst before going home to their families for dinner. *Vive la France*.

As we put on our coats to go, I noticed a framed picture on the table just beside the door. It was the famous black pig, a long dark Tootsie Roll, lolling around on the hay in his pen. He *did* look happy. All the same, I'm glad I didn't see him before we sat down to lunch.

Recipes Inspired by the Bistro Sainte Marthe

SWORDFISH TARTARE
Tartare d'Espadon

I first tasted this appetizer at the Bistro Sainte Marthe. Tartare couldn't be easier. It's essentially small cubes of the raw fish in a gussied-up vinaigrette.

I've toyed around with several versions; these are my favorites. You can make them separately, or serve a tasting portion of each with fresh greens in between. The following recipe is for an appetizer, but a few sautéed potatoes will turn it into a light meal. Served on radicchio or endive leaves, it makes quite the chichi little hors d'oeuvre.

TRADITIONAL

> 250 g freshest swordfish steak (be sure to tell your
>   fishmonger you'll be eating it raw)
> 1 tablespoon plus 1 teaspoon lemon juice
> ¼ teaspoon coarse sea salt
> 2 teaspoons whole-grain mustard
> 2 teaspoons walnut oil
> 2 tablespoons best-quality extra-virgin olive oil
> 2 tablespoons chopped chives
> 2 teaspoons chopped dill

Trim the fish of any skin and red flesh and cut what remains into regular half-centimetre cubes. Set them aside in a glass dish in the coldest part of the refrigerator.

In a small glass jar or airtight plastic container, combine all the remaining ingredients (minus the dill). Shake vigorously to combine. Chill.

Five minutes before you are ready to serve the fish, add the vinaigrette and dill. Stir well to coat. If you leave the fish to marinate any longer, the citrus will start to cook it — and you'll end up with *ceviche*, which does not have the same fresh texture as *tartare*.

Yield: Serves 2 as an appetizer, or makes 4 "tasting" servings

ASIAN

*250 g freshest swordfish steak (be sure to tell your
    fishmonger you'll be eating it raw)*
1 tablespoon plus 1 teaspoon lime juice
¼ teaspoon coarse sea salt
2 teaspoons finely grated fresh ginger
1 teaspoon Thai fish sauce
1 teaspoon sugar
2 tablespoons chopped chives
2 teaspoons sesame oil
4 tablespoons best-quality extra-virgin olive oil
½ cup ripe mango, peeled and diced
A good grinding of mixed peppercorns
1 tablespoon coriander, finely chopped

Prepare the fish and combine the ingredients (lime juice through oils) for the vinaigrette as in the "Traditional" recipe. Five minutes before you are ready to serve the fish, stir in the vinaigrette, mango, pepper, and coriander.

Yield: Serves 2 as an appetizer, or makes 4 "tasting" servings

OVEN-ROASTED PORK RIBS WITH HONEY
Travers de Porc au Miel

I know why bistros love this dish — easy prep, all done in advance. Use fresh rosemary if you can; it makes a real difference. Serve with a mound of crushed potatoes, soaked with the slick honey sauce.

½ cup honey
¼ cup olive oil
¼ cup red wine vinegar
1 teaspoon coarse sea salt
2 cloves garlic, lightly crushed with the back of your knife
1½ teaspoons dried rosemary, or a few sprigs of fresh
2 kg pork spareribs, cut into individual pieces

Whisk together the honey, oil, vinegar, sea salt, garlic, and *dried* rosemary (if using).

Place the ribs in a large zip-lock plastic bag and pour in the marinade. If using fresh rosemary, add the whole sprigs to the bag. Refrigerate for 1½ hours, turning occasionally.

Preheat the oven to 160°C.

Arrange the spareribs in a single layer in a large roasting pan. In a small saucepan, bring the marinade to a boil. Pour it over the ribs and roast in the oven for 2 to 3 hours, turning once or twice. Remove the ribs from the oven and skim a bit of fat from the sauce.

You can let the ribs rest overnight at this point. Reheat them gently in the sauce.

Yield: Serves 4

An ode to coarse sea salt: Since I've moved to Paris, I have a whole new relationship with salt. Coarse sea salt — obtained from the evaporation of seawater — is plentiful and cheap in France. The crystals are dried in snowy mounds, particularly in Brittany (Guérande) and the Camargue. I find the taste more subtle than table salt. If you've never tried it, now is the time. Put it in a small glass jar on the counter and take a pinch as needed. Sprinkling by hand gives you much more control than a shaker or a grinder. I find there's a sensual quality to it as well, like dusting your food with tiny diamonds.

INDIVIDUAL MOLTEN CHOCOLATE CAKES
Moelleux au Chocolat "Kitu"

If you have a chocoholic in your life, prepare to be worshipped. Perfect for dessert for two, this recipe also makes you look a teensy bit like a culinary genius in front of guests. Make the batter in advance, and pop the cakes into the oven right after dinner. As for accompaniments, resist the temptation to go overboard; forget the caramel sauce and raspberry coulis. A dollop of lightly sweetened whipped cream or a golf ball– sized scoop of vanilla ice cream is all that's required.

> 150 g unsalted butter
> 150 g dark chocolate (70 percent cocoa; the quality of the chocolate is essential)
> A good pinch of coarse sea salt
> 2 eggs
> 2 egg yolks
> ¼ cup sugar
> 1 tablespoon flour

Preheat the oven to 220°C.

Melt butter and chocolate together in the top of a double boiler or in the microwave. Add sea salt.

Meanwhile, beat together the eggs, egg yolks, and sugar with a whisk or an electric beater until light and slightly foamy.

Add the egg mixture to the warm chocolate; whisk quickly to combine. Add flour and stir just to combine. The batter will be quite thick.

The unmoulding is the tricky part of these little cakes; the only foolproof solution I've found is to use foil cupcake liners (paper liners don't work, they stick). Use 5 or 6 liners stacked together so they're rigid enough to make a freestanding mould. Make 6 of these moulds. (If you can't the find foil baking cups, use small ramekins, generously buttered.)

Divide the batter evenly among the molds. (You can make the cakes in advance to this point and chill them until you're ready to bake. But be sure to bring the batter back to room temperature before baking.)

Baking time will depend on your oven; start with 7 minutes for a thin outer shell with a completely molten interior, 8 minutes for a slightly thicker crust and a gooey heart.

Yield: Serves 6

Tip: *These also cook well straight from the freezer. Freeze directly in the foil cupcake holders. Take them out of the freezer about 10 minutes in advance. Bake at 200°C for approximately 15 to 17 minutes.*

CHAPTER 3

APRIL IN PARIS

Over the next few months our weekends in Paris took on a lazy routine. Like any proper affair, the first challenge was getting out of bed. There was a backstage tour of the Opera House at twelve thirty every Saturday. With the best intentions, we just kept missing it.

I'd come to cherish waking up in this small room: the futon mattress on the floor, the sunny yellow sheets, the tiny Italian coffeepot that, by some mystery of physics, started with boiling water in its bottom and finished with coffee in its top. The textures and objects in this space began to feel like details in a recurring dream. Gwendal and I had created a little glass bubble, precious and fragile, completely separate from our everyday lives. There was no thinking ahead, no questions. For some people, that might have been normal; for me, it was a small miracle. It might have been the first time in my life that I lived entirely in the present.

While I was still facedown on the pillow, Gwendal bravely pulled on a pair of jeans to go "hunting" for breakfast. He returned from the Tunisian bakery around the corner, not with the head of a freshly killed mastodon, but with a waxed paper bag, neatly crimped at the corners. It was filled with *chouquettes*, nothing more than empty cream puffs sprinkled with tiny pebbles of sugar — like biting into a sweet breeze.

Now that the weather had warmed up slightly and there was less fear for my numb and soggy toes, we spent our days outside, hopping from one café terrace to the next. Paris in the springtime is a different city — every mild day could be just a break in the endless November rain or the true beginning of summer. It was on one of these rambles that I got what I consider to be a glimpse of Gwendal's true character.

There are many things that will tell you the true measure of a man — the way he kisses, the way he holds a fork, the way he talks to his mother on the phone. For me it was something else: we'll call it the infamous bird-pooing incident.

We were on our way down to Bastille to go to a flea market. It was sunny, warm enough for me to be wearing Gwendal's favorite of my summer dresses — blue-and-white gingham with spaghetti straps — that, thanks to some clever engineering, didn't require a bra. He had on his favorite white linen shirt, the one from Australia with the baggy sleeves. We were walking along the boulevard Richard Lenoir in the shade of the plane trees, when I heard a distinct ploop, and saw an enormous green-gray puddle spread across his biceps.

I burst out laughing — no polite pause, no nod of sympathy. It's a reflex. I once pulled a radio alarm clock down on a boyfriend's head in the middle of the night, like the anvil in a Bugs Bunny cartoon. As soon as I saw he wasn't bleeding, the hysterics began — giant tears of laughter rolling down my face. That's what I'm like in a certain kind of crisis. Once the fear of concussion is past, there's just no stopping me.

"Ah, *merde,*" said Gwendal, looking up at the tree. "I see you!" he shouted, shaking a finger toward the sky, as if he knew the pigeon personally. "It's a vendetta," he whispered. "Like the Corsican Mafia. They *know* me." There are so many people in this world who can't laugh at themselves; even fewer who can stomach a girl they are still trying to impress laughing very much in their general direction. I've dated men... this would have ruined their entire day. We would have had to go straight home to change, or straight to a pharmacy to buy some Handi Wipes. There might have been a half-hour tirade on the immediate extermination of all rats-of-the-skies. Gwendal just looked at me, still doubled over on the sidewalk, with a sheepish grin. We went to the café across the street, he washed the sleeve of his shirt in the bathroom sink and let it dry in the Parisian sunshine, and we continued on with our walk.

"Never on a first date," he said, grabbing my hand.

"Never on a first date," I repeated solemnly, still threatening to break into the giggles.

I should have known it right then. A man of grace and humor. A keeper.

Our walks often took us across the river, past the towering facade of Notre Dame and into the flower market on the Île de la Cité. We stopped at the Mosquée de Paris, sipping tea in the shade of their giant oak tree, and lounged in the Arènes de Lutèce, a second-century Roman amphitheater where kids play tag and students study for exams on the terraced stone steps. Much of Paris is actually hidden behind the street, so we followed residents with their two-wheeled shopping trolleys into flowered courtyards and secret gardens. We often spent the whole day doing nothing but walking and talking.

We talked a lot about the future. Not necessarily our future (why burst the bubble?) but the things we wanted, the things we dreamed about.

Gwendal never really wanted to be a computer scientist. He wanted to make movies. He was always inventing stories about people we passed on the street.

"See that man on the bicycle, the way he leans his body forward. He used to ride a Harley-Davidson. All the girls were crazy for him. They promised him his own show on television. Now he dyes his hair and runs a bowling alley."

In fact, Gwendal had just finished a script about a clown named Max who rides around Paris on a bicycle, observing all the strange pieces of stage business that make up life in a big city.

"OK," I said. "When will you film it? How? What's the next step?"

At first he thought these questions were a polite reflex, like laughing at a lover's bad jokes. Now he knows better. This American optimism cheered and puzzled him. He didn't understand my certainty. I didn't understand his hesitation.

I told Gwendal all about my plan to be a museum curator. I would spend my life surrounded by beautiful and precious things. I had it all worked out: master's, PhD, office full of leather-bound books at the Morgan Library. He didn't elaborate on my plan. I made it clear that there was little room for improvement. Instead, he said, "I want to show you the dinosaurs."

All of Paris's natural history museums are in the Jardin des Plantes, a prim flower garden near the mosque. In the foyer of the Paleontology Museum there's a sculpture of a female gorilla, teeth bared, huge hands stretched toward the ceiling. Under her feet is the limp body of a hunter. There's something grand and absurd and slightly comic about it. Is this what we look like when passion gets the best of us?

Gwendal saw me staring. "That's evolution for you," he said. "Survival of the fittest."

Stepping through the turnstile into the great hall was like stepping into a time machine. The place was absolutely silent except for the sharp creak of our steps on the parquet floor.

There were no kids, no educational videos, no interactive computer terminals — just rows and rows of skeletons on wooden stands. The fading paper labels were handwritten in elaborate cursive, slipped into brass frames. The air was completely still, dusty and close, like an attic full of treasures.

I blinked back the strongest memory. My father died several years ago, and when I need to talk to him, I go to a museum. Wherever I've been in the world, museums have been my second homes. The Museum of Natural History in New York was the first building outside my house that I have a conscious memory of knowing my way around. I was proud to lead my parents through the impossibly long corridors toward the *Tyrannosaurus rex* or the giant squid. *Down the stairs, to the left, under the belly of the great blue whale.* When my parents divorced and my father receded into depression, museums were our weekend activity. Dollhouses and mummies and finally paintings filling the blank space where my father used to be.

I was never comfortable with the term "bipolar disorder." My father was diagnosed when it was still "manic depression," and that always seemed to me a better description. It described the years when he would barely speak, wiry thin and smoking menthol cigarettes as we walked the streets of Manhattan. It described the impossible highs, when he would flirt raucously with waitresses, scream at salesclerks, and sue doctors in a desperate attempt to make the world conform to his own grandiose self-image.

Museums became our routine. They were appropriate; and they were cheap (my father wasn't always working). I loved the grand staircase and the ever-blooming flower arrangements in the foyer of the Metropolitan. I relished pinning the smooth tin admission button, a different color every weekend, to my shirt collar. My father would plod dutifully behind me as I retraced our steps — yet again — toward the Temple of Dendur, its stones brought over from Egypt and put back together one by one, a giant jigsaw puzzle.

These rooms became the decor of my imaginary lives. I didn't just want to visit, I wanted to *live* here. I wanted to sleep in the eighteenth-century bed with the satin cover, beneath a ceiling of plaster cherubs. Did they let kids have birthday parties in the American Wing? Even as my interests changed and I let myself be dragged for a few minutes toward the old masters and vintage photographs, the museum itself remained the same. Every object in the same spot. It was an anchor. I like to think my father knew what he was giving me. His offering of order and beauty when he had no other.

I ran my hands along the varnished wooden railing of the museum's balcony, waving to Gwendal on the other side. For a relative newcomer to my life, I got the feeling he knew me suspiciously well. In the space of one afternoon he had unearthed the emotional source of my goals, the pleasure and the comfort of them.

Not the how, but the why.

There were odd moments as well. Tiny pricks of cultural dissonance. After the museum, we strolled in the shade of the neatly trimmed trees, looking for something to drink. The only thing available was Minute Maid fruit juice.

Gwendal took out his wallet. "I hate buying Coca-Cola," he said. "They're everywhere; you don't even have a choice anymore."

I thought maybe it was a translation problem. "It's not Coke," I said. "It's orange juice."

"Yes, but it's made by the Coca-Cola corporation." Ah, the insidious forces of American imperialism at work. Clearly, I was not on the side of the angels in this argument. I didn't even know Coca-Cola made orange juice.

Gwendal and I had been dating for about a year, and one Saturday night just before Easter, he decided it was time for us to take things to the next level: sausage. It's one thing for an American girl to waltz into Paris every few weeks to have sex and eat chocolate, but can she handle a really good *andouillette*?

I'm not queasy in the innards department — I lived in Scotland for a year and did the obligatory haggis dinner without a fuss. Frankly, it tasted a lot like my grandmother's kasha.

It was nine p.m. before we turned into the Passage de la Bonne Graine. I was babbling on excitedly about my latest project, a job at an Internet start-up that sold fine art online. Sure, it was a detour from my studies, but only a minor one, with stock options.

"I have to structure their online magazine," I said, listing the categories: paintings, sculpture, silver, glass. "She gave me her little brother as an assistant." That might have been the most exciting part: "I have an *assistant*."

There was a florist at the corner, closed for the night. I stopped in my tracks. Along with the heavy branches of lilacs and tangled stems of forsythia was a fluffy mound of tiny sleeping chicks — a living, breathing Easter basket. Paris continued to surprise me; instead of the slick consumerism of a twenty-first-century world capital, it was the little things, the living things, that made me smile.

We were greeted at the door of the restaurant by a man with a distinguished bald head, wool vest, and glasses. We slipped into a booth. The ceiling was low, striped with seventeenth-century wooden beams. Empty magnums of wine, large as buoys, lined the walls. I glanced at the menu, clearly a stretch for a student on a budget.

Gwendal had chosen the restaurant because their supplier carried the exclusive AAAAA rating, shorthand for approval by the *Association Amicale des Amateurs d'Andouillette Authentique*, a self-appointed band of *andouillette* lovers who roam the country in search of the best makers and most authentic preparations. *Andouillette* is a peculiar sausage, roughly cut, made from the stomach and intestines of the pig. Mr. Hardouin, the producer of tonight's specimen, was announced on the menu as *pourfendeur de gorets*, which Gwendal translated as the porcine equivalent of "defender of the faith." All my talk about marketing plans and angel investors seemed slightly ridiculous. The immediate question at hand was: did I want my *andouillette* in a mustard cream sauce, or should I opt for the authentic eighteenth-century preparation, with *lardons*, mushrooms, and *ris de veau* — veal sweetbreads?

I have always been enthusiastic about new, even strange, food. My first memories of eating out were yearly "ladies' days," when my mother and my aunt Debbie and I would go for lunch at a fancy French restaurant and out to a Broadway matinee. I must have been four or five the first time we went to *Mildred Pierce*. It was an occasion for white gloves and a tiny patent leather pocketbook. We sat at the Alice in Wonderland table, so called because it was up on a little pedestal and surrounded by mirrors. After my mother explained the menu, I announced that I wanted mussels.

The waiter raised an eyebrow at my mother. "Are you sure?"

Never one to slap down my more precocious tendencies, she nodded. "If she doesn't eat them, we will."

They never got the chance. I didn't share, and I didn't leave a single shell unturned. The waiter cleared the plates with an amused grin and asked me if I enjoyed my meal. Was I allowed to lick my fingers?

My mother turned to me and said, "When you enjoy your lunch that much, you are supposed to go and tell the chef."

"Where's the chef?" I said, not quite sure who that was.

"In the kitchen," said my mother, looking at the waiter. "Can she?"

So I followed the waiter through the swinging doors and offered what I can only imagine were my carefully rehearsed "compliments to the chef." I don't particularly remember the kitchen. What I do remember are the bathrooms. The doors had no pictures, just two brass plaques engraved with the words *Messieurs* and *Mesdames*. Not sure which one to choose, I came back to the table, awaiting instructions.

When the *andouillette* arrived, it was smaller than I imagined — four or five inches at most, a delicate-sized portion for what I imagined was hearty peasant fare. As I tasted the first slice, I understood why. The texture was rich and slightly springy, the gentle patchwork of meats meant to celebrate rather than disguise their humble origins. I made short work of a deep, moist glass of Burgundy. We toasted. "*Dans les yeux*," Gwendal said, meeting my eyes. "It's bad luck to toast if you're not looking directly at someone." The large coins of meat soaked up the mustard.

I felt full and satisfied. We had clearly passed on to a new phase in our relationship; the American girl had proven herself an enthusiastic eater of offal. Gwendal had something else in mind.

He reached past the empty plates and took my hand.

"*Je t'aime*," he said softly.

Nothing says "I love you" like a plate full of sausage.

Weekend Treats

CHOUQUETTES

This was my first and most beloved Parisian breakfast. *Chouquettes* in Paris are dotted with small pebbles of white sugar called *sucre perlé*. You can get the same effect at home with a last-minute dusting of icing sugar. This recipe is adapted from one of my French kitchen bibles: *Lenôtre: Faîtes votre pâtisserie* (Flammarion, 1975).

> ½ cup milk
> ½ cup water
> 160 g unsalted butter, diced
> 1¼ teaspoons granulated sugar
> ¾ teaspoon coarse sea salt (or 1 scant teaspoon fine sea salt)
> 1 cup flour
> 4 eggs (total weight approximately 280 g)
> 3 tablespoons icing sugar, plus more for decoration

Preheat the oven to 220°C.

In a heavy-bottomed saucepan, over low heat, combine the milk, water, butter, sugar, and salt. Bring just to a boil, turn off the heat, and add the flour while stirring continuously, until the flour is incorporated and the dough comes away from the sides of the pan. It will look like a lump of marzipan.

Quickly add 2 of the eggs and stir to incorporate.

Quickly incorporate the remaining 2 eggs and stir until smooth. The batter will be thick and sticky. It can be refrigerated for up to a day.

Line 2 large baking sheets with baking paper. Using 2 teaspoons, dole out heaping dollops of batter, widely spaced. You should have about 24. (If you have room in your freezer, you can freeze the individual puffs at this point. I wouldn't recommend freezing and thawing a big lump of batter.)

Bake one sheet at a time. Before you put them in the oven, sprinkle each puff generously with icing sugar.

If baking immediately: Bake for 12 minutes at 220°C. Then turn down the heat to 200°C and bake for 10 to 12 minutes more with the oven door slightly ajar (I stick a wooden spoon in the door to hold it open just a crack).

If baking straight from the fridge: 15 minutes at 220°C, then 10 to 12 minutes at 200°C with the door ajar.

If baking from the freezer: 17 minutes at 220°C, 12 minutes at 200°C with door ajar.

You'll want to watch the *chouquettes* the first time, as every oven is different. Grab one out of the oven to taste if you like (I always do). It should be fully puffed and highly colored. Don't worry if the sugar caramelizes on top or underneath.

Eat right out of the oven or cool on a wire rack. If you prefer a sweeter finish, dust with additional icing sugar just before serving.

Yield: makes approximately 24 *chouquettes*

CHICKEN AND SWEET PEPPER STEW
Poulet Basquaise

After a flea market near the Bastille or a walk along the Seine to the new national library, Gwendal and I would often end up at Chez Gladines, a student hub in the villagey neighborhood of La Buttes aux Cailles. With a zinc bar, communal tables, and red-checkered cloths, Chez Gladines is cozy in a "love thy neighbor" kind of way. They serve huge salads topped with chicken livers and *lardons*, and heaping plates of this chicken and sweet pepper casserole, a specialty of the Basque region of Spain.

The secret ingredient is *piment d'Espelette*, a smoky red chili pepper. It gives the dish a warming but not overwhelming heat. You can find *piment d'Espelette* in specialty food stores or online. It sometimes comes as a paste; I prefer the powder. You'll find yourself sprinkling it onto omelettes and steak, and in recent years it has become a fashionable addition to chocolate desserts. Espelette truffles — yummm. If you can't find *piment d'Espelette*, you can subsitute with a smoky paprika.

> 1 small chicken (1–1.5 kg), cut into pieces
> Coarse sea salt
> 2 teaspoons piment d'Espelette
> 3 tablespoons olive oil
> 250 g lardons fumés or cubed pancetta
> 4 medium onions, sliced
> 3 cloves garlic, halved
> 2 medium red peppers, sliced
> 2 medium yellow peppers, sliced
> 2 x 400 g cans whole tomatoes, with juice
> 1 bay leaf and a few sprigs of thyme (optional)

In your largest frying pan, brown the chicken on one side, season with sea salt and 1 teaspoon of *piment d'Espelette*. Turn, then season with additional salt and the other teaspoon of *piment d'Espelette*. Remove the chicken from the pan and set aside.

In the same pan, heat the olive oil, add *lardons*, and cook for 3 minutes. Add onions and garlic; sauté for 10 to 15 minutes.

Add peppers and sauté 20 minutes more, stirring occasionally.

Add tomatoes, crushing them between your fingers, and juice. Bring to a boil; return the chicken to the pan with the bay leaf and thyme. Cover, lower the heat, and simmer 30 to 40 minutes, turning the chicken at the halfway mark.

I serve this stew, as Chez Gladines does, with sliced red potatoes tossed in olive oil and roasted in a medium oven.

Yield: Serves 4

CHAPTER 4

A BIRTHDAY CELEBRATION

I get carsick, dramatically, green-around-the-gills carsick. So imagine the knot in my intestines during the five-hour drive to the Brittany coast to meet Gwendal's parents, forty of his nearest and dearest friends — and a leek.

Gwendal and I had been living for the past year in our own little Paris–London bubble. Because of the enchanted but ill-defined nature of our relationship — not to mention my pathetic level of French — we had avoided social occasions. But he was turning thirty at the beginning of May and wanted me to be there.

I was terrified, but I was also curious. Despite a certain nonchalance on my part, we were slowly paddling toward the deep end. I had not exactly *responded* to Gwendal's sausage declaration, but it was there, dangling like a ripe pear on a tree. He didn't pressure me; not for the last time, he seemed to understand my feelings better than I did and was content to wait me out. We had begun to lapse into the comfortable silence of two people who know each other better than they care to admit. Most days ended with the phone to my ear, just listening to him breathe. I needed to know what would happen if we ventured beyond our little weekend world.

Being the studious type, and also scared out of my mind, I was determined to come to this party fully prepared. I resurrected my college French textbook (*why oh why* had I done my junior year abroad in Scotland?) and asked Gwendal for a guest list. I memorized Catherine the biologist; Bastien, the fashion victim. I put a star next to those whom Gwendal had met when he studied in Canada — maybe I could switch to English in a pinch.

I also quizzed him about the first question I should ask when I met someone. He shrugged, thought about it, then shrugged again. Clearly, starting a conversation with a French person was going to be more complicated than "So, what do you do?"

When we arrived at the house in Saint-Malo, preparations were under way for a family lunch. The house was in a grassy new development, a ten-minute walk from the sea. It had the feel of a year-round beach house: white tile floors and an open living room, dining room, and kitchen with doors leading out to the back garden. There was a spiral staircase in blonde wood curving up to the bedrooms.

We were greeted at the door by Gwendal's father, Yanig, who bent to kiss me on both cheeks. He had been a sailor most of his life, the skipper of a boat he'd built with his own hands. With long limbs, watery blue eyes, and a graying beard, he looked like someone perfectly content to sit up all night on a silent windy watch. He shared my own father's towering height, his wiry frame, his walk. As I had with my dad, I took two steps for his every one.

Gwendal's mother was already in the kitchen. As tiny as Yanig was tall, Nicole was dressed in black with a long blonde braid trailing down her back. Did I mention that she's a psychoanalyst? *No pressure there.* Except for the glasses and the delicate creases on her forehead, she could have been sixteen.

Affif and Annick, Gwendal's godparents (or as near to godparents as hippie atheists can get), had come early to help with the cooking. Annick teaches French as a second language. She made sure to speak clearly for my benefit. Affif is an Algerian painter with a disarming grin. As I sat down at the dining room table, he handed me a small paring knife and a leek.

My only previous encounter with a leek was in something called a "soup pack" at our local ShopRite — a plastic box with a few carrots, a stub of leek, some turnips, parsley, and a brittle bay leaf, for those too lazy to cut their own veggies for stew. This thing was as long as a cricket bat, with unruly green ribbons at one end and bristly blonde whiskers at the other. I wasn't one hundred percent sure which end was up. Was I supposed to throw away the white part or the green part? There was dirt between the leaves. Was I meant to ignore it? I stared at the tablecloth while rapid-fire French conversation buzzed in my ears.

I took the SAT, so I know how to make an educated guess: first I took a stab at the green bits; some of the thick outer leaves looked wilted — dead things seemed like a logical place to start. Then I tried cutting down the middle, but the leek bent like a dying tulip, and I was left sawing, one layer at a time. Affif surveyed the situation out of the corner of his eye. *"Pas sous plastique, celui-là."* Not under plastic, this one, he said, winking. Then, as if on cue, the entire room burst into good-natured laughter.

Affif took a leek from the pile, held it firmly by its whiskers (*oh God, those are the roots, you idiot*), and sliced into the white heart of the stalk, ripping straight up to the green tips in a single stroke. He made another slice at a ninety-degree angle and held up the leek like a cheerleading pom-pom, dirt clinging to the inside layers and a faint smell of sweet onion wafting through the air. Lesson over, Affif grabbed a bunch of leeks from the kitchen and presented them to me like a bouquet. The knot in my stomach loosened. I had a vegetable in-joke.

As if finding the business end of a leek was not culinary discovery enough for one afternoon, we then moved on to the mayonnaise. All these leeks were an accompaniment to poached cod — and to accompany the cod, a homemade mayonnaise.

Not to put too fine a point on it, but I *despise* mayonnaise. The smell of the white rubbery gel was enough to dissuade this five-year-old forever, never mind the slimy way it soaks into tuna fish and sogs up a perfectly good tomato. I had a rule against sandwiches as a kid; I wouldn't eat anything stuck between two pieces of bread. In this manner, I had avoided any contact with the stuff for the better part of twenty years. Now I was cornered, hung upside down by the toenails in the name of politesse.

Nicole put a large pinch of sea salt, a dab of Dijon mustard, and an egg yolk in the bottom of a small plastic container. Then she turned on the electric beater while adding a thin but steady trickle of oil.

"*Les femmes.*" Women, mumbled Yanig under his breath. Apparently he beats his by hand.

Slowly, as if by magic, what should have been a mucus-like vinaigrette puffed up into a creamy yellow cloud. It was a little bit of French alchemy — suspicious, but promising.

When we sat down to lunch I faded into the background. I let the conversation wash over me, happy (for once in the life of this only child) not to be the center of attention. But as I picked up my fork, I had the feeling I was being watched. Nicole mashed up a bit of cod with her fork and combined it with a dab of mayonnaise. I did the same. The result was a revelation. The mayonnaise was silky without being oily; it didn't really taste like anything, but it made everything taste better. I felt like Moses, wandering for years in the culinary wilderness, finally come home. Clearly, I was not in the land of Hellmann's anymore.

Nowadays, I am good at parties. This wasn't always the case. Charm, it turns out — like whipping up a good mayonnaise — is very much an acquired skill.

As an only child raised primarily in the company of adults, until the age of thirteen I had very little idea how to talk to kids my own age. I was the kind of shy that came off as haughty, sensitive in the way that allowed smaller, crueler girls (who had presumably spent their childhoods pinned in a headlock by their older brothers) to taunt me between rounds of jump rope. Only children are famously bad at comebacks. We have no experience with smash and grab.

My transformation into a social being was sudden, almost mystical. I had just completed the kind of eighth-grade experience Judy Blume novels are made of: suffice it to say that if there existed a more soul-crushing humiliation than Dave Ware's discovery of my first tampons during math class, I couldn't think of it — until I was up to bat that afternoon for softball (I'm no Josephine DiMaggio to begin with) and Dave led all the boys in a rousing chorus of "GO SUPER PLUS, GO SUPER PLUS." Summer camp was torture for me — *Lord of the Flies* with hair-spray. I begged my mother to let me go to summer school instead. School was what I was good at.

Driving eighty miles an hour in our little Nissan without hubcaps up to a fancy boarding school in Massachusetts, my mother was midway through a pep talk. "It's a fresh start," she said in that overly cheerful tone she trotted out to say something that was true, obvious, and unhelpful, all at the same time.

"Come on," she said, flipping down the visor mirror so I could smile into it, "repeat after me. 'Hi, my name is Elizabeth. Hi! *My* name is Elizabeth. *Hi!* My name is

Elizabeth.'" For three hours, all the way up the Mass Pike. I wanted to open the door and roll under the wheels.

When we arrived at the tree-lined entrance of Northfield Mount Hermon School, I instantly recognized myself in the Greek Revival pillars and white-shingled Victorian houses. This school would turn out to be one of my happiest spots on earth, and I would return not just for a summer program, but thanks to a scholarship and my auntie Lynn, three years of high school. Registration was in the music building. As we waited for the line to inch forward toward the orientation packets and silver coffee service, my mother excused herself to go to the bathroom. I knew it was now or never. So I sucked in my breath and turned to the girl behind me. She was tall with a puggish nose and dark curls:

Hi, my name is Elizabeth.

The universe hung in the balance. The sun swung from a cord above my head.

Hi, I'm Catherine.

I couldn't have been more shocked if I'd split the atom right there on the faded Oriental rug. I wanted a Nobel Prize, a plaque, a medal. *It works*. And suddenly — what felt like instantaneously — I was someone who could talk to anyone.

So how hard could a French party really be? *Bonjour, je m'appelle Elizabeth*. Hi, my name is Elizabeth. I liked my chances.

As the guests started to arrive in the late afternoon, I practiced a more nuanced version of my standard greeting: *Bonsoir, enchantée de vous rencontrer*. Good evening, delighted to meet you. Even as I said it, I realized it might be a little early for *bonsoir*, and I got the feeling that *enchantée* might be limited to State Department cocktail hours.

Kiss or shake? Most went in for the double-cheek kiss just as I extended my hand. We ended up in an awkward tangle of jutting heads and arms, as though we were midway through a good game of Twister. All I really wanted to get across was an old-fashioned "pleasure to meet you," but

Gwendal told me flat out that I couldn't use the word *plaisir* without implying something sexual. Maybe it wasn't going to be such a pleasure to meet these people after all.

Many of Gwendal's friends had come from Paris. Some were staying in nearby hotels, some were camping in the back garden. Everyone was friendly but slightly... vague. No one asked me anything about myself, and no one, even the ones I knew spoke some English, made the slightest effort in that direction. Struggling to piece together a sentence in French, I felt like Harry Houdini, suspended upside down in a glass tank, mouthing words through a wall of water and blowing little bubbles through my nose. Everything was muted. I felt half-funny, half-intelligent, half-charming — half-there.

When I had exhausted my limited stock of French phrases, I tried to move on to the next person. In the States, it is normal to walk up to a stranger at a party and start a conversation. That was my first mistake. There are no strangers at French parties; everyone has known each other forever. Breaking into a conversation is a little bit like starting *David Copperfield* in the middle. You've missed the formative years.

In the States, prefab questions like "What do you do?" or "Where do you go to school?" are an easy way to place people on the social scale. It is assumed that your answer will reveal what you are proud of or passionate about, and of course that all-important American barometer, how much money you make.

A French conversation starter is more subtle. Work is considered boring, money is out of the question, politics comes later (and only in like-minded company). Vacation is a safe bet — it's no exaggeration to say that French people are always going on, returning from, or planning a holiday. But more often than not, social class in France is judged by your relationship to culture. Here's an example:

"What did you think of the new David Lynch?"

The new David Lynch is:

a) a comic book about mice
b) a film about lesbians
c) a brand of toilet paper

Your opinion (or lack thereof) tells them everything they need to know. Turns out, I had seen the new David Lynch. It gave me a headache, but I didn't have the vocabulary to tell anyone why.

Thank God there were dishes to wash.

By ten o'clock my jaw was sore from smiling, and I retreated to a safe spot near the kitchen sink. Nicole was already there. This was really going back to my roots. I was the kid who stuck too close to the counselor at camp; when I'm uncomfortable, I naturally gravitate to the oldest person in the room. Dishwashing turned out to be a stroke of genius. I could be busy, purposeful, silent, *and* ingratiate myself with Gwendal's mom all at the same time. Nicole and I rinsed and dried in silent harmony, nodding shyly at each other.

After dinner, Gwendal's father cleared a space on the living room floor. He had recently given up boatbuilding and taught himself ceramics; he had a studio and a kiln attached to the garage. He was surprisingly talented, especially with the glazes, which he mixed and measured with the same precision that he must have used in front of his navigational charts. Yanig took the huge Moroccan brass plate they used as a coffee table and piled it with tiny parcels, each topped with a metal hook. He handed an improvised fishing rod to Gwendal's high school sweetheart Nathalie, and each of us took a turn trying to catch our prize. Inside each bundle, carefully wrapped in tissue paper, were miniature vases that Yanig had made especially for the occasion. I watched Gwendal as he took his turn, swinging the rod over his shoulder like a kid on his way to the beach. It was easy to see the kind of boy he must have been, quick with a goofy smile, full of intense concentration in front of the task at hand. He fished out a chubby black vase with flecks of blue; I fished out a rose and gray one with a long neck and a big bottom. Hmph.

As everyone admired their prize, Gwendal dragged a large square of plywood out of the garage, put on some fancy shoes, and started tap-dancing. Yup. Right there on the living room floor. I knew he'd been taking lessons, inspired by a love of old American movies — anything with sword-fighting or a top hat and tails. I decided, in the interest of cultural sensitivity, to suspend judgment. He looked like he was having fun, and I already had sufficient evidence that he was heterosexual.

The rest of us started dancing at about midnight; I was grateful for an activity that didn't require me to conjugate any verbs. Things were still going strong at three a.m. when someone turned up "Alexandrie, Alexandra" on the stereo. Suddenly the whole room went into some kind of disco rain dance, whooping and chanting in a circle around the living room. I stood pressed against the wall, like a field anthropologist caught in the middle of a buffalo exorcism. This must be how stupid Americans look doing "Y.M.C.A."

The crowd started to thin at about four a.m. I had barely seen Gwendal all evening; he was busy catching up with old friends. Before we went to bed we finished mopping the living room floor.

I was beyond tired. My brain was fuzzy from the wine and hours of simultaneous translation. Could I really do this? Could these people be my friends? Could this strange life, this language I'd mangled all evening, be mine? I saw myself at the bottom of an enormous mountain, looking up, trying to decide if I was ready for a long, hard climb.

"Want to dance with me?" said Gwendal, pulling me close and turning up the Chet Baker. The French words I'd been fighting with all evening drained from my head to a puddle at my feet.

Let's get lost, lost in each other's arms
Let's get lost, let them send out alarms

A few weeks later, Gwendal called his parents. Nicole mentioned, in that tiny but determined voice of hers, that she was taking English lessons.

A mother always knows.

Recipes for a
Springtime Gathering

MAMY SIMONE'S TABOULEH

Gwendal's grandmother Simone grew up in Morocco, and
although she's been back in France for almost fifty years, her
recipes (and her reminiscences) often nod toward warmer
climes. This recipe uses couscous, a North African staple,
instead of bulgur; it has a lighter consistency and a sweeter
finish. Trust me on the grapefruit juice — it wakes up the
whole dish.

> 2 cups medium couscous
> 2 cups flat-leaf parsley, finely chopped
> 1 tablespoon fresh mint, finely chopped
> 4 tomatoes, seeded and chopped
> 1 cucumber, seeded and chopped
> ½ cup golden raisins
> ¾ cup olive oil
> ⅔ cup freshly squeezed pink grapefruit juice
>   (approximately 1½ grapefruits)
> ⅓ cup freshly squeezed lemon juice (approximately 1½
>   lemons)
> ¼ teaspoon coarse sea salt
> ½ teaspoon ground cumin
> Freshly ground black pepper to taste
> Juice of ½ grapefruit, to squeeze in just before serving
>   (optional)

Put the couscous in a large bowl and add 1 cup boiling water.
Stir and let couscous rise while you chop the herbs and
vegetables.

In a small bowl, cover the raisins with boiling water, let stand.

Whisk together the olive oil, grapefruit and lemon juice, and salt.

When the couscous has cooled a bit, fluff it with a fork and then sift with your hands to separate the individual grains. Add the herbs, tomatoes, cucumber, raisins, and dressing, and toss to combine. Season with the cumin and black pepper and give it a final stir. This dish is best left in the fridge for a few hours before serving, so the flavors have a chance to settle.

I like a bit of extra acidity in my summer salads, so I usually squeeze in the juice of half a grapefruit just before serving.

Yield: Serves 6–8

POACHED COD WITH WILTED LEEKS
AND HOMEMADE MAYONNAISE

Cabillaud Poché aux Poireaux
et Mayonnaise Maison

This is the dish that made a convert out of me. The fish couldn't be simpler; the leeks have just enough mellow sweetness. Add a dollop of silky mayonnaise to the side of your plate, and grab a tiny bit with each forkful.

POACHED COD

1 bouquet garni (a mixture of fresh herbs — parsley, coriander, bay, thyme, dill — still on the stem, tied with kitchen string or left loose)
A few black peppercorns
Coarse sea salt
1½ kg boneless cod fillet, at least 2 cm thick
Lemon wedges

ROASTED LEEKS

12 small leeks, the skinnier the better
3 tablespoons olive oil
Coarse sea salt

HOMEMADE MAYONNAISE

The key to success is to have everything, from the bowl to the eggs, at room temperature.

1 egg yolk (only the freshest, preferably organic — remember, you're eating it raw)
Scant ¼ teaspoon coarse sea salt
1 tablespoon Dijon mustard
½ cup safflower, sunflower, peanut, or mild vegetable oil

For the cod: Partially fill a frying pan large enough to comfortably hold the fish fillets with cold water and add the herbs, pepper, and enough salt so you can taste it. Bring to a boil.

Turn down the heat, add the fish, and simmer (tiny bubbles will rise to the surface) until the flesh is firm, about 4 minutes per centimetre of thickness. Discard the herbs. Remove the fish with a slotted spoon to a serving platter. Serve warm or at room temperature with lemon wedges.

For the leeks: Cut off the hairy base (root) of the leek and the tough dark green leaves (you can use these for stock). You should be left with a white stalk and just a hint of pale green at the top. Starting a few centimetres below the top, slice up through the center, turn the leek ninety degrees and slice again, separate the inner layers with your fingers, and wash thoroughly. The result will look like an oniony feather duster with a solid handle and some stringy fringe.

Line a large baking sheet with aluminium foil and arrange the leeks in a single layer. Drizzle with olive oil, rubbing it around to make sure all the leeky fringe is well coated. Cook at 200°C for 30 minutes, until the leeks are tender when pierced with a fork. Sprinkle with sea salt. Serve warm or at room temperature, alongside the fish. Each diner will end up with two soft leeky feather dusters on their plate. Bon Appetit!

Yield: Serves 6

For the mayonnaise: Combine the egg yolk, mustard, and salt in a small mixing bowl. Using an electric beater, beat the yolk mixture while adding a few drops of oil at a time. When the mixture begins to thicken and set, add a thin but steady trickle of oil. The mayonnaise will not take more than a minute or two to puff up.

It's never happened to me, but apparently there are days when the mayonnaise just won't take. There are old wives' tales about not making this while you have your period — or maybe it was just my father-in-law's theory. It is important to add the oil drop by drop at the beginning, to make sure the emulsion holds.

Yield: Makes about ½ cup

Pregnant women or anyone with an allergy to raw eggs should be advised.

FENNEL SALAD WITH LEMON, OLIVE OIL, AND POMEGRANATE SEEDS
Salade de Fenouil

The morning after Gwendal's birthday party, we all went for a walk on the old customs trail, which hugs the cliffs of the Brittany coast. Gwendal's dad picked some wild fennel, rubbed the fronds between his fingers, and held them under my nose. The earthy licorice smell is one of my purest memories of France. Fennel is one of the few vegetables in Paris that is available year-round, so I serve this with fish in the warmer months and with roasted chicken when the weather turns chilly.

> 2 medium bulbs fennel
> Juice of ½ lemon
> Best-quality extra-virgin olive oil, or truffle oil
> Coarse sea salt
> Fresh dill, chopped, to taste
> Freshly ground black pepper
> A handful of pomegranate seeds (optional)

Slice the fennel as thinly as possible. Arrange it in a thin layer on a platter, squeeze over half a lemon, and drizzle with olive oil. Sprinkle with sea salt, dill, and a grinding of black pepper. In the fall, when pomegranates appear at the market, I add a handful of the ruby red seeds.

Yield: Serves 6

CHAPTER 5

PIXIE DUST

Where the hell is Tinker Bell when you need her? As anyone who has ever read *Peter Pan* will tell you, little girls can't fly all by themselves. They need help, they need magic. Up until now, I've been fortunate in that department. It's not that I can pull a rabbit out of a hat or make a quarter appear from behind my ear, but among my family and friends I have a certain reputation for making hard things look easy. Some people call it mojo, my grandmother calls it *beshert*. I've heard it described as panache, charm, or just dumb luck. My mother calls it "pixie dust." I'd always had a healthy supply. And now it was gone.

Gwendal and I were in New York for Christmas, staying at my auntie Lynn's apartment in Manhattan. A blizzard had smoothed the hard edges of the city, blanketing the streets in silent white. In preparation for the storm, we had gone out for supplies: all the ingredients for pancakes, plus *The Band Wagon* and *All About Eve*. It's just as well that it was snowing, because after three months apart, sightseeing was just something we did between sex. Truth be known, if Gwendal hadn't been there, I probably would have been hiding under the covers anyway.

My five-year plan was at an all-time low. The Internet start-up had collapsed; my master's thesis was finished but my adviser had rejected my subject for a PhD. Every job I'd interviewed for in London wanted to know if I had a work visa. I was out of ideas and very nearly out of money. I'd come back to New York in mid-October to do some consulting for the first museum I worked for out of college. Back in the fluorescent-lit basement office where I had photocopied as an intern, I felt like my life was moving in reverse.

The only thing moving forward was us.

Gwendal was definitely on an upswing. He had just defended his PhD and, finally inching away from engineering toward the world of movies, had found a job at a Paris cinema archive, in charge of the digitization of their collection of films.

We had been *not* talking about me moving to Paris for months. I was having trouble imagining the free fall — no school, no job, no idea how to pick up my dry cleaning. Nothing but love. It sounded crazy, even to me.

The only thing that seemed more impossible than going to Paris was staying in New York. I saw the smug faces of family and friends, heard the self-satisfied recitation of twenty years' worth of "innocent" chatter: Elizabeth, the flaky one, the pretentious one. *Elizabeth with her head in the clouds and her nose in a book. Elizabeth, with her fancy education and English ball gowns and French lovers.*

Right back where she started. And she still can't earn a living.

I wanted to cover my ears and stamp my feet like a four-year-old. Clearly, coming back to New York would be a sign of defeat. They would be vindicated and I would be miserable. I needed a handful of pixie dust. I wanted to throw it in their faces and run.

High above the city streets, Gwendal was making things sound irritatingly simple. *I know what I want. What do you want? Next.* True, I had started writing for a few art magazines before I left London, and although the start-up had burst with the Internet bubble, I still had a nice "online editor" credit on my résumé.

"You can write from anywhere," he said as I leaned into him. *Here's good*, I thought. *Right here.* Even as I let the tension ease from my body, I could hear the "but" rising in my throat. What was I trying to tell him? That I loved him, but he wasn't part of the plan. That I was creeping toward thirty — all right, creeping toward twenty-eight, but still — and soon there would be an *accounting*. An invisible tally: all the sour cherry martinis and little black dresses in one column, everything I was supposed to have accomplished in the other.

As I hid my face in his shoulder, I couldn't see forward or backward. I couldn't think about what dream I wasn't chasing or whom I might be disappointing.

It is amazing how you can make the right decision for all the wrong reasons.

When the woman behind the counter at JFK saw the size of my suitcases, she smiled. "Going on vacation?" she said. "Study abroad?"

"I'm going to live there," I answered, and her face did this weird, twisty thing around the mouth.

"That's so *brave*," she replied as she loaded me up with extra luggage tags — in case I wanted to come home and forgot my real address.

In the departure lounge of the airport, my stepfather, Paul, gave me a hundred dollars in cash. "Just in case," he said. I imagined myself running through the forest, slipping under barbed wire, dogs on my tail, forced to bribe the border guards in order to get a first-class seat on the Eurostar. The money was clearly meant to buy an emergency supply of Americanness — the financial equivalent of a three-pound sack of Tater Tots.

As the plane took off I realized I was gripping the armrest, my knuckles white. It's hard to say exactly what I was afraid of.

I am afraid that this is my last chance to make my life extraordinary.

I am afraid that I have strayed from my trail of breadcrumbs, that I will be lost.

Like a Spanish explorer with a map where the continents end and the oceans are marked with dragons and winged monsters, I am afraid I will fall off the edge of the world.

I arrived in Paris at the beginning of April, just as the song instructs.

I tapped the code into the keypad outside, and the blue door made its characteristic click. *My door, my click.* My suitcases were wider than the spiral stairwell, but we managed to twist and turn them up to the second floor. Gwendal had already made me a key, and when I opened the door, the apartment was spotless. There were roses on the table and yellow index cards suspended from the ceiling with pieces of string. They fluttered like bright birds in the breeze from the hallway. Each card described what we would do in a particular place, some of it innocent, much of it not. There was one above the stereo: *This is where we will dance.* One near the couch: *This is where you will distract me while I read.* One in the shower... There was one on the refrigerator, held up with a magnet like a Chinese take-out menu: *Amour, baisers, tendresse — livraison 24h/24 — 7j/7.* Love, kisses, and tenderness, delivered twenty-four hours a day, seven days a week. *My refrigerator, my new life.*

"Welcome home, *mon amour.*" For all my castles in the air, in this moment I felt like Gwendal had laid the world at my feet. My universe expanded and contracted at the same time. He had built me a two-room Taj Mahal.

"I already put your name on the gas bill."

How thoughtful.

"Trust me. In France, if you don't have a gas bill, you don't exist."

When Gwendal left for work on Monday, I was on my own. I lay in bed, looking at the ceiling and listening to the new weekday sounds. In the courtyard, I heard a television, some high-pitched voices and familiar theme music. It took me a minute to place it — a rerun of *Beverly Hills 90210* dubbed in French. For the first time in my life, I had nothing to do, nowhere to be. My only fixed appointment was every Tuesday and Thursday, between eight a.m. and one p.m., at our local market.

Our nearest open-air market is at the intersection of a North African and Asian district on the boulevard de Belleville. It's one of the cheapest in Paris, and though it lacks the wicker basket charm of the boulevard Raspail or the rue Mouffetard, the produce is fresh and the banter lively.

I got the impression that at ten a.m. I was already late. As I walked up the rue du Faubourg-du-Temple, it was clear that the neighborhood had been up for hours. Delivery trucks blocked the cobblestone street, butchers in white coats chose whole sides of beef suspended on hooks like enormous dangling earrings. An African woman with a baby tied to her back looked through a bin of lacy underwear outside a shop. On the pavement, plastic tables and chairs were full of North African men drinking coffee, smoking cigarettes, and watching the soccer highlights. Three Chinese women with strollers gossiped outside an herb shop selling ginseng tea, birds' nests of rice noodles, and pirated DVDs. Every third store there was something called a *bazar,* where pastel laundry baskets, frying pans, and shiny new aluminium garbage cans were set up on the sidewalk. There was a line outside the shop that sold African groceries: yams as big as footballs and tiny red chili peppers, still on the vine. I walked up the block, an immigrant among immigrants. An immigrant with an American Express card, but even so.

When I reached the intersection, the boulevard de Belleville looked like a shantytown, with white canvas tarps and fruit crates as far as the eye could see. The aisle between the stands was crowded, the vendors screaming for customers' attention.

As I made my way down the street, a man shoved a strawberry in my path. "*Mademoiselle, goûte, goûte*" (taste, taste), he said, trying to catch my eye. This was not the French I learned in high school. It was loud and fast and filled with the guttural click of Arabic. "*Ça va, princesse?*" He handed me a slice of melon, broke open a pod of sweet peas. I knew it was ridiculous, but after two years in England, it felt so good to hear this caressing tone of voice, to smile and lower my eyes, even if the guy was just trying to sell me a tomato.

On the next table were barrels of olives — wrinkled black, shiny green, and mauve — and small pickled lemons, bobbing to the surface like rubber duckies. There was a patchwork of cardboard boxes filled with spices: paprika, cinnamon sticks, and something called *graines de paradis* — seeds of paradise. They looked like caraway seeds, but when he held the metal scoop toward my nose I smelled a spicy hint of pepper. I bought some, figuring no dish could be made worse by a pinch of paradise.

Behind the next stand was an older man, white bristles poking out of his beard, still bundled in a hat, scarf, and his winter overcoat on this warm day. He was almost entirely hidden behind a wall of greenery, small bundles of fresh parsley, coriander, and mint stacked in dense, neat rows like a garden hedge.

I passed piles of carrots with their bushy green leaves, radishes sold in bunches like roses. There was something near the leeks that looked like a prop from Dr. Frankenstein's laboratory, a knobbly root shaped like a brain, with dimpled ridges and tiny coiled stems. *Céleri*. It looked like something you might dissect rather than eat. I bought one, just to have a look inside.

There was clearly an event up ahead. Shoppers were stacked three-deep under a blue-and-white-striped awning, pushing their way toward the front. I had arrived at the fishmonger. As I approached, I took in the mildest whiff of the sea (a quality fishmonger is never smelly). I nudged myself toward the corner of a large table packed with ice as water dripped on my shoe. Behind the counter, there was a man with large red hands and close-cropped hair, his apron tied across one shoulder like a toga. In a booming voice he abused the customers as he plunged his hands into a pile of sardines. I stared at the fish, and for the most part, the fish stared back at me. There were mounds of mackerel and trout with glassy eyes and shiny skin. There was an ugly one, fat and gray with a gaping red mouth that looked like it should have had teeth. There were piles of mussels, whole octopuses, long strips of squid, as thick as foam-rubber insulation. Nothing was square or breaded or in a cardboard box. I bet these shoppers had never seen a fish stick.

Clearly, I was too close to the table to be a mere spectator. The man with the big hands was getting impatient. A woman rolled her shopping trolley over my toe. I pointed to the mackerel, said, *"Deux, s'il vous plaît,"* and handed him a twenty-euro bill. He gave me a look that said: "If you were older and uglier, I'd be grumpy right now," and he deposited seventeen euros in small coins into the palm of my hand. I took my blue plastic bag. "*Merci.*"

So there I was: an immigrant with an American Express card, seventeen euros in small change, a bouquet of radishes, Frankenstein's brain, and two mackerel.

When I got home, I took the first mackerel out of the bag. His skin was slick and iridescent, with black spots that fanned out in a pattern on either side. *This would make a nice handbag,* I thought, as I lost my grip and he fell into the sink. *Slippery little bugger.*

I got hold of him again and put him on a plate. I knew there were things I had to do to him. Dirty, violent things. I'd seen Gwendal gut a fish; I'd seen people skydive too, that didn't mean I was ready to do it myself. I thought about all the things I knew something about — eighteenth-century bookbinding, Victorian photography, Renaissance painting. Somehow I had missed this particular skill on my carefully groomed résumé.

The little guy was still looking at me. It was a superior stare. I'm on to you, he said. You're nothing but a New York princess. You have no idea how to turn me into dinner. He was speaking French, so it was hard to tell, but I think his last words were something like, *Pixie dust, my ass.*

I took the knife and pressed its pointed tip into the belly of the fish. I hesitated, searching for something civilized to think about during my upcoming act of brutality. Had Jane Austen ever gutted a fish?

The knife made a ripping sound, like an uncooperative zipper.

It is a truth universally acknowledged,...

I had hold of something now, soft and dense, like a clot of blood.

... that a single man in possession of a good fortune,...
I pulled out the tiny heart and liver.
... must be in want of a wife.
I yanked out the final membrane, guts dripping from my hands.
Tell Tinker Bell to put that in a pipe and smoke it.
After the initial carnage, the rest was easy: white wine, onions, and a sizzling hot frying pan. I felt like a lean and dangerous individual, a creature of the wild. The fish tasted terrific, though I've no idea if it was the wine or the adrenaline.
"*Ça va?*" asked Gwendal, wrapping his arms around my waist while I rinsed the pot in the sink. He loves to catch me in the kitchen when my hands are busy. "*Ça va,*" I said emphatically. A-okay. I squealed as he sank his teeth into my neck. "Good dinner."

Over the next few weeks I became a regular customer at the market, walking with my head held high and throwing my melon rind on the ground.
The fish man was expecting me. I picked out my own mackerel, two the same size, slick but not slimy, wiping my hand on the apron wrapped around the pole. There was a flicker of recognition in his eyes as I handed over my three or four coins.
"*Vous avez un copain?*" You have a boyfriend? he said, holding on to one end of my blue plastic bag.
"*Oui,*" I answered with a half smile.
"Does your boyfriend work on Mondays? Because me, *non.*"
I looked my mackerel straight in the eye.
One slippery little bugger at a time.

A Market Day Dinner

MACKEREL WITH ONIONS AND WHITE WINE
Maquereaux au Vin Blanc

Mackerel is perfect for a weekday, because it doesn't really improve with fancy treatment.

> 1 medium onion, thinly sliced
> 5 black peppercorns (or a good grinding of mixed peppercorns)
> A few sprigs of parsley
> 2 whole mackerel, approximately 180 g each, gutted and rinsed
> Dry white wine (approximately ⅔ cup)
> Coarse sea salt

Preheat your grill.

In a shallow roasting pan, place the onions, peppercorns, and parsley. Top with the fish, add white wine until you've got about half a centimetre in the bottom of the pan. Sprinkle generously with sea salt.

Cook under the grill for 5 minutes. Gently turn the fish and continue to cook for an additional 5 minutes. If your fish are slightly larger, give them an extra minute or two.

Serve topped with the onions and a few spoonfuls of sauce.

Yield: Serves 2

Whole fish are sometimes hard to find in supermarkets. I encourage you to go a bit out of your way. If you don't have a fish market or fishmonger nearby, look for an Asian supermarket, which will often stock many varieties, sometimes still swimming in their tanks.

Cooking whole fish has many advantages. They are not as

fragile as fillets; the skin protects the flesh from drying out and makes methods like grilling a real option. They look spectacular on the plate; suddenly you feel as if you are eating something luxurious as well as virtuous. Check whole fish the same way you would a fillet; if the flesh is opaque and flaky down to the bone, it's done.

POTATO AND CELERIAC MASH
Purée de Céleri

Behold, your new favorite mashed potatoes. Though celeriac may look like Frankenstein's monster's brain, it is among my most smug Paris discoveries. With a light celery scent and a turnip texture, this mash satisfies both the French passion for smooth buttery taste and the American vigilance about carbs.

> 1 kg (4 medium) potatoes, scrubbed and chopped into 2 cm cubes
> 1½ kg celeriac (1 large or two small), peeled and chopped into 2 cm cubes
> 2–3 tablespoons butter
> Salt and pepper to taste

Fill a stockpot with cold, lightly salted water. Add the potatoes and bring to a boil. Add the celeriac and continue to boil until both are tender, 20 to 30 minutes. Drain well.

Return the celeriac and potatoes to the pot, and over a very low flame, mash the two together. (The heat will help evaporate any water left in the celeriac.) Aim for a chunky consistency. This is a rustic purée, so there's no need to get obsessive-compulsive about the lumps. Add butter, salt, and pepper to taste. Serve at once or put in a gratin dish, dot with additional butter, and pass for a minute or two under the grill.

Yield: Serves 6

Variation: Mix in chopped dill or chervil, or a handful of freshly grated Parmesan or Gruyère just before serving.

YOGURT CAKE
Gâteau au Yaourt

If I'm going to make dessert on a weekday, it has to do double
duty — something comforting before bed with enough left over
for breakfast or tea the next day. Yogurt cake fits the bill
perfectly; it's tender, moist, and not too sweet. This is the first
cake Gwendal learned to bake. French children use the empty
yogurt pot to measure the rest of the ingredients. The version
I've found works best comes from blogger turned cookbook
author *extraordinaire*, Clotilde Dusoulier. For more of her
wonderful recipes, check out *Chocolate & Zucchini* (Broadway
Books, 2007).

> 1 cup plain yogurt (full fat, please!)
> 1 cup sugar
> A large pinch of sea salt
> 1 teaspoon vanilla extract
> ⅓ cup vegetable oil
> 2 large eggs
> 1⅔ cups flour
> 1½ teaspoons baking powder
> 1 teaspoon baking soda
> Zest of 1 lemon
> 410 g can apricots, drained and quartered

Preheat the oven to 180°C. Lightly oil a 25 cm round cake pan
and line it with baking paper. In a medium mixing bowl,
combine the yogurt, sugar, salt, and vanilla, whisking until
smooth. Add the oil in a steady stream, whisking to combine.
Add the eggs one by one, whisking to incorporate after each
addition.

Sift together the flour, baking powder, and baking soda; add to
the yogurt mixture; whisk lightly to combine. Stir in the lemon
zest.

Transfer the batter to your cake pan; top with the chopped
apricots. Bake on the center rack of the oven for 45 minutes,
until golden brown and slightly risen. A toothpick in the center
should come out clean.

Lift the cake by the baking paper onto a wire rack to cool. Serve slightly warm or at room temperature. This cake actually gets moister with age, so it tastes great the next day. Simply cover the fully cooled cake with aluminium foil; an airtight container or plastic bag will make it soggy.

Yield: Makes one 25 cm cake

Seasonal tip: Yogurt cake is like a blank canvas. Feel free to experiment. Instead of the apricots, try fresh raspberries or chopped pears mixed with a bit of brown sugar. If I'm feeling homesick, I sometimes add a streusel topping as well.

CHAPTER 6

VOCABULARY LESSONS

I am trying to improve my French. It is unnerving to live in an apartment full of things I can't identify. Familiar objects have become exotic strangers. As I do the dishes, or make the bed, or put away the shopping from the market, I try to give myself little vocabulary tests: *casserole* (pot), *évier* (sink), *poussière* (dust). "Pillow" is killing me. The word in French is *oreiller* (or-RE-ay) — but I can't keep hold of it. It doesn't look like a pillow, doesn't sound like a pillow, and it certainly doesn't bring anything pillowy to mind. The rolled "r" sticks at the back of my throat, to say nothing of all those silent vowels waiting like wallflowers for me to ask them to dance. How hard would it be, I wonder, to sleep without one?

The radio has become my new best friend. I keep it tuned to France Info, a station that repeats the same news report every fifteen minutes. What I don't catch the first time, I catch the second, or the third. I make a point of being home between two and two twenty p.m. for a program called *2000 ans d'histoire.* Every day the show explores a different subject — a two-thousand-year history of the pyramids or a two-thousand-year history of the sandwich.

Inevitably, someone has written a book on the subject. The interview is cut with songs and clips from old movies. Charlton Heston has an even sexier voice dubbed in French.

For the purposes of speaking to actual people, Gwendal and I have divided things roughly into two categories, "*Chez la Marquise*" and "*Pas chez la Marquise.*"

"*Chez la Marquise*" are the polite things, the things you could say if you were invited to lunch with the Queen of England: *Je vous en prie* (No sir, after you). *Tout le plaisir est pour moi* (The pleasure's all mine).

"Pas chez la Marquise" is what Gwendal says when he drops a raw egg on the carpet or stubs his toe: *Putaindebordeldemerde* (@#%$#$!!).

I try out my phrases, haltingly, in the neighborhood. I wave to the Italian man in the window of the pizzeria, mouthing *bonjour* through the window. I put exact change into the hand of my dry cleaner with a flourish and a *Voilà*! On the rue Saint-Maur, there is a fruit and vegetable stand run by a lovely man from Senegal. He has a cousin in New York (doesn't everyone?). I go almost every day to buy fresh mint, a cardboard basket of raspberries, or a slice of *halva*, the sweet sesame seed paste that he sells by the kilo. "*Bonjour, je prends des framboises, s'il vous plaît.*" Really, I go just to say hello. I don't even know his name, but for better or worse, he is my first friend in Paris. The only person other than Gwendal and my mother who knows if I'm alive from one day to the next.

While I am trying to piece together a vocabulary that will allow me to buy raspberries without sounding like a mentally challenged walrus, Gwendal is expanding his range in English. Although he is used to giving straitlaced scientific papers at international conferences, his colloquial English is a mix of spaghetti Westerns, Fred Astaire, and early Beatles lyrics.

One evening, while I was making dinner, Gwendal decided to scrub down the bathroom. He emerged with a bottle of Ajax in one hand and a sponge in the other. "That was *some* dirty bathroom," he said, leaning against the door like John Wayne surveying the landscape from the porch of a saloon.

It's like living with a toddler; I have to censor myself. I never noticed the bizarre way I spoke English until I had someone mimicking me like a parrot. My vocabulary is a disorganized closet full of fifties slang and phrases plucked from my favorite nineteenth-century novels. Why be funny when you can be "deeply amusing" instead?

I'll be on the phone with Amanda in California, gossiping about an old friend. "I don't know what *she* thought of him, but clearly *he* thinks he's the cat's pajamas."

"The cat pajamas," said Gwendal later that night. "Can I use that?"

"Not unless you want to get your ass kicked."

Now that I was a full-time resident in Paris, it had become a ritual for *me* to get up on Saturday mornings and go to the bakery. Gwendal, as most men would, chose his *boulangerie* by which one was the fewest number of steps from his bed. Turns out, another hundred paces in the opposite direction, there is an infinitely better *boulangerie*. The kind of *boulangerie* dreams are made of, with a big glass window displaying neat rows of lemon tarts and chocolate éclairs, and an open kitchen door, so you can smell the *pains aux chocolats* even before you turn the corner. They also make what I consider to be the perfect croissant.

She just got there, you say. How would she know? The glorious thing about France is that it takes no time at all to become a snob about these things. Falling deeply in love with a pastry is easy.

Where croissants are concerned, I've found two principal schools of thought. Some prefer a brioche-like model, with a golden hue, a little spring, and an eggy chew. Not I. I like flake, a croissant with an outer layer so fine and brittle that you get crumbs all over yourself from the very first bite. When you pull it apart there should be some empty space, pockets of air between the buttery layers of dough. When you finally do rip off a hunk to dip in your coffee, it stretches a little before it breaks. More crumbs, but utterly, completely worth the mess. I've abandoned my *chouquettes*. Pastry love is fickle that way.

My first trips to the *boulangerie* are not all ogling. I have to keep my head about me as I place my order. First there is the gender issue; every French noun is assigned a sex, masculine or feminine. Personally, I think my croissant is a woman, as tender and fragile as a Brontë heroine. But apparently, the Académie Française, the guys who make the dictionary, have decided that "croissant" is masculine, *un croissant*. I have been outvoted.

Along with his croissant, Gwendal usually requests a *financier*. These mini almond cakes were traditionally made in the form of a gold ingot. Here they are round, like an giant one-pound coin. Gwendal always gives me a piece of the crisp exterior and keeps the humid center for himself. I strain to hear the amount I owe as I take my bag. There is no time for repeats. There's a line out the door and three women weaving behind the counter to avoid a collision.

"*Bonne journée*," I say to no one in particular as I walk out the door.

If I'd been able to read the paper those first few weeks in Paris, I would have been more aware than I actually was that the world was coming to an end. I had landed in France in the middle of a heated presidential election. The Left couldn't seem to get its act together, and in the confusion the extreme Right candidate Jean-Marie Le Pen had made it past the primaries to face the sitting president Jacques Chirac in the final runoff for the presidency. Paris was up in arms. Saturday morning was May Day — French Labor Day — and I was about to be initiated into a national sport: *la manif*.

With a fervor left over from the heated strikes and student protests of 1968, the French like nothing better than to take to the streets. Doesn't much matter what for; one thing you learn quickly in France, there's always something to be against: the new government, the old government, the European Union, fewer teachers, fewer holidays, regulations about how much bacteria you can put in your cheese or how much wax you can put in your chocolate. You name it, someone thinks it's a terrible idea. Nobody is offering a viable solution. That, presumably, is next week's job. Today it is just the joyful frenzy of a collective "*non!*"

Suddenly everyone had become a political activist. You couldn't pass a café table without hearing the rustle of a newspaper and the shaking of heads. "*C'est la vraie merde*" — we're in the shit. That much I understood.

The place de la République is a five-minute walk from the house. When we arrived at the base of the giant bronze statue representing the Republic of France (a toga-clad damsel holding an olive branch), there were already thousands of people grouped around brightly printed banners as music blared from flatbed trucks. There were students in tank tops and sunglasses, women in veils, and older lefties with rounded shoulders and light jackets (clearly those who had done these protests the first time around), their graying hair stuck upright on their heads as they smoked a last cigarette under the banner of their local union.

The atmosphere was casual, even upbeat. Maybe this is just what they do on Saturdays, like we go to the movies or get our nails done.

As the dragon's tail of people began its descent down the boulevard toward Bastille, the crush was overwhelming. By the end of the day more than a million people throughout France would be marching.

There was a man in front of me holding a sign: PLUTÔT ESCROC QUE FACHO. "What does that mean?" I said, pointing up at the hand-painted letters; my French slang was very limited.

"'*Escroc*' means 'crook,'" said Gwendal, "and '*facho*' is short for 'fascist.'"

"Better a crook than a fascist." Talk about the lesser of two evils.

There were quieter times. Chirac won the election with eighty-two percent of the vote, and instead of ranting about a political apocalypse, people could get back to grumbling about the status quo. As the weather warmed up, the café terraces filled with girls in dark glasses and flowered dresses. I felt the pace of the city slacken as workers and tourists and children seemed to ease into summer vacation.

While the rest of France was starting to think about going on holiday, I was trying to get back to work. Just before I left London, I'd been named new media editor of a small arts magazine. They needed someone to cover emerging trends — art projects on the Web, that sort of thing. I was an art historian who had worked for an Internet start-up and presumably knew how to use a computer — that seemed to be enough to make me an expert in this nascent field. The pay was wooden nickels, but it meant I would have my name on the masthead and some shiny new clips to show around. Plus it was an ideal beat for my new location. While I explored the art scene in Paris, I could surf the Net for international artists. It wasn't much, but it was a beginning.

I had bought Gwendal a picnic basket for his thirtieth birthday, wicker with a leather shoulder strap, real glasses, and (very practically, I thought) plates in heavy blue plastic of the kind I imagine they sell only at Bed Bath & Beyond. We were about to give it its first outing.

A picnic is about as far back to nature as I go. When I was growing up, my auntie Lynn had a house on a lake near Danbury, Connecticut. With her two sons we would stage "Pirates' Picnics," complete with a map hastily sketched on the back of a brown paper bag. There was a toadstool of an island in the middle of the lake, but to me we might as well have been in Nam. My mother planted soda cans and key chains for a scavenger hunt. We ate bologna sandwiches and potato chips and drank juice out of cardboard boxes poked with a plastic straw. As an adult, I progressed to the Jane Austen version — plaid blanket, long flowered dress, and somebody else to carry the overstuffed basket.

We walked up to the Buttes Chaumont, my new favorite park in Paris, sculpted from the ruins of one of Napoleon III's old gypsum quarries. In that uniquely nineteenth-century attempt to do nature one better, the park is filled with stucco rocks, fake rolling hills, an artificial waterfall, and a man-made lake stocked with swans and topped with a Grecian temple. Paris from up here looks like a toy village, jagged rooftops and the dome of Sacré-Coeur peeking over the trees. In addition to the theatrics, it has a unique advantage over all the other parks in Paris: you can sit on the grass.

We put down our blanket (a flowered flannel sheet, but hey, give me a little time) and started to unpack.

A picnic basket in Paris is like a treasure chest — untold riches in a limited space. The first apricots had appeared at the market, their skins fading from speckled red to glowing orange to burnished gold, like the sun-bleached walls of an Italian villa. There were tiny cucumbers, as thick as my thumb and curled like a ribbon. I'd become obsessed with a new fruit called a *pêche plate*, a flat peach. Imagine a perfectly ripe white peach that someone has sat on. Gwendal picked up a tomato and bit into it like an apple. I did the same.

At the bottom of the basket was a carefully folded square of waxed paper. Inside was a small mound of *rillettes*, shredded pork cooked in its own fat until meltingly smooth. Gwendal ripped off a piece of bread; I dusted the remains off his shirt. I've started calling him *le roi des miettes*, the king of crumbs.

I watched the couples walking around the lake. "Maybe it's the New Yorker in me. I'm too used to rushing around. But everyone here is so relaxed, it's like they're moving in slow motion."

"Why should they rush? They're not going to get anywhere."

Sometimes I really have no idea what he is talking about.

"You will never understand. You come from a place where everything is possible." We lay side by side on the grass, our eyes half closed.

"It's Henry Miller that said, 'In America, every man is potentially president. Here, every man is potentially a zero.'"

And then he told me a story.

"When I was sixteen it was time to decide what kind of studies I would pursue. I was the best in the class in Math and Physics, but also the best in Literature. I went to the school library and the woman behind the desk gave me a book. It was called *All the Jobs in the World*. I looked through it. I found two things I liked: scientific researcher and film director. I brought the book to the front and showed her my choices. '*Ah, non*,' she said. 'You forgot to look at the key.' And she pointed to the top of the page. Next to each job there were dollar signs — three dollar signs if the job paid a lot of money, one dollar sign if it paid very little. Next to the dollar sign was a door. If the door was wide open it was very easy to get this job, if the door was open just a little bit, it was very hard. '*Regarde*,' she said. 'You have picked only jobs with no dollar signs and a closed door. '*Tu n'y arriveras jamais.*' You will never get there.'

"'You should become an engineer,' she said. My parents had never met anyone who did these other things. We don't come from that world. They had no friends they could call to get me a job. They were afraid I would fail and they couldn't help me. They were afraid I would have no place in the society. And I didn't have the force to do it myself. I didn't want to disappoint them. So I became an engineer.

"It's just like that here. If you want to do something different, if your head sticks up just a little, they cut it off. It's been like that since the Revolution. You know the saying, *Liberté, égalité, fraternité. Egalité*, equality, is right in the middle. Everyone has got to be the same."

Of all the stories Gwendal has told me, before or since, this is the one shocked me the most. Never in my life, not once, had anyone ever told there was something I couldn't do, couldn't be.

By the time he finished talking, I was sitting straight up, ready to pick a fight. I was furious on his behalf. He was so smart, so focused. He could do anything. Gwendal was still lying on the grass, enjoying the sunshine. He didn't look bitter or enraged. That's just the way it was, and it wasn't going to keep him from taking an after-lunch siesta.

"What kind of country makes a deliberate policy of squashing the best and brightest in favor of mediocrity?" I said, brow furrowed and mind racing. "And what kind of guidance counselor is *that*, who tells you you're going to fail before you even *start*!"

I was off to the races, my own little monologue. "But you're doing it," I said. "You work with films every day now."

He opened his eyes and looked at me. "When I finished my PhD, I had a thought for this woman and her book. How do you say it? 'One down, one to go.'"

The sun was fading as we folded our flannel sheet and stowed the glasses in the pocket of the picnic basket.

It occurred to me as we walked down the hill toward home, hands lightly intertwined: if I chose Gwendal in part to confound expectations, maybe he chose me for the same reason.

Three Recipes for a French Picnic

SAVORY "CAKE" WITH BACON, CHERVIL, AND FIGS
Cake Salé aux Lardons et aux Figues

Somewhere between a tea cake and a quiche, *cake salé* is a marvelous invention; it often graces buffet tables at parties. You can vary the filling as you choose — olives, hazelnuts, feta, bacon, artichokes, and sun-dried tomatoes have all gone into the mix at one point or another. This is one of my favorite combinations, adapted from *Cakes Salés et Sucrés* by Christian Ecckhout (Editions Aubéron, 2007).

> $1\frac{1}{4}$ cups flour
> 1 tablespoon baking powder
> 225 g lardons, *pancetta, or bacon, cut into* $\frac{1}{2}$ cm cubes
> 4 eggs
> $\frac{1}{4}$ teaspoon fine sea salt or table salt
> $\frac{1}{2}$ cup olive oil
> $\frac{1}{2}$ cup milk
> 8 dried figs (the tender, partially rehydrated kind)
> 2 packed tablespoons chervil, chopped
> 1 cup grated Comté cheese, lightly packed

Preheat the oven to 160°C.

In a small bowl, sift together flour and baking powder. Line a 23 by 13-cm metal loaf pan with baking paper (I use a brilliant red silicone version instead).

In a small frying pan, fry the *lardons* until they have rendered their fat; drain on a paper towel.

In a medium bowl, whisk together the eggs and salt. Add the oil and milk; whisk until light and foamy.

Add the flour mixture to the egg mixture and whisk until just combined. Don't overwork the batter — a lump or two is fine.

Add the remaining ingredients and stir lightly to combine. Transfer the batter to your loaf pan. Bake for 1 hour, until a toothpick comes out clean. Cool for a few minutes in the pan, then unmould onto a wire rack and cool completely. Place the loaf on the picnic blanket (or coffee table) and let your guests cut themselves a slice. Store wrapped in aluminium foil.

Yield: Serves 8–10 as an hors d'oeuvre

POTATO AND GREEN BEAN SALAD
WITH PASTIS VINAIGRETTE
Salade de Haricots et de
Pommes de Terre au Pastis

Pastis is a refreshing summer *apéritif*, particularly beloved in the south of France. Here it adds a licorice kick to crunchy beans and creamy potatoes.

> 2 teaspoons white wine vinegar
> 1 tablespoon lemon juice
> 1 tablespoon pastis or anisette
> 1/4 teaspoon coarse sea salt
> 1/4 teaspoon freshly ground black pepper
> 1 teaspoon Dijon mustard
> 1/3 cup extra-virgin olive oil or more, up to 1/2 cup, to taste
> 750 g small red potatoes, halved or quartered
> 375 g haricots verts, *extra-thin French green beans*, blanched
> 1 small red onion, minced
> 1/2 cup flat-leaf parsley, finely chopped
> 1 tablespoon fresh thyme (if you can't find fresh, skip it)
> 1/2 cup tiny black niçoise olives

Combine the first seven ingredients for the vinaigrette in a glass jar or other airtight container. Shake vigorously to combine. You can make the vinaigrette several days in advance.

Place the potatoes in a pot of lightly salted cold water, bring to a boil, and cook them until tender (20 to 30 minutes).

Meanwhile, trim the beans and blanch them in lightly salted water for 3 to 4 minutes. They should remain bright green and retain their snap. Drain and rinse them under cold water; pat them dry with a paper towel.

Drain the potatoes. While they are still warm, place them in a large bowl with the onion, parsley, thyme, olives, and green beans. Add the vinaigrette and toss to coat. Leave in the fridge for an hour so that the flavors have a chance to blend. This salad is best served at room temperature.

Yield: Serves 4–6

MINI ALMOND CAKES WITH
A RASPBERRY BUTTON
Financiers aux Framboises

With a raspberry in the center and crisp golden edges, these little cakes are pretty enough for a *pâtisserie* window. This recipe comes from my Argentinean friend Fernanda, who has the looks of a beauty queen and the sweet tooth of a five-year-old. She once brought an entire batch of these to a lazy Sunday picnic — they disappeared before sunset.

> *¾ cup demerara sugar*
> *¾ cup plus 2 tablespoons ground almonds*
> *⅓ cup flour*
> *200 g unsalted butter, melted*
> *4 egg whites*
> *A pinch of salt*
> *1 egg yolk*
> *½ teaspoon vanilla extract*
> *150 g raspberries*

Preheat the oven to 220°C.

Pulse the sugar in a blender or food processor to obtain a fine powder. (Sometimes I just bash it in the bottom of the bowl with a potato masher.) Combine with the ground almonds and flour.

Meanwhile, melt the butter over gentle heat; let cool.

Whip the egg whites and salt into what the French call a *mousse,* just till they're frothy. This takes no time at all, 10 seconds max. You should stop when you have liquid underneath and bubble-bath-like foam on top. Gently fold the egg whites into the dry ingredients.

Fold in the egg yolk and vanilla. Then add the melted butter. Don't panic; this will look like a flood — just continue to fold gently and the butter will incorporate itself.

Spoon large, drippy tablespoons of batter into nonstick mini muffin molds; I use flexible silicone ones. Gently place a raspberry in the center of each *financier*. Don't push it in too far, or it will sink completely during baking. Bake on the center rack for 10 to 11 minutes, until the edges are crisp and golden, the insides tender.

Let the *financiers* cool 10 minutes in the pan. Transfer them to a wire rack to cool completely.

Yield: Makes 25 mini *financiers*

CHAPTER 7

FIG FEST

Gwendal was away at tap-dance camp (you heard me) and I was left to my own devices in Paris for Bastille Day. My friend Courtney had recently moved to London to write a book, and we decided to make a girlie week of it.

I've known Courtney since my senior year of college, when we bonded over being stranded back on a snowy hilltop in Ithaca after spending our junior year abroad in Europe. Smart and bitingly funny, she is also modest to a fault. She was a reporter for the *Miami Herald* at the tender age of fourteen, and by the time I got around to visiting her in DC a year after graduation, she was a staff writer for a local news magazine. When we got to her apartment — a perfect storm of books, papers, empty Diet Coke bottles, and other feminine debris — I noticed a small blue and white package on the bookshelf.

"What's this?" I asked.

"Oh, those are the M&Ms from Air Force One," she said, not looking up from what she was doing. I still haven't gotten the full story.

Courtney arrived on Monday. With Gwendal gone, we could do all the things you can't do when boys are around — namely, shop, flirt, and totally pig out.

Actually, the pig-out would have to wait, because our first destination was a party for Paris Fashion Week. If New York fashion parties were an accurate predictor, we would be drinking heavily, but no one would be eating anything at all. I'd been invited by Wendy, a PR person I knew back home; the label she represented was hot with the art crowd, and I was thinking of writing a story. In the three months since I'd moved to Paris, I hadn't been to a single party. I was eager to get dressed up and *go somewhere*, dying to talk to somebody other than the guy who sold me my courgettes.

When a non–fashion person gets dressed for a fashion party, there's no sense in straying too far from the obvious — black with a little cleavage and the highest shoes in the closet. Balanced precariously on one of our two folding chairs, I wrested my black lizard sandals from the crawl space in the hall, where I had stored nonessentials that I didn't want to trip over every morning. I had managed to squeeze two of my mother's vintage handbags into my luggage allotment. I popped in lipstick and ID — not for bars, no need here, but Gwendal told me I should carry identification at all times. Unlike England or the United States, the police in France have the right to randomly stop you on the metro and ask for your paperwork.

The party was on the other side of the river, in a residential district behind the Luxembourg Gardens. This, I'm guessing, is the Paris equivalent of how-the-other-half-lives. We heaved open a set of cathedral-sized double doors that revealed not a courtyard but a private *street*. It was like walking onto the closed set of a movie — Paris 1900. Narrow two-story houses lined either side of a cobblestone lane. Wisteria vines hung from the roofs and small cherry trees littered the ground with white blossoms. Without a single glass of champagne between us, Courtney and I were already stumbling around like drunkards.

"There must be special lessons in French high school," muttered Courtney, almost turning her ankle. "On how to walk down a cobblestone street in stilettos."

"Yup," I said, grabbing her arm to steady myself for a graceful entry. "Right after Balzac."

It was easy to see where we were going. The front garden was lit with candles; there was a table stacked with empty bottles and someone playing the guitar, very badly. I had a brief thought for the French neighbors, whose families have probably owned these houses since Napoleon. They must love it when the Americans come to town. It was the designer's birthday, and I arrived with an elaborately ribboned box of chocolates from Gérard Mulot, a fancy pastry shop in Saint-Germain.

"Thanks sooo much!" She looked at the box like a bomb that was about to explode in her hands and hastily dumped it on a side table.

The house was the kind of country chic you find only in the city, with a long wooden table and armoires bigger than my bathroom. Presumably Wendy was still upstairs getting dressed. These are the kind of (nauseating) people who don't even need a room at the Ritz, because whatever city they happen to be in, they always have somewhere fabulous to "crash." We had been there for a half hour (we were an hour and a half late) when she finally appeared from her bedroom in white tights, Marc Jacobs sandals, and a skirt whose circumference rivaled my mother's prom dress. "Hiii. It's *so* great you came." She kissed me on both cheeks (at least I had that down) and promptly disappeared.

After that no one spoke to us — in French or in English — and I made one too many trips back to the dimly lit kitchen to refill my glass. As we milled around, doing our best to look casual, the thought occurred to me more than once: *What in the name of Karl Lagerfeld am I doing here?* I was wearing the same clothes, holding the same drink, as a night out in New York, but everything felt wrong. I didn't belong to this amped-up jet set. Certainly Gwendal would think these people were shallow and ridiculous. Only three months out of Manhattan, and my sense of destiny, of arrogant momentum, was beginning to desert me. I was trailing my old life into my new life like toilet paper stuck to the bottom of my black lizard heels. I was trying too hard. It was conspicuous and embarrassing, and I wasn't having any fun.

We managed to find a taxi back to the canal, taking off our shoes for the final flight of spiral stairs. In less than twenty-four hours, Courtney and I had transformed the apartment into a college dorm room. There were clothes strewn over chairs and overstuffed cosmetic bags balancing on the ledge above our fishbowl-sized bathroom sink. The futon frame in the living room was broken, so once the bed was open it was just easier to leave it that way. Since the mattress took up most of the room, we ended up walking back and forth across the pillows to get from the bathroom to the hall.

I could tell that Courtney was a little surprised by the apartment. Just as I had my vision of her as Roving Reporter, Next Great American Novelist, she had this thing about me as Glamour Girl — vintage coats, pearls, and opera tickets. The last time she'd seen me I was sharing a cavernous house in Islington with double-height ceilings and a *sitting room*. Sure, a love nest in Paris sounded glamorous as well — very *La Bohème* — but I don't think she was expecting the mattress on the floor or a metal coatrack for a closet. How could I explain that curled up on the broken futon, inches from the matted blue carpet, I was more at home than I'd ever been in London. That on the two-burner electric hot plate I'd made some of the best meals of my life. As Courtney wedged herself past the toilet to step up and into our Lilliputian shower, I saw her glance at Gwendal's tatty green robe on the back of the bathroom door. I had adopted it, my equivalent of a high school letterman's jacket.

"That's the great thing about living with somebody," I said. "You only need one bathrobe."

The next morning I took Courtney up to Belleville. Summer is showing-off season at the market. Pyramids of apricots and peaches are piled high like the treasures in Ali Baba's cave. Boxes of tiny *fraises des bois* — wild strawberries — glow like edible rubies, and teardrop-shaped figs are nestled in pallets of straw. We weren't really awake; after hanging out with the fashionistas, getting up before noon seemed a bit of a stretch. The market packs up at one p.m., so we were late enough to be in competition with the Asian grannies, shopping at the last minute in hopes of reduced prices. When they steal, which I'd witnessed more than once — one peach in the plastic bag, one in their purse — the vendors shout at them in mock Chinese gibberish and hit them on the hands with cardboard fruit cartons.

After three months in France, I still hadn't quite mastered the numbers — or the quantities. Still foggy from one too many *kirs royals,* the language came at my head like a hail of bullets *doekillo, doekillo dekillohewnhurosankant deux kilos, deux kilos, deux kilos un euro cinquante, 2 kg, 1.50 €.* Fractions were always a problem for me... is a kilo half a pound, or double? We stood mute in front of the mountain of fruit. The man behind the counter was itching to unload his stock. Before I could protest, he filled up a hefty bag: *dekillohewnhurosankant.*

It is in this manner that Courtney and I ended up with a hangover *and* four and a half pounds of overripe figs.

We ate them for breakfast and as a midnight snack — three days in a row. On the fourth day we still had an entire paper bag full of figs, and the bottom was starting to get soggy.

I remember a wholesale market my mother used to take me to in Paterson, New Jersey. She would buy trays of overripe peaches and plums and we would go home and make compote. How hard could it be? Eager to give it a French twist, and in keeping with the booze-infused tone of the week, I decided we should add some alcohol. We went to the supermarket and found some Sauternes. Did I read that in a magazine? We soaked the fruit and added honey; a vanilla bean may have fallen into the mix. We stewed and stirred and waited for the juices to thicken. Never quite happened. It wasn't what you'd call a raging success, but spooned over vanilla ice cream it wasn't half bad.

All this culinary creativity was exhausting. We went back to bed.

I had an itinerary all planned out. We made a good faith effort to go to the decorative arts museum — only to find that it was closed for renovations. The semi-annual sales were on, so we did a little shopping. I'm a tallish size ten, but the disparaging look from the bitty-breasted salesgirl seated behind the counter (on what I can only imagine was her concave ass) was enough to tell us that the sweaters would strain across our chests and the pants would barely get past our knees. After that, we concentrated on food.

I wanted Courtney to taste everything I'd tasted these past few months, and although I didn't have the city entirely figured out, I had a number of culinary landmarks on my mental map that I could display with the authority of a native.

Our first destination was Berthillon on the Ile Saint-Louis. Berthillon is France's most celebrated ice cream maker.

Although it was the middle of July, the owners were on vacation. They sell their stock to other shops and restaurants and, in the true measure of French success, take the entire summer off. There are a number of Berthillon stands to chose from; avoiding the hordes of tourists while maintaining a broad selection of flavors requires insider savvy. I walked us to the other side of the island, as far as possible from the gardens behind Notre Dame. There was still a line, but a bit of waiting is a good thing; you need time to choose between pink grapefruit and raspberry sorbet or cinnamon and honey nougat ice cream. They serve golf ball–sized scoops, so you have to be a real purist to walk away with just one *boule*. Courtney and I both got doubles — pear and cacao amer (bitter chocolate) for her, peach and rhubarb for me.

You don't have to give women ice cream to get them to talk, but it helps. Down at the tip of the Ile Saint-Louis, our feet dangling over the Seine, we started one of those endless conversations, like two ten-year-olds at a sleepover. Ah, girl talk. We would sit there until every morsel of information had been observed and chewed over and observed again, the carcass picked dry by a couple of lipsticked vultures. It felt so good to be speaking English, I could have gone on for a month.

A year's worth of details came tumbling out. Courtney was trying to decide if an almost-kiss at a London bus stop constituted a seduction attempt by one of her editors. "We were both so drunk, it was hard to tell. Was it leaning, or *leaning* leaning?"

She didn't know much about Gwendal. Until very recently, he was referred to in e-mails as "The Frenchman," the kind of anonymous nickname we gave to the passing men in our lives: Dumb Dave, Patrick the Pathological PhD Student, Stubble Boy. It felt good to be breaking down my relationship with Gwendal as if it were just another first date instead of the rest of my life, the analysis of minutiae covering for the real questions.

Minutia: He doesn't even own a suit. How did he survive thirty-one years on this planet without a suit?

Real question: How is it possible that a man this smart, this cultivated, never went anywhere — a wedding, a funeral, a job interview — that required a tie?

Minutia: Paris is amazing, but the whole city feels a little bit like a museum. Everything seems a bit stuck — and everyone seems to think that's normal.

Real question: Do I really want my children to grow up in a country where the first answer to every question seems to be "no?"

Minutia (OK, not really): Isn't marriage the last great way to change your life?

Real question: Is this the change I want?

The fact is, Gwendal was simply not who I'd been expecting (and I'd been expecting who I'd been expecting for quite some time). Like most women I know, I was born with a Prince Charming checklist: Is he tall enough, smart enough, rich enough? Has he been places? Is he going places? The list goes on and on. I am fully aware that this kind of musing grinds the feminist movement back to the Stone Age. Though I was raised by an independent single mother, I always fantasized that my husband would be some practical banker type who would earn enough for me to pursue my artistic interests and still send the kids to a decent college.

"How are we supposed to be two creative people in a couple? We'll starve to death," I continued crunching into the tip of my cone.

"He has a job. And a PhD." Courtney stood up, crumpling her napkin.

"He's practically a Communist."

"You'd prefer a Republican?"

"He tap-dances."

She shrugged, as if to say, That one, you're on your own.

All these things whirring around in my head didn't quite get to the bottom of it. There was something else about Gwendal that made me uncomfortable. I couldn't quite put my finger on it.

Yes I could.

"He's just so fucking happy all the time. It's weird."

It was as simple as that. He's a happy person and I am fundamentally suspicious of happy people. In the America I grew up in, little kids don't say, "When I grow up, I want to be happy." That's not the appropriate end to that sentence. We say, "When I grow up, I want to be a doctor, an astronaut, a fighter pilot." Happiness to me was something very abstract, the end of a long equation: initial self-worth multiplied by x accomplishments, divided by y dollars, z loans, minus f hours worked, plus g respect earned. Happiness, I assumed, would be the end result of a whole list of things I hadn't gotten around to yet.

Plus, I have lousy genes for happiness. My father's depression is like a shadow, some days it walks in front of me, some days behind. I've learned to watch myself. Is this *a* bad day, or *the* bad day? The one I never quite recover from.

I worried that Gwendal was too contented, that if he wasn't constantly striving (and therefore constantly dissatisfied) like myself, that there was something wrong, something missing.

"How is he ever supposed to be successful? He needs to be a little bit miserable, like us. It's how you get to the next thing."

There was something else.

"When I'm with him, everything is wonderful and I can't imagine being anywhere else. But when I'm on my own — there's just... nothing. I can't work, I can't study, I can't even read a magazine on the metro. I've always known that by living abroad I made the choice to be a little bit uncomfortable, one-sixteenth of an inch out of step. That's the price I pay for not being bored at home. Still, you have to wonder if there isn't something wrong with me."

I looked down at the river lapping at the stones beneath our feet. "How can anyone choose to be this lonely?"

Saturday night was the 13th of July. The fireworks at the Eiffel Tower were for tourists; we were going to a fireman's ball. The *bal des pompiers* is a French Independence Day tradition; each Bastille Day the local fire stations throw a party, open to the neighborhood.

The French love their firemen; they are truly the first responders. Whether it's a gas leak or a heart attack, in France you don't call a plumber or an ambulance; you dial 18 for the *pompiers*.

I don't know if they select on looks, but I certainly wouldn't rule it out. They are also the only people in Paris you will see openly exercising, running through the Tuileries Gardens in tight standard-issue navy Ts. You need to be in pretty good shape to run up six flights of spiral stairs with a stretcher.

We got to the entrance at around midnight — me and my fabulous sense of direction had underestimated the distance — climbing the hill into Ménilmontant for what seemed like hours.

Even at this time of night, there was a line. We paid our three euros and got our hands stamped. "I thought we said we'd never go to another frat party," said Courtney as we walked inside. This particular fire station had a parking lot in the interior courtyard, and the place had been completely transformed. Streamers and flags hung from the bandstand. There were tables selling wine and beer and fries and little plates of *saucisson*. There were *pommes d'amour* and *barbe à papa* for the kids. Personally, I never met a candy apple I didn't like. I wondered if I could buy one without a five-year-old to hand it off to. The *bal* was the only event I'd attended in France where I'd seen wine served in plastic cups.

There was a swing band on the stage and dozens of couples turning like tops. Courtney got whisked way. Fathers swayed back and forth with kids on their shoulders.

It was only a matter of time before the striptease began. One of the firemen, with a blonde crew cut and the cuffs of his pants still tucked into his regulation boots, jumped up on the bandstand, whipped off his shirt, circled it slowly above his head, and tossed it into the cheering crowd.

It was three a.m. before we headed down the hill toward home. We walked along the boulevard de Belleville arm and arm, singing old camp songs at the top of our lungs.

Miss Lucy had a baby.
She named it Tiny Tim.
She put it in the bathtub
To see if it could swim.

We were loud, raucous, totally inappropriate. And anyone who had seen us on the boulevard that night would have smiled. Just a couple of happy idiots, drunk on life. It felt so good to be acting out instead of trying to fit in.

When Gwendal turned the key in the door on Sunday afternoon, we had just gotten out of bed. "Having fun?" he said, surveying the wreckage. "Mm-hmm," I mumbled with my mouth full. We'd been caught red-handed: two American college girls in our pajamas at three p.m. with the freezer door open and our spoons in a container of pear sorbet.

Recipes for Summer Fruit

GOAT CHEESE SALAD
WITH FRESH FIGS
Salade de Chèvre Chaud aux Figues Fraîches

Fresh figs and snow-white goat cheese are a match made in heaven. Walk by any café terrace in Paris during the summer months and you'll find someone eating this simple green salad topped with a *tartine* of crusty bread and fresh melted cheese. The figs are my special touch of late summer sweetness.

> 1 small head of red Batavia or lollo rosso lettuce
> 4 fresh figs
> 2 tablespoons best-quality extra-virgin olive oil
> 2 teaspoons balsamic vinegar
> ¼ teaspoon coarse sea salt
> 1 teaspoon Dijon mustard
> 250–300 g soft goat cheese, cut into 1 cm slices
> 2 large, thin slices sourdough bread, cut from a round
>   boule (pain Poilâne is the gold standard in Paris) or
>   3 slices of whole grain toast

Preheat the oven to 240°C. Wash the lettuce and dry it thoroughly. Rinse the figs and gently pat them dry; cut into quarters. In a small bowl, whisk together the oil, vinegar, salt, and mustard. Toss with the lettuce and figs.

For the goat cheese toasts: Place the goat cheese rounds on top of the bread. I like to make 1 large or 3 smaller toasts per person. If using bread from a square loaf, cut slices in half on the diagonal so you have 6 triangles. Bake on the middle rack of your oven for 5 to 6 minutes, until the cheese is softened and beginning to color.

Divide the salad between two plates. Top with the goat cheese toasts and find yourself a sunny spot!

Yield: Serves 2

DUCK BREASTS WITH BLACKBERRIES
Magret du Canard aux Mûres

When I moved to France, Nicole introduced me to a beautiful series of brightly colored pamphlets printed on handmade paper with uncut edges — mini cookbooks with ten recipes for a single ingredient. This is especially helpful in a Parisian market, where blackberries or white asparagus might appear for three weeks and then disappear until the following year. This recipe is adapted from *Le Canard, dix façons de le préparer*, by Pierre Dubarry and Georges Audabram, 2002. Duck breasts are wonderful with seasonal fruit — try the same sauce with sliced mango.

> 2 duck breasts
> A good pat butter (about 2 teaspoons)
> 1 tablespoon sugar
> 1½ cups blackberries
> Splash (½ teaspoon) of sherry vinegar (or red wine vinegar)
> 1 tablespoon chicken broth

Place the duck breasts, skin side down, in a nonstick frying pan. Cook over low heat until they render their fat and the skins are golden and crisp. If you are being really French, reserve the fat to sauté some potatoes you've parboiled and drained.

Meanwhile, melt the butter in a small frying pan, add the sugar and the berries, and stir, crushing the berries lightly with the back of a wooden spoon, until they release a bit of juice and begin to bubble.

Deglaze the pan with a splash of sherry vinegar. Add the chicken broth, reduce a tiny bit, and set aside.

Finish cooking the duck breasts, skin side up, for 3 minutes; they should stay deep pink in the middle. Pour any juice from the duck breasts into the sauce. Reheat lightly.

Serve the duck breasts, topped with sauce, with some skinny *haricots verts* and roasted potatoes.

Yield: Serves 2

STRAWBERRY RHUBARB CRUMBLE
Crumble Fraises Rhubarbe

Crumble has crossed the Channel. This traditional English dessert now graces the menu of every trendy French bistro. The topping is a slight variation on the crumble from Jane Stimpson's *New Food for Thought* (André Deutsch, 1994), the cookbook of a wonderful cubbyhole of a vegetarian restaurant near London's Covent Garden. The rhubarb — as far as I know the world's only hot pink vegetable — is a personal passion.

COMPOTE

½ cup vanilla sugar (or ½ cup sugar plus ½ teaspoon vanilla extract)
1 tablespoon cornflour
750 g rhubarb (the thinner and pinker the better), cut into 2 cm pieces
Zest and juice of 1 organic orange

CRUMBLE TOPPING

½ cup light brown or raw sugar
2 cups rolled oats
Scant ½ cup whole-wheat flour
½ cup plus ⅛ cup ground almonds
160 g cold butter

1 cup strawberries (halved or, if large, quartered)
2 tablespoons water

For the compote: Preheat the oven to 100°C. Combine sugar and cornflour in a bowl. Spread the rhubarb in a baking dish (I use a 25 cm oval casserole). Sprinkle it with the sugar mixture; zest and juice the orange directly into the dish. Stir to combine. Cook for 45 minutes, stirring once, until the rhubarb is tender. Let cool completely so the juices have time to thicken.

For the topping: Combine the dry ingredients in a bowl. Cut in the butter, first with two knives, then with your hands, until the mixture is crumbly. Everything up to this point can be done in advance and refrigerated.

Add the strawberries to the cooled rhubarb mixture. Add the water to the crumble mixture, 1 tablespoon at a time, stirring to combine.

Layer the topping over the fruit; bake on the bottom rack of the oven for 25 minutes, until golden and bubbly.

Tip: To make vanilla sugar, split 1 plump vanilla bean lengthwise, down the middle, and add to 1 kilogram white sugar. Let it sit for a few days. I use it as a substitute for regular sugar in most of my baked goods.

Yield: Serves 6–8

CHAPTER 8

THE LONG WINTER

I spent my first winter in Paris under the covers reading *War and Peace*. No better way to avoid making a decision than burying yourself in a big fat book. These were the grayest days of February, when the sky in Paris feels so close to the ground you can almost step on it. Nearly a year had passed since I put my toothbrush on the shelf above our tiny bathroom sink, but in many ways I still felt like a stranger in Paris. My name was on the gas bill, but I didn't have the right to work. I took the entrance exam for the Sorbonne, but failed because I didn't understand the directions at the top of the page. We talked vaguely about buying an apartment, but I didn't even have a French bank account. As I read about Napoleon's retreat across the Russian tundra, I thought more and more about going back to New York. There were two things standing in my way. One was a fear of going home with my tail between my legs; the other was a marriage proposal.

It happened one Sunday in August, just before I went back to the States for the Jewish New Year. Gwendal said we were going out for dinner; I put on a sundress and grabbed an umbrella, just in case. He told me, his voice on edge, to put it back. It wasn't going to rain.

We walked up to the Buttes Chaumont, enjoying the last of the pink-gray light, taking a winding path through the trees. We stopped in front of the waterfall (extra points for a waterfall, even a fake one), and that's when he pulled out the ring.

I am an impossible person to surprise, but this was not the first time, or the last, that he managed it. Tucked into a slip of black velvet was a light blue, almost violet sapphire, surrounded by tiny diamonds. It was old-fashioned and unusual. In other words, perfect for me. I held the box in my hand like a newborn bird, afraid that I might drop it.

"I want things to be clear," he said quietly. "I don't want us to be in a situation later on where we decide to get married so you can have a work visa or because we buy an apartment. I know what I want. I want to spend the rest of my life with you."

There it was, that phrase again. *I know what I want.* How was he always so damn *sure*?

As had so often been the case since I arrived in France, my emotions were upside down and backward. Here I was, at one of the defining moments of my life, and instead of twittering cartoon doves and a crescendo of Tchaikovsky in my head, my whole life flashed before my eyes, like the scene in a movie a split second before the fatal car crash.

"I just got here," I managed to stumble out, touched by his words and more than a little impressed with his bravery. "I need to have a life of my own."

And then, the dillydallying kiss of death: "I just need a little time."

I have no idea what we had for dinner; the proposal had obliterated my normally excellent memory for food. Strangely enough, Gwendal seemed perfectly composed. As we walked out of the restaurant he turned to me. "I know you're going to say yes. So you take all the time you need."

Now it was February. Six months had passed, the ring was stashed on top of a bookshelf in the hall, and I still hadn't made a decision.

The apartment that seemed like a charming love nest in July was now more like a giant icebox. The lack of central heating lost its *La Bohème* appeal when Gwendal wasn't there to snuggle in bed all day. We had worked out a system for the morning showers: Gwendal took the space heater from our bedroom to the bathroom when he went to work; by the time I got up the tiles had thawed from deep freeze to just plain cold.

The winter had taken away much of the pleasure of going to the market; the selection dwindled to onions, potatoes, gnarly roots, and some unnatural-looking strawberries from Jordan. So now I was stuck, like so many French peasants before me, with pantry staples: rice, lentils, canned tomatoes, alcohol.

Our two electric burners turned out to be extremely effective for this kind of hearty, slow-cooked food. I started with a French nursery favorite, *riz au lait*, classic rice pudding. The English recipe said to bake it for three hours in the oven, but lacking the necessary appliance (and the necessary patience), I decided to make mine a sweet risotto. I stirred and stirred, going around in circles in my head.

For the record, I'm not an indecisive person, and I'm not a coward. I just have a very detailed imaginary life, and it sometimes takes precedence over what's actually happening around me.

When I was seven, my mother let me wear lots of rhinestones and walk up the grand staircase at the Metropolitan Opera. She had reserved a table at the café for intermission — I still have the card somewhere. I had rum-raisin ice cream; I didn't like the taste, but I liked the *idea*.

My imaginary life has been getting in the way of reality ever since.

I spent my teens and early twenties dating boys with Waspy last names, a suspicious number of whom came from Westport, Connecticut. They represented the things I thought I wanted: wealth, status, security. They were the castles in my head, the done deal, the sure thing. My situation in Paris was pure potential.

Monet once said he wished he'd been born blind and suddenly recovered his sight, so he could see things as they really were, instead of how they were supposed to be. I needed to see Gwendal with fresh eyes. It was so difficult to peel away all the layers of cultural expectations and look at what was in front of me. Here was the smartest, kindest, happiest man I'd ever known. A man who wanted to build something, and he wanted to build it with me.

Holy matrimony. Like everything else, marriage was something I was convinced I had to be *good at*.

In fact, I didn't know very much about marriage at all. I didn't grow up around happily married people, and I wasn't sure what they looked like. I knew that my mother, in the opinion of her family, had "married down." My father was many wonderful things — funny, creative, charming, handsome — but he was not well educated, not well off, and perhaps this was the fatal one — not as intelligent as my mother. She loved him, but she also wanted to change him. And it didn't work. My father's very real struggle with mental illness aside, their marriage had set him up to fail. I didn't know a lot, but I knew this: what you see is what you get. People grow, but they don't change.

All those boys from Westport were so reassuring, like a kit with all the pieces numbered and the small screws sealed in tiny plastic bags. I knew they weren't going to turn out like my father. I didn't know how Gwendal was going to turn out. Neither did he.

There were many things he wanted to do, many things we could do together. But I felt deep down that if I wasn't prepared to spend the rest of my life with the man in front of me *right now* — the poorly paid French civil servant with no tie, an unheated bathroom, and a principled grudge against the Coca-Cola Corporation — I had no business marrying him at all.

And then there was Paris — beautiful, slightly inaccessible Paris, like the girl who lures you close with her ruffles and her scent, then leaves you in the doorway, cold and alone, with the barest hint of a good-night kiss. I felt like I was standing on the doorstep of a culture, and I wasn't sure if anyone was ever going to let me in. I couldn't just say yes to Gwendal. I had to say yes to Paris too.

The spoon made a milky path through the rice; with each stir the path disappeared, the mix felt a bit more solid. The settling aroma of vanilla filled the room. I'd been brave enough to get on the plane. What was stopping me from landing? I could still taste the sharpness of the rum-raisin ice cream melting on my tongue. I kept stirring and stirring.

One icy Sunday morning, Gwendal and I went for a walk in the neighborhood. The winter had put me in some kind of fashion Big Chill; it was simply too cold to be chic. I pulled on a fraying turtleneck sweater, jeans, and a pair of bulbous white Nikes that, because of my aversion to exercise, had survived from high school gym class. We walked down to the rue Oberkampf, stopping into a few *brocantes*, bric-a-brac shops selling old shaving mirrors, fifties furniture, and martini glasses.

We were standing in the middle of the street. "What do you want to do now?" I said, glancing briefly at the cover of *Paris Match* on a nearby newsstand.

"I want to marry you," he answered, cool and regular as if he were saying, "I want to go to the movies" or "I want to grab a coffee."

Somehow at that moment, the wonderful inevitability of it hit me. My imaginary life was through, and my new life, my real life, was standing in front of me on the Paris sidewalk. I stepped up and looked happiness in the face for the first time.

"I want to marry you too," I said.

Nobody decides her whole life in a single moment. But you *can* decide what you are unwilling to do without, and it was impossible for me to give up on this happiness. I wasn't sure I understood it, or was even capable of it. But I wanted it.

If Gwendal loved me in part for my sense of entitlement, for the arrogant optimism that said the world was mine for the taking, I loved him for his smile, his core, his sense that he was right with the world. I wanted every day for the rest of my life to grow from that first weekend in Paris — tender, alive, and *free*.

Turns out, I did want to be happy when I grew up.

"Let's go home and get the ring."

When we got back to the apartment Gwendal took the ring down from its hiding place and slipped it on my finger. "I cheated, you know," I said sheepishly. "I tried it on every day, right after you left for work. Didn't you notice there was no dust on the box?"

It was just getting dark as we pushed open the door to the Bistro Sainte Marthe. The place was empty; the staff were wiping down tables and chopping vegetables for dinner. I showed the barman my hand and said, in my best French accent: "*Champagne, s'il vous plaît.*"

We spent the rest of the evening on the phone — parents, grandparents, and friends. When I spoke to my friend Betsy in Boston, she sounded happy, but incredulous.

"You were wearing those sneakers?" she said.

"Yup."

"Wow, he must really love you."

Recipes to Substitute for Central Heating

RICE PUDDING WITH DRUNKEN RAISINS
Riz au Lait au Calvados

The ultimate cozy food, rice pudding is one of my childhood favorites. My mom once dated a man who managed a restaurant; he would bring back an industrial-sized sheet pan with a mottled cinnamon crust, which we would demolish practically overnight.

This recipe is essentially a sweet risotto. All the stirring is ideal for pondering boy problems. The Calvados gives it a distinctly adult kick.

> 6 cups milk
> ¼ cup sugar
> 1 vanilla bean, split and seeded
> ½ cup golden raisins
> ¼ cup plus 1 tablespoon Calvados (apple brandy)
> 1 heaping tablespoon butter
> 2 tablespoons light brown sugar
> 1 cup Arborio rice
> 1 heaping tablespoon crème fraîche, sour cream, or whipping cream
> Cinnamon and additional brown sugar to finish

Heat the milk over low heat; add the sugar and the vanilla seeds and pod. Keep the milk over a low heat; do not boil or let a skin form.

Soak the raisins in a bowl with the ¼ cup Calvados.

In a second, thick-bottomed saucepan, melt the butter with 1 tablespoon brown sugar over low heat. Mix in the rice and stir 1 minute, until it is slightly translucent. Keeping the heat relatively low (you want lazy bubbles rising to the surface), add a ladleful of milk, about ½ cup, stirring until the milk is almost absorbed. Continue in this manner, adding milk a ladleful at a time, stirring constantly for 40 to 45 minutes. Add the raisins and Calvados at the 20-minute mark.

The pudding is done when the rice is tender but there is still a good amount of creamy liquid in the pot. If you evaporate all the milk, the pudding will dry out when cooled. I usually have about ½ cup of milk left over. You can add it at the end, just for extra creamy security. Add the remaining brown sugar and Calvados. Let the pudding cool slightly, then add the *crème fraîche*. Spoon into six 180 g ovenproof ramekins and chill. The pudding can be made to this point a day ahead.

Before serving, sprinkle the pudding with a bit of cinnamon and brown sugar; put the ramekins under the grill for 2 minutes, until the sugar has caramelized.

Yield: Serves 6

LENTILS WITH WHITE WINE, HERBS, AND TOMATOES
Lentilles au Vin Blanc

This recipe has become one of my favorite solo suppers. I make a big pot when Gwendal is away on business and chip away at it all week. Simple, hearty, and healthful, all you need is a green salad, some crusty bread, and an oozy cheese to feel like you never want to leave the house again.

> 2 tablespoons extra-virgin olive oil
> 1 carrot, roughly chopped
> 4–5 small shallots or 1 medium onion, roughly chopped
> 2½ cups dried Puy lentils
> 6 cups chicken broth
> 410 g can whole tomatoes, drained and chopped
> 1 cup dry white wine
> A handful of fresh flat-leaf parsley, including some of the
>   stems, chopped
> 1 bay leaf (fresh, if possible)
> Fresh ground black pepper to taste
>
> Sour cream or crème fraîche
> Chopped fresh coriander
> 3 limes, halved

In a large stockpot, heat the oil over medium heat. Add the shallots and carrot and sauté for 5 to 10 minutes, until the onion is translucent.

Add the lentils and stir to coat with the oil. Add the broth, tomatoes, wine, parsley, bay leaf, and a good grinding of pepper. Leave to simmer over a low heat with the cover ajar until the lentils are tender and most of the liquid has been absorbed, about 1 hour.

Serve in shallow bowls with a dollop of sour cream, a sprinkling of chopped fresh coriander, and (essential!) half a lime for squeezing.

For easy entertaining: Top the lentils and sour cream with a pan-fried or grilled salmon fillet, squeeze the lime over the fish, and sprinkle with coriander.

Tip: The leftovers freeze well. They also make great soup: just throw in a bit of extra broth and a dash of white wine and puree. Serve the soup with the same condiments.

Yield: Serves 6

BRAISED BEEF WITH RED WINE, GARLIC, AND THYME
Daube de Boeuf

Warning: this is not your grandmother's pot roast. It's infinitely better, with silky sauce and big chunks of meat that fall apart with the touch of a fork. I leave you to fight over the bone — the marrow is heaven spread on a piece of fresh baguette.

> 2 kg rump or chuck pot roast, or brisket, cut into 6 large pieces
> 1 marrow bone
> Coarse sea salt and fresh ground pepper
> 1–2 tablespoons olive oil
> 6 large shallots, whole
> 6 large cloves of garlic, whole
> 1 carrot, chopped
> Zest of ½ navel orange, peeled in two long strips
> 400 g can whole tomatoes
> 1 cup full-bodied red wine
> 1 cup chicken broth
> 1 bouquet garni (6 sprigs parsley, 1 bay leaf, 8 sprigs thyme, tied with string)
> 4 carrots, halved
> 12 cremini or button mushrooms
>
> A handful of flat-leaf parsley, chopped

Preheat the oven to 160°C.

In a large casserole dish, brown the meat and marrow bone on all sides, sprinkling generously with sea salt and black pepper, 15 to 20 minutes. Remove the meat and bone; set aside.

Add the olive oil, shallots, garlic, chopped carrot, and orange zest; cook until softened, about 10 minutes.

Return the meat and bone to the pot and add the tomatoes (crush them between your fingers) with juice, wine, and broth.

The sauce should come about three-quarters of the way up around the meat. Add the herbs. Bring to a simmer.

Cover and put in the oven for 1½ hours. Turn the meat and cook for another 1½ hours. Add the carrots and mushrooms and cook for another 40 minutes, until the vegetables are cooked through and the meat is fork-tender. Discard the bouquet garni.

Serve the beef surrounded by the vegetables. Sprinkle with chopped parsley. Make sure you have some boiled fingerling potatoes or egg noodles to soak up the sauce.

Yield: Serves 6

Tip: This stew tastes great, possibly even better, the next day. Chill it overnight, skim off the fat, and reheat it for dinner. If you need extra liquid to reheat, use equal parts chicken broth and red wine.

Equipment: There is only one pot in my kitchen that I could not live without — my casserole dish. A pot that goes easily from the stovetop to the oven is essential for braised dishes like this one. I use a cherry red Le Creuset. For all but the most formal dinners, I take it straight to the table.

CHAPTER 9

MEET THE PARENTS

My parents came to Paris in March to meet their future in-laws and help us look for an apartment. Mom wasn't buying my bullshit about *La Bohème*. An apartment without heat is an apartment without heat.

I call them my parents, but in fact I mean Mom and Paul. Paul is what most people would call my stepfather, but I call him my fairy godfather, because he sort of fell out of the sky one day and lots of wonderful things happened.

If we're comparing first dates, in many ways my parents' story is more of a whirlwind romance than Gwendal's and mine. They were introduced by mutual friends at the end of my sophomore year in college. Paul was recently widowed with two grown children. My mother had just returned from a six-week trip to Tibet, a lifelong dream. Her suitcases were still lying half-unpacked on the living room floor when he came to pick her up on a Friday evening. Paul's grandson Lucas was born that night, and while Paul was at the hospital on Saturday morning my mother called me, a little too early, in my Ithaca studio: "If this man is still around on Monday, I'm going to marry him." He moved in on Wednesday, and has been with us ever since.

As my grandmother never hesitated to remind her, Paul was the kind of man my mother should have married the first time around: smart and kind, stable and successful. Jewish, but not too Jewish. A born techie who worked for IBM in the 1960s before starting his own business, Paul now spends most of his time researching mother–daughter long-distance calling plans.

Nicole and Yanig's first date was a product of the high hippie days. They met not during the "Summer of Love" but during the "summer of strikes" — the student protests of 1968. They met through a mutual friend, one evening at the local cinema. She thought, in case of a riot, it would be a good idea to be going out with someone tall. Their wedding picture is telling: Nicole in a flowered micromini, Yanig with a long beard and a short tie. (He kept the beard, lost the tie.) He looks as though he came straight from one of his meetings of the anarcho-syndicalists. (It's hard to explain. In France, even the anarchists want a union.) There are wonderful photos of toddler Gwendal and his parents walking in the woods, Yanig smoking a pipe, Nicole with her waist-length blonde hair flowing over a particularly shaggy sheepskin coat.

Now these two couples were coming together for the most important first date since their own.

If Gwendal and I had been the producers of a reality TV show, we couldn't have rigged the setting more carefully. In a narrow passage in the residential 12th arrondissement, Le Picotin spills over warmth from the moment you walk in the door: bright yellow walls and red checkered curtains, the only music is the animated clinking of silverware and glasses. We called ahead for the restaurant's specialty, *épaule d'agneau confit,* slow-roasted shoulder of lamb. Real estate agents will tell you to bake cookies when you are trying to sell your house. It makes buyers feel as though they are already home. Le Picotin smelled like a farmhouse before a big holiday dinner. If you can conjure up the feeling of "home," why not "family"?

As on any first date, everyone had dressed carefully, my mother in black with one of her vintage brooches, Nicole with a brightly colored scarf slung just so over her shoulders. The contrast was striking: Nicole, tiny and blonde, capable of sitting in silence with a volume of Lacan and a pot of herbal tea for hours at a time; my mother, tall, with jet-black hair and hands always in motion, the kind of person who talks to strangers on planes and trains.

We sat down at the narrow table against the warm leather banquettes, one couple on each side, Gwendal and I in the center. I imagined a Bedouin tent, two families from different clans coming together to negotiate a dowry. Gwendal and I are both only children, so it was clear that each side was offering up their most prized possession, hoping the others knew what a precious gift they were receiving.

When introducing future in-laws, a language barrier can be a very useful thing indeed. No one can say anything insulting, on purpose or otherwise, and everyone has time to warm up to one another gradually. Gwendal and I began the slow work — a life's work, it turns out — of translating back and forth.

In the year I had been in France, I had learned first to detest, and then to appreciate a certain amount of awkward silence. All this translation was wearying, but I knew it was better that they couldn't fully engage right away. I was sure that they would come to like one another, but not if my parents stormed the ramparts like typical Americans, loud and laughing and talking about very personal things. It would take time for my parents to absorb Nicole's intellectual formulations and Yanig's reserve.

One thing everyone could actively participate in was the food. The lamb had been cooked for hours, till it fell apart with the touch of a knife. Generally speaking, the French do two things to meat: eat it raw or bloody, or cook it for so long it begins to melt, turning into an unctuous, fragrant, childhood memory-inducing stew. *Saignant*, the word for "rare," literally means "bleeding." "Medium" or "well done" smacks of indecision, or worse, disrespect for the animal. Why would you kill an innocent creature just to eat it ashy and gray? At Le Picotin, the tender lamb is served on a wooden carving board, surrounded by sautéed potatoes and mushrooms.

Normally, I would be against an all-brown meal. A meal of a single color usually signals "school cafeteria," but in this case there was something festive, medieval, abundant, about the homogeneous palette of meat, starch, and vegetable. Portions here were generous — we were easing my parents in slowly, trying not to shock them with the comparative restraint and expense of a French dinner plate.

Except for approving ums and ahs, conversation ceased. Gwendal and I were glad to take a break from the translation.

Along with the fading awkwardness, I felt a sense of relief. As halting as this meeting was, it was easier than others I'd rehearsed in my head. I had allowed myself to imagine a dinner like this only once before in my life, with the parents of my college boyfriend, and even the imaginary version had been a disaster. Like almost every boy I'd been out with since high school (who says I didn't have a rebellious streak?), he was Catholic (I am Jewish). When would we discuss getting married in church? Before the appetizer, or after? Except for the Christmas tree, Gwendal's family was as atheist as they come.

The two couples sitting across from each other tonight were so different that there was no possible way they could pass judgment. My mother was a bobby-socked sorority girl who saw Elvis in concert at the Brooklyn Paramount. Paul grew up speaking Yiddish in the Bronx. Nicole was born in Casablanca when Morocco was still a French protectorate, and Yanig was raised in a small fishing village in Brittany, where he learned to sail on his grandfather's boat. I tried to think of some common point of reference. Maybe they all watched Neil Armstrong take his first steps on the moon? (It was broadcast live in France in the middle of the night.) Did they all remember where they were when President Kennedy was shot? When the Berlin Wall fell? They had seen so few of the same things, led so little of the same life, yet here they were, about to become family.

At least there would be no postgame wickedness. No arguing about the check (Gwendal and I took it), no spending the taxi ride home talking about who would pay for the rehearsal dinner ("What's that?" said Gwendal), and no haggling over how many great-aunts each side got to invite (none). Everyone was swimming, not so much out of their depth as in a different pond. Curiously, it made things easier.

"Mo-re wi-ne?" Yanig refilled Paul's glass with Brouilly. Yanig, I'd begun to suspect, understood more English than he let on. I'd been watching his brain work under the crease of those bushy eyebrows all evening. All those years of sailing back and forth across the English Channel and the Irish Sea, surely he knew how to do more than competently order a beer.

The waiter came back to see about dessert. Normally dessert is a bit of a nonstarter in this place, owing to the quantity and richness of what came before, but Paul is a committed chocoholic and the profiteroles had attracted his attention. Yanig and Nicole ordered espresso. My mother, still searching in vain for a big mug of black decaf coffee, settled for a cappuccino.

The profiteroles arrived, three golden, lopsided puffs of choux pastry, filled with vanilla ice cream just starting to melt from the heat of the kitchen. The waiter poured the dark chocolate sauce from a small copper pitcher and, watching Paul's eyes widen in delight, left it at the table. He also brought several extra spoons. I thought back to the Bedouin tent; eating from a shared plate is a mark of both hospitality and trust. Paul pushed the dish into the middle of the table and everyone picked up a spoon. No more translation necessary.

The next day, we met Nicole and Yanig at a flea market. Walking was better for everyone, less conversation, lots of opportunities to nod and point. After half an hour, we left the men at a café, sipping a beer and watching the world go by. I continued with my mother and Nicole.

They inspected the stands at the same leisurely pace. My mother picked up a silver strawberry spoon, looked at Nicole and smiled. Nicole picked up a teacup and a saucer, raised her eyebrows, and smiled back.

I think this might work out just fine.

We rented my parents an apartment for their stay, and it didn't have cable. In the year and a half since September 11, my parents had become politically unrecognizable news junkies. My mother, who used to watch TV only when she did the ironing on Sunday afternoons, now kept CNN going 24/7. The Four Horsemen of the Apocalypse might be tonight's guests on *Larry King*, and she didn't want to miss it.

September 11, a moment of terrible unity for most Americans, had been a moment of exile for me. I wasn't home, and in the months that followed it was made clear to me, I would never be entirely home again. I was living in London at the time. I watched my home city crumble on the BBC while my parents watched the local news. They were with the widows of firefighters and men holding pictures of missing fiancées, I was with the evenhanded political analysts and smug pundits. I was watching history on somebody else's channel, and in that moment I became, for them, slightly less American.

As George Bush ordered the first bombers over Baghdad, we were waiting for the metro on our way home from dinner. My parents kept looking around, like maybe they could get a mini Panasonic TV out of one of the vending machines. "They keep showing this video," said my mother, "of Saddam Hussein's brother torturing dogs." Gwendal didn't say a word; he is smarter than I am. "Which is what to do with anything?" I snapped, steam coming out of my ears. Like so many formerly reasonable people, my parents were now convinced that Saddam Hussein and Osama bin Laden were childhood friends who sat in the sandbox together pounding GI Joes over the head with a plastic shovel. "They have WMD. Colin Powell said so." When my parents finally accepted, along with millions of Americans, that Colin Powell had presented faulty intelligence to the United Nations, they reacted as if their own perfect child had betrayed them, broken curfew, decided to get a sex change operation without telling them. They were personally, achingly, head-shakingly disappointed.

"I just wish we could get some real news," grumbled Paul as we stepped off the train. It was one of many times over the next few years when I heard the American version of things described as the truth, everything else as just commentary.

Thus far the apartment search was yielding nothing but tired feet. My parents, unused to ambulating without a car, were now forced to tramp up five flights of spiral stairs to dim apartments with sinks at odd angles and the occasional view of the tip of the Eiffel Tower (if you stood on the toilet, looked left, and leaned out the window until you almost fell out).

After one particularly bleak morning of visits, Paul went back to the flat to take a nap and my mother and I walked over to the bric-a-brac shops on the rue Oberkampf. We looked at an art deco vanity with a pond-sized circular mirror, and a set of ceramic pantry jars lined up in descending-size order like Russian dolls: *farine, sucre, café, thé, sel, poivre*. They were so much more civilized than the plastic wonton soup container I'd used to store my sugar in New York.

We both saw it at the same time, as we turned into our street. There was a cardboard panel in the window, nothing official: *à vendre* and a phone number. An apartment. For sale. On our very own street. I wouldn't have to change my dry cleaner, my *boulangerie*, my fruit man, my pizzeria. I felt my salivary glands go into overdrive. I leaned forward like a jungle cat ready to pounce.

And then I saw him, out of the corner of my eye. A man across the street, twenty yards up, cell phone cocked, also staring up at the window.

I've looked for an apartment in New York, so I know what it is to act fast — to shove your rival to the pavement and offer up cash, drugs, *duck à l'orange*, and your firstborn child all for a studio on East 62nd Street.

Although I stopped dating before whole relationships were conducted by text message, I can be a dial demon when I need to be. The phone rang. *Oui, allo*. I looked at the guy up the street. He put his phone back in his pocket and walked on. No doubt he was going to do something foolish, like *call back later*, by which time if there was anything up there worth having, it would be mine.

The phone was answered by Natacha. Yes, she was in the apartment. Sure, we could come right up. We climbed one flight, noting the paint flaking in the hallway and the smell of fried fish hanging in the air. Natacha met us at the door in tight black pants and stilettos utterly unsuited to climbing the spiral staircases of Paris. Her hair was streaked blonde like a lion's mane, escaping in wisps from behind her huge sunglasses.

The entry was dark. "Welcome, we just finished the renovations," she said, flipping on the lights. This was already a good sign. Apartments in Paris are sold by the square meter, and whether the thing has recently been burned out in a fire or has brand-new granite countertops makes very little difference in the price.

There was a small bar that separated us from the empty kitchen. I leaned on it with my elbow and my shirt stuck to the wood. The varnish wasn't even dry. There was no refrigerator, no oven, no stove. I long ago stopped looking for the washing machine. In Paris, most apartments, even rentals, come with no appliances. These are bought and lugged around (and I thought my books were a pain to move) or given as unsexy but very practical wedding gifts. Beyond the bar was the living room: shiny hardwood floors and a cast-iron fireplace that resembled a taller, flatter version of a potbellied stove. Above it was a tiny marble mantel, dusky pink veined with gray. The room was flooded with the early afternoon light. It was everything I imagined a Parisian apartment to be: intimate and a little bit eccentric around the edges. Natacha pointed toward the bedroom door. A real door, with a handle and everything. I peeked in. It was small but gleaming white, with a recess just begging for bookshelves. And what was that over in the corner? Wonder of wonders, a *dressing* — that's French for "hot diggety dog, a closet!"

There were also, my mother noted with emphasis, radiators.

I dialed Gwendal and told him to extend his lunch hour and come right over. Fifteen minutes later we were down to business. The apartment was at the tippy-top end of our price range. Was there anything, I said, mentally placing my dog-eared copy of *Paradise Lost* on the soon-to-be-built bookshelves, that she could do?

"*Bien*," said Natacha, seeing in our eyes an early finish to her day's work and a long vodka tonic. "I can knock the price down ten thousand euros if you can pay ten percent in cash." I looked at my mother; she had on her "I found a Prada gown at Marshalls" face. Gwendal looked panic-stricken. I gave him my best "stick with me, kid" smile.

"Take the sign out of the window," I said. "Sold."

We arranged for the signing, which is split into two parts — the *promesse de vente* (sealing the offer) and three months later the *signature* (exchanging the title). Suspecting that Natacha worked for a muscled and mustached man named Boris, we negotiated to deliver the cash in two parts.

Gwendal was in shock. Had we really just made the decision to be homeowners in less time than it takes to finish a beer? My mother and Paul were over at the bar, scribbling numbers on the back of an envelope.

Gwendal was about to be introduced to a unique and quite possibly earth-shattering new theory: Bard Economics.

Bard Economics has two central principles:

1. Money not spent on item A is money saved, thus making item B half price.
2. You regret only the things you *didn't* buy.

Money in my family has always been a fairly abstract concept. Usually, this kind of abstraction applies only to very wealthy people, like the saying "If you have to ask, you can't afford it." That wasn't precisely our case. More like, "Why ask, we can't afford it anyway." My auntie Lynn calls my mother "the richest poor person I ever met."

Paul, an accountant by training, still insists my mother must have done it with mirrors, multiplying the zeros at the end of our bank account like the fun house at the end of Orson Welles's *Lady of Shanghai*. My mother spent her career at the New York City Board of Education, first as a special education teacher, then as an administrator. How did she send a kid to college (home equity loan), the opera (she took lunch to work), and summer camp (she sold her first engagement ring — it wasn't the cut she wanted anyway), all while maintaining a home and a fabulous collection of vintage handbags.

Growing up, I never had my own money. When I worked during the summer the money went into "the kitty," and when I wanted to go to the movies with my friends or buy a new CD, I just took it out again. I guess I never did anything unreasonable, because we somehow never got to the bottom of the kitty. I have a very distinct memory of the first time I used an ATM in high school. It fit in very well with my airy-fairy understanding of finance. Money may not grow on trees, but it does come out of brick walls.

Gwendal couldn't quite fathom all this. Debt, it turns out, is not universal. As hard as this is for Americans to believe, most of the world does not live life off of borrowed money. Most French people do not possess a credit card as we know it. Nicole and Yanig didn't buy their first home until Gwendal was eighteen. I know that being a psychoanalyst conjures visions of a comfortable Manhattan apartment with lots of potted plants, but there is no such thing as a $300-per-hour shrink in France. Yanig was away on the boat for weeks, and there were many times when things came up short at the end of the month. Gwendal took money out of the bank the same way he added pasta to boiling water, one small handful at a time.

There's a Billy Wilder movie from the 1960s called *One, Two, Three*. James Cagney plays the regional manager of Coca-Cola in postwar Berlin. His mission is to bring America's greatest beverage behind the Iron Curtain. One day, the boss's daughter arrives from Atlanta, falls for a Communist, and gets pregnant in the bargain. James Cagney has twenty-four hours to get them married and to transform the new son-in-law into a respectable capitalist. As they're driving to the airport to meet Big Daddy, Cagney adds up the tab for his protégé — new suit, aristocratic title, fancy car.

"Total: Ten thousand two hundred and fifty-five dollars."

"You mean, I have been a capitalist for three hours and already I owe ten thousand dollars?"

"That's what makes our system work. Everybody owes everybody."

All this to say that my future husband had never seen anyone take fifteen thousand euros out of a cash machine.

My parents caught their plane to New York the morning we signed the *promesse de vente*. We had carefully hidden the cash all week in Gwendal's two-volume copy of *Maus*. I didn't quite know what to do with the envelope on the way over. Just putting it in my purse seemed like an invitation for trouble, so I stuffed it into my bra. Seven thousand euros looks like less money than it is. One cup size at best.

My Jewish mother said Hail Marys all the way to the airport. They wouldn't know until they landed in New York that "Boris" was in fact a balding middle-aged Frenchman from the staid 16th arrondissement. He had polished loafers, a respectable linen blazer, and, of all things, an American wife. I bet the *dressing* was her idea.

A Meal to Warm Everybody Up

WILD MUSHROOM TURNOVERS
Chaussons aux Champignons

500 g cremini *mushrooms*
250 g *mixed wild mushrooms (I use chanterelles and black trumpets)*
2 tablespoons olive oil
2 tablespoons butter
1 large clove garlic, sliced
1 teaspoon fresh thyme leaves (or a handful of flat-leaf parsley)
2 tablespoons Armagnac or Cognac
2 tablespoons crème fraîche *or whipping cream*
2 sheets frozen puff pastry, thawed
½ teaspoon coarse sea salt, or more to taste
A good *grinding of fresh pepper*

Preheat the oven to 200°C.

Clean the mushrooms by wiping them with a damp paper towel rather than running them under the tap; the less extra water they absorb, the better. Slice them.

Heat the oil, butter, and garlic in a large frying pan. Add the *cremini* mushrooms and sauté over medium heat for 5 minutes, until they start to release a bit of water. Add the wild mushrooms and thyme and cook another 5 minutes, until they're wilted.

Deglaze the pan with Armagnac. Lower the heat, add the *crème fraîche,* and simmer for a minute or two. Add salt and pepper to taste.

Roll out the puff pastry rectangles to half their original thickness; cut them into 10 cm squares. Place the pastry on a baking sheet covered with baking paper. Leaving a 1 cm border, place a tablespoon of the mushroom mixture in the lower right-hand corner of the square. Fold the upper left-hand corner over the top and press the ends together with a fork to seal. You should have a nice stuffed triangle. Repeat with the remaining pastry and mushrooms. Bake at 200°C for 20 to 25 minutes, until the pastry is puffed and golden brown.

Serve with drinks.

Yield: Serves 6–8 as an hors d'oeuvre

LAMB SHANKS WITH ORANGE AND STAR ANISE
Souris d'Agneau à l'Orange et à la Badiane

Unless I'm dealing with a tried-and-true vegetarian, this is probably what you'll have for dinner the first time you are invited to my home. This recipe was inspired by *Un Rôti pour Dimanche* by Emmanuel Renault (Larousse, 2007). The combination of orange and star anise fills the kitchen with a spicy gingerbread scent, so you are almost guaranteed to hear, "Wow, something smells good" as your guests walk in the door. If you've never tried making lamb shanks, please do. They are inexpensive, easy to serve, and very forgiving with timing. So if your in-laws (or whomever else you are trying to impress) are caught in traffic, you can just turn off the oven and let them sit, no harm done.

> 6 meaty lamb shanks
> Coarse sea salt
> Freshly ground black pepper
> 1–2 tablespoons extra-virgin olive oil
> 1 medium red onion, diced
> 1 head garlic, cloves peeled and left whole
> 3 whole star anise
> 1 organic navel orange, cut into 6 sections
> 1 teaspoon sugar
> 1 cup best-quality tomato and basil sauce
> 1 cup chicken broth
> 1 cup white wine

Preheat the oven to 180°C.

In a large casserole dish, brown the lamb shanks, seasoning generously with salt and pepper. Remove and set aside.

Add olive oil to the pot. Add the onion, garlic, star anise, and orange; sauté until the mixture is slightly colored, 3 to 5 minutes.

Add the liquids and sugar; bring to a boil. Add the meat back to the pot. Cover tightly and transfer to the oven. Cook for 1½ to

2 hours, until the lamb is tender and the sauce is slightly reduced. If anyone is running late, just shut off the oven and leave the shanks to rest. (They should rest for 10 to 15 minutes out of the oven in any case.)

To serve, transfer the shanks to a large shallow casserole dish. Surround them with boiled new potatoes and pour the sauce over everything. Top with the cooked orange sections, cloves of garlic, and star anise.

Yield: Serves 6

CHOCOLATE PROFITEROLES
Profiteroles

This is a warm and wonderful ending to a get-to-know-you meal. It is also relatively stress-free. You can make the choux puffs a few hours in advance, and leave the chocolate sauce in its double boiler on the stove, ready for a quick reheating. For easy assembly, make the little ice cream balls in advance and store them on a baking sheet or waxed paper in the freezer.

CHOUX PUFFS

½ cup milk
½ cup water
160 g butter, diced
1¼ teaspoons sugar
*1 level teaspoon coarse sea salt, or 1 scant teaspoon fine
    sea salt (I know it seems like a lot, but I like to
    taste the salt here; I find it's a nice counterpoint to
    the chocolate)*
1 cup flour
4 eggs (approximately 280 g)
3 tablespoons icing sugar

DARK CHOCOLATE SAUCE

¾ cup milk
*225 g dark chocolate (70 percent cocoa; I use Valrhona
    or Green & Black's), chopped*
*1–2 teaspoons rum, dessert wine, cognac, raspberry
    liqueur, or any other alcohol that catches your
    fancy (optional, but recommended)*

1 litre vanilla ice cream

Preheat the oven to 220°C.

For the choux puffs: In a heavy-bottomed saucepan, over low heat, combine the milk, water, butter, sugar, and salt. Bring just to a boil. Turn off the heat and add the flour while stirring continuously, until the flour is incorporated and the dough comes away from the sides of the pan. It will look like a lump of marzipan.

Quickly add 2 of the eggs and stir to incorporate.

Quickly incorporate the remaining 2 eggs; stir until smooth. The batter will be thick and sticky. It can be refrigerated for up to a day.

Line 2 large baking sheets with baking paper. Using two teaspoons, dole out heaping dollops of batter, widely spaced. You should have about 24. (If you have space in your freezer, you can freeze the individual puffs at this point. I don't recommend freezing and thawing a big lump of batter.)

Bake one sheet at a time. Before you put them in the oven, sprinkle the puffs generously with icing sugar.

If baking immediately: Bake for 12 minutes at 220°C. Then turn down the heat to 200°C, and bake for 10 to 12 minutes more with the oven door slightly ajar (I stick a wooden spoon in the door to hold it open just a crack).

If baking straight from the fridge: 15 minutes at 220°C, then 10 to 12 minutes at 200°C with the door ajar.

If baking straight from the freezer: 15 minutes at 220°C, then 12 minutes at 200°C with the door ajar.

You'll want to watch the puffs the first time you make them, as every oven is different. Grab one out of the oven to taste (I always do). It should be fully puffed and highly colored; don't worry if the sugar caramelizes on top or underneath.

The puffs can be made several hours in advance. Leave them on the wire rack, uncovered in a dry spot.

For the chocolate sauce: Gently heat the milk in the top of a double boiler, mix in chocolate, stir until thoroughly combined — the sauce will be thick and glossy. Add alcohol and stir to combine. You can make this sauce before dinner and gently reheat it in the double boiler just before serving. Add an extra dribble of milk to loosen it if necessary.

To serve, cut each puff horizontally, but not all the way through, like a little Pac-Man. Place a small scoop of vanilla ice cream in the opening. I usually serve three puffs per person, but — as this is part of a dinner meant to inspire a feeling of welcome and abundance — who would protest if they were served a fourth? Like the waiter at the Le Picotin, I like to bring the chocolate sauce to the table in a little pitcher or copper pot and let each guest serve according to his whim.

Yield: Makes about 24 profiteroles

CHAPTER 10

FAMILY HEIRLOOMS

We didn't want to wait a year to get married. I had been in visa limbo long enough. I wanted the right to work and to open a bank account and to travel through the European Union with one of those flimsy plastic identity cards instead of my U.S. passport. Health insurance would be nice. July Fourth weekend was four months away — ambitious, but not impossible.

Anyone who has ever planned a wedding will tell you that suddenly *everyone* has an opinion. What was peculiar about planning the wedding in Paris was that everyone's opinion — from the band-leader to the restaurant owner — was more important than mine. The fact that there was money involved only made matters worse. As far as the chef was concerned, he was not paid to follow my instructions, he was paid to do what he did best, and who was I to tell him how. The restaurant hostess refused to clear a dance floor among the tables; I was making a party in *her* space, and she knew best how to use it. I understand that living in another culture is partly about learning to put aside the perfect in favor of the possible. But is her wedding really the time to ask a girl to learn this lesson?

The choosing of the hors d'oeuvres alone was like the Indy 500. We went round and round in circles, interrupted only when we crashed into a wall. But I didn't *want* white toasts with the crusts cut off spread with a millimeter-thin layer of salmon purée and topped with a slice of black olive. "What about chicken liver purée?" the chef said. I finally went out and bought a book, with lots of pictures. I pointed to the polenta triangles topped with roasted peppers and said, "What about this?," crossed my fingers, and left.

There was also the small matter of securing the date — an equally circular process, only slower. Getting married in France requires a stack of paper the size of a dictionary, double spaced. Apparently, I needed a proof of residence in order to apply for a marriage license, but I had no legal right to be residing in France until I was married.

Hence the gas bill.

We had already decided against a formal sit-down meal. Nobody really enjoys their chicken/fish option, and I wanted to retire to bed with a cold compress at the very thought of a bilingual seating chart. It would be a small reception, only eighty people. Gwendal has very little family, and only my closest friends and relatives would be making the trip.

If we weren't serving dinner, it seemed logical to me to have the wedding in the afternoon. I might as well have suggested that Gwendal's grandmother spend the day skinny dipping in the Seine. French weddings are all-night, get-down-and-boogie affairs — none of this "rent the room till one a.m. and then the waiters start pushing you out with a broom." The last French wedding we went to began with champagne at three in the afternoon and ended with the traditional French onion soup and bad French disco music (also traditional) at four in the morning.

"If it's in the afternoon, no one will dance," said Gwendal, looking as if I had just killed his hamster. "And if people don't dance it's not a real wedding."

I had a birth certificate to translate. The music would have to be next week's problem.

One of the great gifts of an intercultural relationship is that when you fight, you never quite know if you are mad at the person, or at their culture: Is he really too bum-ass lazy to call back the band at eight p.m. on a Monday evening (are they in the middle of dinner?), or is he just being *French*? Is she bombarding me with lists and timetables and questions about the color of the wax used to seal the invitations because she is a manic control freak (or General MacArthur's granddaughter), or is she just being *American*?

It's like the UN: things escalate, but then everybody calms down for a minute while they look over the transcript for a mistranslation.

We were fine until we got to the cake.

America may have landed a man on the moon, but the French have the coolest wedding cakes on earth. It's not really a cake. It's called a *croquembouche* — a "crunch in the mouth" — or, more regally, a *pièce montée*. It's like you climb the ladder to your new life on a four-foot pyramid of individual vanilla cream puffs, held together with glossy praline — caramelized sugar that shatters in your mouth like glass and sticks in your teeth like toffee. It's glorious and magnificent, and I guess also the cultural equivalent of dry fruitcake and chalk-white icing with a plastic bride and groom on top.

"But it's *cheesy*," moaned Gwendal. I had recently authorized him to use this expression.

"I don't care," I said, giving up on UN-style diplomacy in favor of a unilateral strike. "I *want* one."

While I was working out the international cake treaty, Gwendal was busy shooting a short film with friends. That is, when he wasn't writing, directing, and rehearsing for a full-scale musical comedy with his tap-dance school. Part of me admired his enthusiasm, part of me thought it was childish. Since he had finished his PhD, Gwendal had settled into one of France's most cushy situations, a glamorous public service job. Working for a movie archive was sexy but socially conscious, with none of the dirty implications of actually turning a profit.

Like most French people, I don't think Gwendal ever expected fulfillment or recognition for his work. When he finally asked for a raise for hiring and managing the team of five people that executed his digitization project, the director told him he had taken on the extra responsibility *pour plaisir* — for fun.

When he was bored or frustrated (which was more and more often), instead of looking for a new job, he simply funneled his energy into other things. I just couldn't keep my big American mouth shut. "If you put all the time and effort you spend on your hobbies into your job, you'd have the cinema career you've always wanted."

"You are right," he said calmly. "At least in the United States. But here, working harder, faster, and better just makes people hate you."

"I have to go," he said, kissing me good-bye. Coming from an American man, this would have been a blow-off, a clear signal not to mention it again. But Gwendal didn't function that way. Our cultures were starting to leak into each other's brains. I knew he was filing it away for further consideration.

I went back to New York at the beginning of May for my wedding shower. I tried in vain to explain the concept to Gwendal.

"When you get married, people give you things."

"You mean we get our wedding presents in advance?"

"No, these are other presents."

"Oh." Then he added, still not quite with me, "But why is it called a shower?"

"I don't know, maybe because the gifts rain down on you like a shower."

As I watched CNN in line for immigration at JFK, I was reminded that 2003 was not a good year for an American to be marrying a Frenchman. President Chirac may have donned his NYPD cap after September 11, but since then, France, along with much of the population of Europe, had been critical of the invasion of Iraq. In 2003, "French fries" became "freedom fries." I was sleeping with the enemy.

Since I was not yet official in France, I'd kept my American health insurance. My gynecologist had a particularly strong opinion on the subject. "A Frenchman," he said, when I told him I was getting married. "They've got their heads up the pipe." It was an echo of what I'd been hearing on the street and reading in the newspapers: *Sure, they like to talk. If it wasn't for us, they'd all be speaking German right now.* An awkward conversation to be having, particularly in sight of a speculum.

My other appointment that week was with my editor from the *New York Times*.

I know. I was excited too.

My first article for the paper of record had been a stroke of luck; they needed someone to interview a French artist who was having an exhibition at the Guggenheim. I was ecstatic. I thought I was a made woman — a real journalist. I patted myself on the back and checked one more thing off my life's to-do list.

I allowed myself to enjoy this bloated feeling of accomplishment for a full ten minutes. Then, in classic Elizabeth fashion, I began to belittle it. I started worrying about the next thing. How long would it take me to get an article into the *Times Magazine?* When would they put me on staff in Paris? This was a pattern I'd repeated so often, I hardly noticed it. No sooner was something done than it meant nothing at all.

I quickly realized that getting my second story in the paper might actually be harder than it was to land my first. Though most people imagined that I was living in the art capital of the known universe, Paris is a city of great *dead* artists. The live ones are in New York or London or Cologne or Shanghai. What was worse, with the tension between the two governments, nobody in the United States wanted to hear about what was happening in France. Europe in general was kind of *persona non grata*.

Even so, it felt so good to be a professional again, to have a *meeting.* As I waited outside the Times Building with my cardboard cup of coffee, scalding hot and milky sweet, I absorbed the energy coming up off the pavement, the people rushing past. I wished I could plug in, recharge my batteries, take some of this whirl of activity and promise back to my little desk in Paris.

The wedding shower was supposed to be a surprise. Fortunately I did enough acting in high school to swoon and start and even cry a little when Sarah opened the door. Sarah is my oldest friend, more like a sister, really. I've known her since before my second birthday. We finger-painted together with chocolate pudding. We learned to roller-skate in my backyard. When we went to day camp together, she was my partner in the licorice-eating contest, each of us on one end of a long red yarn of candy, trying to chew our way to the middle. I haven't always been the most constant friend. I forget birthdays, leave too many months between calls. And yet we always seem to find each other again.

Wherever I go in the world, she is there, on the other end of that piece of licorice.

With the invitation, Sarah included two recipe cards to be sent back by each guest, whether they were coming or not. Afra, my best friend from college, lives in San Francisco. Her family is Persian, and she sent along her mother's recipe for *sohaan-e asali*, tiny sweets made with ground almonds and pistachios. The first time I went to her house for the traditional Persian New Year, I ate so many that I couldn't button my pants on the plane home.

Coincidentally, the wedding had inspired this same gesture from Gwendal's family. A few weeks after we announced our engagement, Gwendal's great-aunt Jane sent us several family recipes, neatly copied by hand in blue ink on white graph paper. One of them was *le bon jeune homme*. Gwendal described it with rapture as an island of chocolate custard floating in a sea of *crème anglaise*; I could see him, nose barely higher than the tabletop, standing on tiptoe to peek over the edge of the dish. I scanned the directions; the first paragraph alone involved forty-five minutes of continuous stirring. It was a taste of Gwendal's childhood, something I was now responsible for preserving and passing on.

Sarah had included her grandma Vicky's recipe for sugar cookies, and her gift to me was a set of cookie cutters. She found a ballerina, to commemorate our years of matching tutus, and a camel, like the one we rode on our trip to Israel and Egypt when we were twelve.

I was so moved that I wanted to crush her lungs in an enormous hug. At the same time, part of me was thinking:

But the French don't eat cookies. My first winter in Paris, Gwendal and I were invited to a holiday party at the home of another American. She made Christmas cookies in the shapes of trees, candy canes, ornaments. She made sky blue and cherry red icing, decorated each one — the works. When Gwendal saw them, all he could say was this: "Why would anyone want to eat blue food?"

The rest of the afternoon was lost in a sea of pastel wrapping paper, tea sandwiches, and heat-resistant spatulas. But the best present, the one I would run back into a burning building to get, was a hot pink plastic binder from my aunt Joyce. Aunt Joyce, my mother's younger sister, is the best cook in our family — equally enthusiastic about a dinner at the Culinary Institute of America and a breakfast of cold pizza and Diet Coke.

The binder is a family heirloom, a collection of recipes that my mother made for Joyce when she got married in 1972. It includes some of my parents' early dinner-party classics: my father's fettuccine Alfredo, "French toast" cream cheese and jelly sandwiches, my grandmother's mandel bread. My mother, ever the schoolteacher, made each page into a mini collage with illustrations cut from magazines. One shows a young woman, still in her wedding veil, sitting on a piece of lettuce the size of a magic carpet, pulled along by a single dove. Underneath is the heading "The Bride Makes Salads." Joyce had added to it over the years, and written an inscription inside: *This book was made with love. It was used with love. It starts the cycle again, with love.*

As I got up from the living room couch in my silly paper hat covered with ribbons, I caught sight of myself in the mirror across the room. The girl who lived in Paris might not have recognized me. I looked at myself among this well-meaning and loving bunch of people, and I knew that for all I carried with me, my life would be radically different from theirs. I hoped these recipes would be enough to link me to my past, and open the kitchen cupboard to my future.

When I got back to Paris it was time to look for a wedding dress to accommodate those other family heirlooms, a pair of 34-DD boobs.

Nicole and I went to Galeries Lafayette. France's most famous department store is the Saint Peter's of shopping, topped with a splendid glass dome and probably traversed by an equal number of tourists.

We bypassed the bridal department without a second look. I hardly needed to be walking up the seedy boulevard de Magenta on the day of my wedding in a satin train. Gwendal's only request was that I be able to dance. Searching among the endless racks of size thirty-sixes (that's a small American four) left me feeling, at five seven and a slim size ten, like the Jolly Green Giant. French women are, there is just no other word for it, *petite*. They have little bones and little noses and they wear little jackets with little shoes. Not to put too fine a point on it, there's just nothing in the tits-and-ass department. The cannonballs with which Napoleon conquered all of Europe probably didn't amount to a 34-DD.

This was torture. Everything seemed to have a cap sleeve (out of the question) or a skirt designed to lie beautifully over the hips of an eleven-year-old boy. After an hour, I was ready to throw myself off the Belle Epoque balcony. Nicole was mute; I think I was scaring her. We were heading toward the escalator to make a quick escape when I spotted a dress in taupe chiffon. It looked a little like a costume from a Fred Astaire movie, a flapper dress, with delicate beading along the neckline and below the bust. I tried it on. It landed lightly just below my knees and billowed slightly when I turned. It was simple, elegant, a perfect match for my grandmother's silver prom bag, which I wanted to carry. Naturally, I was falling out of it a bit, but the right bra ought to solve that.

With a surprising lack of hesitation, I paid for the dress and left. I felt human again. My American body and French fashion had been reconciled.

Temporarily.

Two weeks before the wedding I was walking down toward the canal wearing a long navy blue sundress with an Empire waist. My path was blocked by two men on a motorcycle parked in the middle of the sidewalk. As they revved up the engine, a cloud of black smoke belched right into my face. The friend turned to look at me. "*Attention*," he said to the driver, "not in front of the pregnant lady."

Three Family Heirlooms

CHOCOLATE CREAM WITH CRÈME ANGLAISE
Le Bon Jeune Homme

I didn't muster the will to try this recipe until several years after our wedding. The first time, I burnt the chocolate. The second try, I stirred for an hour and ended up with chocolate milk. Desperate for a solution, I turned to Nigella Lawson, Britain's sexiest hausfrau. Her chocolate pots from *Nigella Bites* (Chatto & Windus, 2001) achieve great results with a minimum of fuss. Topped with Tante Jane's *crème anglaise*, I hope I've done justice to the original.

CHOCOLATE CREAM

1 egg
180 g best-quality dark chocolate (70 percent cocoa)
½ cup whipping cream
½ cup milk

CRÈME ANGLAISE

5 egg yolks
½ cup sugar
3 cups milk
1 vanilla bean

Fresh mint for garnish

For the chocolate cream: Lightly beat the egg in a small bowl.

Chop the chocolate and place in the top of a double boiler with the cream and the milk. Heat, stirring to combine, until just below boiling. Turn off the heat.

Quickly whisk the beaten egg into the chocolate mixture until smooth. Divide the chocolate cream among six tall glasses. Refrigerate for at least 6 hours or overnight.

For the *crème anglaise*: beat the egg yolks with the sugar in a medium bowl until the mixture is a light lemon yellow. Set aside.

Pour the milk into a medium saucepan. Split the vanilla bean lengthwise down the middle; scrape the seeds into the milk, and throw in the pod as well. Heat over a low flame, until just below boiling.

Slowly add the hot milk to the egg yolks, whisking continuously. Pour the mixture back into the saucepan and cook over low heat, stirring continuously, until the *crème anglaise* coats the back of a spoon, about 10 minutes.

Cool the sauce briefly in an ice bath; store it in an airtight container in the fridge. Like the chocolate cream, the *crème anglaise* can be made a day ahead.

Just before serving, top the chocolate cream with a layer of *crème anglaise* and top with a sprig of mint.

Yield: Serves 6

Tip: This is a wonderful dinner party or holiday dessert. It is terribly elegant in its black and white simplicity, and because you must get it in the fridge the night before, there's less hassle on the day!

BURT BARD'S FETTUCCINE ALFREDO

I made this pasta meal recently for the first time in almost twenty years. It was not until I started grinding the pepper over the pot that the memories came flooding back. Something about the smell. It was a real Proustian moment... my dad must have been standing over my shoulder.

> 250 g salted butter
> 2 cups heavy cream
> 180 g freshly grated Parmesan cheese
> 1½ teaspoons fresh ground black pepper (don't skimp!)
> 2 egg yolks, unbeaten
> 750 g De Cecco fettuccine or orecchiette

In a large stockpot, boil water for the pasta. Add enough salt so you can taste it.

In a heavy-bottomed saucepan, over low heat, melt the butter.

Add the cream and stir to heat through. Add the cheese, stirring to combine.

Add pepper. I know it seems like a lot, but my original recipe card says, "When you think you've covered the whole thing, add more — really!!"

Stir and cook 5 minutes.

While the sauce is cooking, toss the pasta into the boiling water.

Whisk the egg yolks into the sauce, continuing to whisk until slightly thickened — this will happen pretty quickly.

Cook the pasta until *al dente* — with a slight bite. Drain and quickly return to the pot.

Toss the pasta with the sauce. Serve immediately.

Yield: Serves 6

Variation: I now often stir in blanched broccoli florets or fresh peas for a bit of color.

GRANDMA ELSIE'S MANDEL BREAD

To give credit where credit is due, this recipe actually comes from my grandmother's friend Sadie. My grandma Elsie Kishner tweaked it a bit over the years on her yellowing recipe card. The result is slightly crumbly biscotti studded with nuts and mini chocolate chips. Perfect with a cup of tea.

> ½ cup walnuts
> ⅔ cup vegetable oil
> ½ cup sugar
> 2 eggs
> 1 teaspoon vanilla extract
> 2 cups flour
> 1 teaspoon baking powder
> ½ cup mini chocolate chips
> Cinnamon and sugar to garnish

Preheat the oven to 180°C. Toast the walnuts until lightly browned and fragrant. Let cool completely. Chop coarsely.

In a large bowl, whisk together the oil and sugar. Add the eggs one at a time, combining after each addition. Add the vanilla.

In another bowl, sift together the flour and baking powder. Stir the flour mixture into the egg mixture.

Add the nuts and chocolate chips; stir to combine.

On a baking sheet covered with aluminium foil, form the batter into 3 loaves (each about 8 by 15 cm). Leave some space between them, as they tend to spread. The batter will be quite sticky to work with. I pat it into shape with lightly oiled hands.

Sprinkle generously with cinnamon and sugar.

Bake for 25 minutes. Remove the baking sheet from the oven but keep the heat on.

Allow to cool for 5 minutes, then cut into 2 cm slices.

Lay the slices on their side on a wire rack and return them to the oven; toast for 10 minutes.

Flip the mandel bread and toast for 8 to 10 minutes on the other side.

Cool directly on the wire rack.

Yield: Makes 20–25 cookies

CHAPTER II

BIG BAND, SMELLY CHEESE

Whenever people talk about my wedding, they remember two things: the band and the cheese.

In order to get people to dance in the middle of the afternoon, Gwendal decided we should blow the budget (was Bard Economics rubbing off on him already?) on a big band. They had sky-blue blazers and matching ties. There were eighteen of them. If people wouldn't get up and dance to this, they were just being grumpy.

As usual, I was more concerned with what we were going to eat. Having dispensed with the hors d'oeuvres and the cake, I turned my attention to the meal we weren't serving. I took an imaginary survey among my friends: what are the things you most long for when you visit France? Two items kept coming up at the top of the list: great wine and great cheese. Easy enough.

But a year in France was long enough to make me wary of "easy." As I suspected, there was one final obstacle: simply put, our cheesemonger didn't want to sell us smelly cheese.

I went to see Monsieur Gilot on Sunday morning at the small market just around the corner from our house. He is balding, with a well-trimmed mustache and black-rimmed glasses. Central casting would put him up for the role of the high school social studies teacher. Instead, he and his wife drive into Paris every Sunday from Normandy to sell cheese, fresh eggs, and breasts from ducks they've raised themselves.

"Les américains, ils n'aiment pas les fromages qui puent." But Americans don't like smelly cheese, he insisted. Nothing too strong.

His implication was clear. There was something bland, flaccid, in the American character, unable (by dint of historical unripeness) to muster the gastronomic courage to try a hunk of *roquefort artisanal*, so potent it made everything you dared to eat afterward taste like laundry detergent. He might as well have challenged me to a duel.

To be fair, the French are rightfully proud and even a bit pedantic about their cheese. The *fromages* of France are as individual as the field of grass that fed the cow (or sheep, or goat) who gave the milk, not to mention the fellow who mixed, molded, and aged it. Certain bacteria, like those that produce the blue in *roquefort*, are a well-guarded secret, protected with the same fierceness as a set of nuclear launch codes. In an interview with *Newsweek* in 1961, President Charles de Gaulle famously commented, "How can you govern a country with two hundred and forty-six kinds of cheese?" What he meant was, "How can you govern a country with two hundred and forty-six kinds of *French*." Cheese is an apt expression of the French character. There may be a hard, crusty, even a stinky, exterior. Up to you to cut through to the dense, melting (sometimes piquant) heart.

But the arrogance and enthusiasm of youth have their own advantages. What Monsieur Gilot didn't understand, though he'd been happily selling me my cheese for over a year, was that in the short time this American had been in town, she had become a bona fide cheese connoisseur. True, my palate had a long way to go. Like many Americans of my generation, I was raised on Kraft Singles and macaroni and cheese made with orange powder and a pat of butter. I never quite descended into the gooey inferno of Velveeta, but I wasn't far. I certainly didn't encounter anything as sophisticated as Cracker Barrel cheddar or Brie before college, and even then it was in the guise of tiny toothpicked chunks surrounded by seedless grapes and pale water crackers.

When I arrived in France, I started with names I recognized. There was something in his case labeled *Munster*. That must be the "monster cheese" of my childhood. It was softer and creamier than the vacuum-packed rectangle I remember my mother slicing (I liked the ends, marked in paprika with a pattern of tiny squares). That evening after dinner, I unwrapped the Munster from its protective waxed paper and lifted it onto a plate. Gwendal caught a whiff from across the room. When I got up the next morning to take a shower, my hand smelled as though I'd slept holding a wet gym sock.

I soon graduated to Comté, a hard, fruity cheese that when aged has the sweetness and flake of Parmesan, and tête de moines (literally, "a monk's head"), made from sheep's milk. Bleu d'Auvergne, my favorite blue cheese, had nothing much in common with the crumbs I'd seen at home on a California Cobb salad. It was so dense it resembled a hunk of butter, coursing with violet veins.

For the wedding, Gwendal also wanted Salers, a cheese from Cantal with an almost peppery after-bite. It is made in huge *tommes* that, when you cut a slice, leave crags as in the side of a cliff. Monsieur Gilot kindly suggested a milder *Entre-deux* (literally, "in between"), but Gwendal held his ground.

As a last choice, we took a *tomme de chèvre frais,* a round of fresh mild goat cheese the color of newly fallen snow. It is always prudent to follow a little of your *vendeur*'s advice, if only to be polite.

Our new couch arrived for the wedding four hours before my mother. We moved into our apartment at the end of May and, this being France, the couch we ordered was (without explanation, refund, or regret) six weeks late. I had just finished stuffing the plastic wrap into a garbage bag when I heard the taxi pull up in front of the building.

The neighborhood put on its best face for my family's arrival. It was laundry day at the building across the street; there were undershirts and housecoats and a velour blanket printed with a giant tiger hanging out the window. The streets around the canal, for all that the area was up and coming, still had as many socks on the windowsills as geraniums. That morning, directly across the street *chez* our neighbors on the second floor, there were neither undershirts nor geraniums: just a skinny guy, stark raving naked, smoking a cigarette. I opened the door as Gwendal leapt in front of the window. Arms stretched wide to block as much of the view as possible, he put on his sunniest grin. "Welcome! How was your flight?"

My mother came in with Paul, kissed us hello, and handed me a long rectangular box. "I carried this all the way over on my lap," she said. "It's from your father."

A wedding present. From my dead father. *This oughta be good.*

The box was as big as a trombone case, and filled with several layers of bubble wap. I picked my way through the intricate packing job to reveal the top of a shiny ceramic head. *Oh God.*

"You *bought* Lladró?" I said, my heart sinking like the hull of the *Titanic.*

"No, I *brought* Lladró."

And sure enough, when I looked closely at the glazed porcelain statue of the seated milkmaid and her elongated shepherd playing his lute, I recognized it. It had been on the mantelpiece in our living room for my entire life, right next to the portrait of the old man that I thought was a lion until I got glasses in the first grade.

"Your father and I bought this on our first trip to Europe. I thought you'd like to have it."

I knew I was being hurtful, but I just couldn't think of anything nice to say. I couldn't think of an object that reminded me less of my father. Our friend Diego grew up in Peru. His mother, for her wedding, had received not just Lladró, but *fake* Lladró, from a number of elderly and easily insulted relatives. In 1974, there was an earthquake in Lima. Isabelle quickly took Diego outside, then ran back into the house, up to the first floor, and knocked the statues, one by one, *clink*, *clink*, *clink*, off the mantelpiece.

Where is an earthquake when you need one?

The thought must have registered on my face, because my mother clammed up and looked as though she was about to cry. Paul said they were tired from the flight and would see us later. Perfect. My mother had been here for ten minutes and already I'd put my foot in it. A record. A personal best.

On Thursday afternoon, I left Gwendal with Paul and Gary, Auntie Lynn's husband, to install the kitchen cabinets. There are not a lot of comedy acts I'd pay good money to see; one of them is a PhD in engineering sitting on the living room floor forty-eight hours before his wedding trying to put together a set of Ikea cabinets.

Since we were having thirty people over for brunch on Sunday morning, this was not a chore that could wait. My mother (who was, for whatever reason, still speaking to me) decided this would be a good time to go out and buy a coffeepot. We left Gwendal balancing a four-foot cabinet on his head while Paul and Gary stood across the room with their arms crossed, muttering.

"A little to the left, no, up, up up, now down."

Gwendal, like Atlas holding up the globe, stood perfectly still, muscles tensed, hammer poised.

"I wouldn't do it like that," murmured Paul under his breath. "Would you?"

"No," said Gary, with the slightest shake of the head, "not like that."

They have a name for this in French. *Inspecteur des travaux finis* — inspector of finished works. It's the guy who walks behind you and tells you what you did wrong. Gwendal, too gracious to tell his future father-in-law and uncle to go jump in a lake, just moved a little to the left and started banging away. I'm surprised he didn't come to the ceremony with a nail in his thumb.

I'm not sure what everyone was expecting.

If someone had asked me, ten years ago, to picture my wedding in France, my first thought would have been a château in Burgundy (just a few turrets, nothing over the top) with a horse-drawn carriage to take us to the twelfth-century parish church (Grandma, it's a very small crucifix). A tiny stained-glass window would cast a kaleidoscope of colors on my white satin gown. A tiara (it's very precise in my head, the tiara) would hold my veil. If the wedding were in Paris, why not the Grande Galerie of the Louvre? It has a lovely view of the Seine, and we could take some pictures later riding the elevator in the Eiffel Tower.

Our wedding took place in the town hall of the 10th arrondissement, not far from the Gare du Nord. In France, because of the strict separation of church and state, only a government official can perform a wedding. Religious ceremonies happen afterward or often, not at all. We were just thankful there was no rugby game that weekend. When there is, the singing and bagpipes wake up the natives. The Brits swarm the *brasseries* around the station, drunk at eight a.m., right off the Eurostar.

Our town hall is grand in its own way, a hulking nineteenth-century building with lots of towers and spires, Neuschwanstein meets Notre Dame. The neighborhood is better known for the passage Brady, a street of cheap Indian restaurants, and the rue du Château d'Eau, an entire street lined with African hairdressers. This Saturday morning, like any other, the sidewalks teemed with people. The smell of cocoa butter and peanut oil flowed out of the shops, as women spent the day getting their hair braided for a night on the town. There are three huge guys who stand all day at the exit of the metro at Château d'Eau, harassing the girls on their way out. All of my English friends in big hats passed that way.

Inside the town hall is a grand staircase, made slightly less grand by the plastic bulletin board with announcements about recycling and nursery schools. My friend Oscar, a fashion designer, was straightening Gwendal's silver tie when I met them on the front steps.

If the groom was having doubts, the décolletage of my dress squashed them right away. Despite my best efforts in the lingerie shop, my wares were conspicuously on display, like the Christmas windows at Saks.

I could say I was nervous, but that would be a lie. My inner control freak had taken the day off, and in her place appeared a perfectly relaxed young woman, kissing friends, directing traffic. I had descended from the mountain of the perfect, into the valley of the possible, and was now on the happy shaded trail, dappled with sunlight, of the present. It was the most wonderful walk of my life.

That may have been because I didn't understand a word of what I was committing myself to.

In France, before you sign any kind of legal contract, they read it out loud to the assembled parties. I'm sure it's an excellent idea; it lets you prick up your ears for little words like "illegitimate," "disinherit," "obey." But the effect is limited when the person signing is still learning the word for "turnip." At one point the intonation raised slightly to indicate a question, and I said, "*Oui.*" I think that was it. Since we had our backs to our family and friends, I gave a little thumbs-up to the peanut gallery. They didn't understand anything either.

Like so many other rituals in France, this one involved paperwork. We turned the pages and kissed, knocking noses on the way. Then Gwendal's godmother Annick got up to sing a song. It was a love poem, but again, the words didn't penetrate. Carefully applied mascara started rolling down my cheeks. They weren't tears of sadness, or even tears of joy. I was just overflowing. Like so many things since I'd been here, I didn't yet understand it, but I felt it.

The reception was in the Buttes Chaumont, the park where Gwendal had proposed. The restaurant was lovely in an old-fashioned way, with two huge terraces, one in front, one in back. It was a sunny day, which was a relief, as there was no place for an eighteen-piece band inside. The city disappeared behind a curtain of chestnut trees.

When we arrived, the hostess handed us each a glass of champagne. The chef had done his level best with the polenta triangles (a little thick and sticky, but what do you expect when you ask for something foreign). I could see the *tommes* of cheese, stacked like the ends of barbells on the serving table inside. Rachel, Gwendal's witness, had brought *saucisson* and smoked duck breast from Toulouse. I had bought medjool dates and plump dried apricots and tiny grapes, so red they were nearly black, which hung over the edge of the serving dish with Dionysian abundance.

We had hidden the big band on the back terrace; only four of them, a perfectly polite jazz ensemble, greeted us at the front door. But I've been known to surprise people, so as the guests filed through to the back terrace, the remaining brass let out an astounding honk, and the saxophone players stepped up in unison as they broke into a swingin' version of "Stompin' at the Savoy."

Gwendal pulled me onto the dance floor. There was no time for speeches or formalities or introductions.

He was right about the music. It was barely noon, and the terrace was full of twirling couples. It was an instant form of communication. On the dance floor, you couldn't tell who was who, or who spoke what.

Admittedly, lunch itself may have been a little confusing. Americans tend to eat cheese as an hors d'oeuvre at the beginning of the meal and the French eat cheese at the end of the meal, just before dessert. We had skipped the meal altogether. I was beginning to see the beauty of an intercultural marriage — things were so mixed up that we could get away with anything. Instead of doing it the American way or the French way, we did it our way. Our guests caught on soon enough.

In the end, the U.S. contingent did me proud. They inhaled the cheese like they'd been born eating it — not a wrinkled nose in sight.

Afra asked if she could perform part of the Persian wedding ceremony. During a traditional Persian wedding, the bride and groom sit under a piece of white silk, and all the married women grind two cylindrical cones of sugar over their heads to wish them a sweet life together. My mother came up, and then Nicole, then Sarah and Rachel and on and on till the cloth was heavy with sugar and Gwendal and I started to taste it on our cheeks.

There was no way Gwendal was going to get away without tap-dancing. Hervé and Axelle, two friends from his class, had already done a routine, and my American friends had been hearing rumors for months. Gwendal strapped on some borrowed shoes and went to it. The band struck up "Cute," and the saxophone players stood up and made a swift forward bow. Gwendal shuffle-stepped and turned and slid, and our friends hooted and cheered as if they were at the Super Bowl. As usual, by being exactly who he was and doing exactly what made him happy, Gwendal had charmed the pants off of everyone. I stood to one side, hands clapping in time to the music, thinking to myself: *I'm going to spend the rest of my life in Paris with a tap-dancing Frog.*

In that moment, it sounded like the best idea I'd ever heard.

On Sunday night, we organized a small "family" dinner at the Bistro Sainte Marthe. Only one person there was actually related to me, but I had always had the good fortune to choose my family. They set us up at a long table outside. The men started off with vodka rocks. Normally the French don't drink hard alcohol before dinner, they insist it dampens the palate, but the Yanks were in town, so normal etiquette was suspended. With more than a dozen guests and only two translators, I think everyone saw the advantage of more, rather than less, social lubrication.

We were a big group for a small kitchen, and the *raviolis d'escargots* were slow to arrive. What we lacked in food, we soon made up for in wine. Bottle after bottle was uncorked by the bar. By the time the pork ribs with honey and bloody steak topped with foie gras began trickling out toward the table, Yanig and Affif were speaking to each other in English: "Kahn you pleeze passs ze zalt. *Tu ne peux pas parler anglais, comme tout le monde?*" Why can't you speak in English like everyone else?

We decided that dessert for fourteen might cripple the kitchen permanently; there was plenty of leftover *croquembouche* in the fridge. We walked woozily back to the flat. As if English and French weren't trouble enough, Paul had decided to introduce some Yiddish into the mix. He had Yanig by the elbow trying to explain the word *Machatunim*.

"In English there is no word to describe the direct relationship between the two sets of parents." He called Gwendal over to translate. Auntie Lynn took a pillow off the couch and plopped down on the floor. I gathered various plates and saucers from the kitchen. I didn't have enough cake plates for everyone. It was a bit of a motley crew, but I guess I'd always preferred my life this way. Sprawled across our living room eating leftover wedding cake, we became a family.

On Monday morning, Gwendal and I went to my parents' hotel room to say good-bye. I noticed, for the first time, that the management had put a welcome basket in everyone's room for the Fourth of July — wine and fruit topped with a miniature American flag.

Paul zipped the suitcase and did a final sweep to see if they'd left anything in the bathroom. My mother, who had been good up until this point, finally burst into tears. "I just don't know if I can leave you here."

As she hugged me, hanging on for dear life, I realized she was hanging on for all the other times she unselfishly let me march out into the world — sleepaway camp, boarding school, college, junior year abroad, grad school in London.

I'd been so far away for so long. I pressed my forehead against her cheek and thanked her again, silently, for letting me go.

Three Recipes for Summer Goat Cheese

COURGETTE FLOWERS STUFFED WITH GOAT CHEESE AND MINT

Fleurs de Courgettes Farcies au Fromage de Chèvre

Early July, right around our wedding anniversary, is the brief season when courgette flowers appear at our local market. These delicate bright yellow blossoms have a surprisingly concentrated courgette flavor. In Italy they are often stuffed with ricotta. Here I've used local goat cheese and fresh mint.

> 1 egg
> 90 g fresh goat cheese
> Salt and pepper to taste
> 2 packed teaspoons chopped fresh mint
> 12 courgette flowers
> Extra-virgin olive oil

Preheat the oven to 180°C.

Lightly beat the egg, crumble in the goat cheese, and mash them together with a fork. Add salt, pepper, and mint. Stuff the flowers (no need to take out the stamen) with a small amount of cheese mixture. Twist to close.

Cover a baking sheet with aluminium foil. Pour a small amount of olive oil onto the sheet and spread it around with your fingers. Roll the stuffed flowers through the oil until lightly coated.

Bake for 12 to 15 minutes, until lightly browned and fragrant.

Yield: Serves 3–4 as an hors d'oeuvre

GOAT CHEESE, TOMATO, AND ANCHOVY TARTS

Tarte au Fromage de Chèvre et aux Anchois

Call me crazy, but I love a good anchovy. I could be one of those cartoon cats who dangles the fish above his mouth and comes away with nothing but the skinny skeleton. Puff pastry is an easy base for impromptu tarts like this one. Here, the salty zing of the anchovies gives the mild goat cheese a kick in the pants. Serve as a summer lunch or light dinner.

> 2 sheets frozen puff pastry, thawed
> 500 g soft goat cheese, cut into 1 cm slices
> 4 small tomatoes, cut into ½ cm slices
> 12 whole anchovies packed in oil, drained
> Oregano
> Black pepper

Preheat the oven to 200°C.

On a sheet of parchment paper, roll out the pastry until it is about half its original thickness. Using a small plate as a guide, cut out four 15 cm rounds. Transfer parchment paper to a large baking sheet (or two smaller ones).

Decorate each round of dough with slices of goat cheese in the shape of a flower (1 in the middle, 5 or 6 petals), leaving a 2 cm border of pastry all around. Top with 4 thin slices of tomato — use the larger center slices (keep the ends for your salad). Drape over 3 anchovies so their tails meet in the middle of the tart, like the spokes of a wheel. Drizzle with a tiny bit of the oil from the anchovy jar. Finish with a pinch of oregano and a grind of black pepper.

Bake on the lower middle rack for 25 minutes, until puffed and golden. Serve with a green salad.

Yield: Serves 4

PASTA WITH FRESH PEAS, ROCKET, AND GOAT CHEESE

Pâtes aux Petits Pois, Roquette, et Fromage de Chèvre

This dish is full of bright contrasts — hot and cold, raw and cooked. Five years ago, if someone told me I would take this much satisfaction in shelling my own peas, I would have laughed out loud. How times have changed.

> *500 g bow tie pasta (I use whole-wheat)*
> *2 cups fresh peas*
> *¾ cup good-quality Italian pesto sauce, or more to taste*
> *2 large handfuls of rocket leaves*
> *250 g soft goat cheese, crumbled*
> *Freshly ground black pepper*

Bring a large pot of salted water to the boil. Add the pasta.

When the pasta has 1 minute left on the clock, add the peas. Make sure the heat is extra high, so the peas don't drastically lower the temperature of the water.

Drain the pasta and peas, then return them to the pot. Add the pesto and stir to combine. Add the rocket and toss lightly.

Divide the pasta among four shallow bowls. Crumble the goat cheese on top and add a grind of pepper. Serve immediately.

Yield: Serves 4

CHAPTER 12

FAMILY VALUES

I know the real reason why "French Women Don't Get Fat."
It has a lot to do with stern looks from your mother-in-law
— and the annual return of *le bikini*.

I haven't been in a bikini since Afra and I went to Jamaica
for three days after she graduated from law school. In
between were two years in England, a bazillion vodka tonics,
and ten pounds. Now I was facing my first August vacation
with Gwendal's parents on the island of Belle-Ile, off the
coast of Brittany. Nowhere to run, nowhere to hide.

Since I arrived in France, I've looked around me with
wonder. How do all these women, often with several young
children in tow, look as though they just graduated from high
school? Is there a slender gene? As someone who left
"slender" behind with her last pink tutu, I was hoping that
nurture, rather than nature, played a dominant role. Maybe
now that I'm married to a Frenchman, I will be initiated into
the cult. There must be secrets, rituals, passed down from

mother to daughter. Since I don't have a French mother, but I'd very much like to look like Nicole when I'm fifty-five, I set about observing her behavior with an almost scientific interest.

Gwendal's mother is a near perfect specimen of French womanhood: five foot two, hair a becoming shade of graying blonde, and an even hundred pounds. She had Gwendal when she was twenty-two, and well into his teens people would ask him on the beach if they could scam a date with his older sister. She doesn't diet; she just doesn't eat.

Like most French women, Nicole is descended from Joan of Arc types — waiflike blondes who can halt an army with a single withering glance. I, on the other hand, come from hearty Russian peasant stock, and although I've always been relatively tall and slim, you can tell my hips were designed to give birth squatting in a field, digging potatoes. In addition to my natural endowments, Gwendal and I had just returned from a two-week honeymoon in Italy, which always does wonders for the figure.

We arrived by the early ferry, docked in the small port, watched by vacationers sipping their coffee and reading the paper. From the port you could see the seventeenth-century fortress dominating the hillside. I was not the only American on the island. The fort was hosting a classical music festival, organized by a U.S. tenor who had visited the island twenty years before and fallen in love. It was easy to see why. The port was lined with narrow stone houses, their shutters brightly painted in reds, blues, and greens. We were staying with family friends, who have a graceful house on the town square. Marie-Chantal was standing outside to welcome us. She was tiny, bird-like, with a pinched nose, short dark hair, and wrists like the pterodactyl skeletons you see in museums.

She, like Nicole, hasn't gained an ounce since she was twenty-five.

From the moment I walked in the door, it was clear that she thought there was a giantess in her house. I'm conscious that I'm a larger person than your average French woman, but despite the glossy magazines and the after-school specials, I grew up with a pretty great body image. Maybe it was being raised in a house with all women (even the cat). I've never been overweight, nor am I obsessed with being model thin or Madonna toned. Afra used to call me her Botticelli, because it's hard to tell if I have any bones. But looking at myself through Marie-Chantal's eyes, those postcollege pounds suddenly felt like a fat suit.

We unpacked our bags and went for a walk in the village. Nicole was on the lookout for a famous Parisian psychoanalyst who vacations here every year. She had just read his latest book and thought, maybe, *maybe*, she would have the guts to approach him if we saw him in a café. We ate lunch by the water, big bowls of mussels swimming in white wine. Nicole sipped a glass of Sancerre, and I noticed, not for the first time, that she didn't finish her French fries. She got a good way down, but you couldn't see the bottom of the bowl. I made a mental note. She ordered an espresso and drank it slowly, admiring the view.

After lunch we packed up to go to the beach. I had something to prove. My mother-in-law could be a very respectable member of a Vermont polar bear club. The house in Saint-Malo is a ten-minute walk to the sea, and she swims from April to October. Nothing hard-core, just a quick dip. The water is freezing, and the air outside isn't all that hot either. The water in Belle-Ile, Gwendal promised, was slightly colder. But I was going in, whether I liked it or not. I was not going to be the sissy American.

I'm completely in tune with the French attitude toward exercise: in my view, sweating is reserved for sex. I've never met a French person with what an American would consider a "workout routine." I don't know anyone here who belongs to a gym, except Fernanda, but she's Argentinean, and has that trickle-down Brazilian thing to deal with. Our French friends might take a dance class or spend their holidays hiking in the Pyrénées, or bike to work or walk up four flights of stairs with their groceries. But nothing specifically designed to get your heart rate up to 462 beats per minute.

When we arrived at the beach, I scanned the small groups of people dotting the sand. Something was odd. Then I realized, with considerable shock, that almost every woman, from sixteen to sixty, was wearing a bikini. Obviously, they didn't all look as if they'd just stepped out of the *Sports Illustrated* swimsuit issue. That would be unfair. There were wrinkles, some cellulite, less than perky breasts, a few flappy arms where muscle used to be. But in almost every case, you could see the body (with a few minor adjustments) that they must have had at seventeen. There was a distinct lack of things jutting out at odd angles. Very few jelly rolls, very few thunder thighs. The immediate impression was one of comfort and ease. They weren't perfect, but these people didn't hate their bodies. They had no reason to.

Looking around me on the beach that day, I began to formulate a theory. We've heard it all before: the French eat cheese and drink wine and somehow live longer and look better than Americans. What if the X factor is the vacation itself ? If every year, *every* year, you know you are going to spend at least two weeks in a bikini, maybe you pay attention. The five pounds of winter flab disintegrates with a few weeks of well-chosen meals, and by August you can bear to look at yourself in the mirror again. Think about how many five-pound winters there are between the average American and a two-week beach vacation.

I left my skirt and sunglasses in a pile. I wouldn't say I was feeling svelte, but it was impossible to feel self-conscious when there was a woman the age of my grandmother, not three feet away, wearing basically the same bathing suit.

Gwendal seemed to approve. As far as he was concerned, the more time I spent in something that resembled a black bra and underwear, the better.

Nicole had a one-piece, but this was no L. L. Bean granny special with superstraps and a skirt. It was a high-cut black number, with spaghetti straps and a plunging neckline. She took down her hair, which still falls halfway down her back. As she bent to take off her sandals, I caught a brief glimpse of the woman Gwendal must have played with on the beach twenty-five summers ago. She looked elegant, appropriate, beautiful.

We ran down to the water and plunged in, squealing. It was glacial.

The things we do for love.

As Nicole changed back into her skirt and braided her hair, I noted the contents of her bag: book, scarf, tube of sunscreen, bottle of water. I made another mental note. French women drink an extraordinary amount of H_2O. Nicole is never without a blue Vittel bottle. It's not that she totes it around — the French rarely eat or drink on the run — but wherever she stops, there's a liter close at hand. There is bottled water on the table at every meal, and she takes a smaller bottle (fortified with magnesium) up to bed with her every night. Even when she's not drinking water, she's drinking water: she drinks a big pot of tea in the morning, and *infusions* — herbal teas — in the afternoon and evening. She'll have the occasional beer, but I've never seen her within sight of a soda.

What was conspicuously absent from her bag were snacks. If an American family goes to the beach for the afternoon, chances are there's going to be a box of Fig Newtons in mom's tote, or at least money for a drippy ice cream cone. Nicole *never* eats between meals. She drinks wine at lunch;

she usually has dessert or a square of dark chocolate with her coffee. Sometimes, when she sees patients till ten o'clock, she'll come down and grab a plain yogurt with a spoonful of jam. But she doesn't *graze* in the kitchen, ripping off a hunk of baguette before dinner. She doesn't pick while she cooks, popping one green bean into her mouth for every one she puts in the pot.

The non-snacking thing must take practice, because by the time we got back from the beach I was starving. There was no way I could ask to stop by the bakery on our way home; we were past the hour of *le goûter* — the French four o'clock tea — when it might have been acceptable to have a *crêpe* or a *financier* to tide us over until the evening *apéritif*. There was no question of my going into the kitchen to grab a glass of juice or a piece of fruit; it was clear that the area was off limits except for strictly observed mealtimes, like banker's hours.

Dinner did not disappoint. Marie-Chantal had been to the market that morning and had come back with shiny aubergines and a basket of tomatoes for a ratatouille, and a large (but not enormous) sea bass.

Ratatouille holds a special place in my heart because it's the first French dish I learned to make by myself. Funnily enough, my introduction to French cooking was also my introduction to French women; I was taught by Agnès, the first Frenchwoman I ever met.

Agnès was an exchange student in Scotland the same year I was. She wore her hair pulled back into a bun, white blouses, and navy blue cashmere sweaters with a silk scarf tied neatly around her neck. Since I had a single room and she had a double, she once "sexiled" me, for a tall German guy who also wore a navy blue cashmere sweater. Even in the dorm, we threw dinner parties together, taking the mismatched knives and forks down to the study room with the big table in the basement.

Agnès was from Toulouse, in the south of France, so she knew a thing or two about sun-soaked veggies. She taught me how to sauté the onions until they turned translucent with a pale caramel around the edges. Then she added the slices of aubergine, but no more oil — because aubergine soaks up every liquid within reach. We served it over pasta; we were students, after all.

Marie-Chantal brought out the fish. Or, rather, she brought out a solid white mountain with the fish hidden inside. She had baked the bass in a crust of coarse sea salt, which she cracked open at the table with a knife and a hammer. It was spectacular really, like serving baked Alaska for a main course. She deboned the fish at the table, and if I had to guess I would say there was no more than two to three ounces per person. There were no leftovers, no seconds, just the memory of the *apéritif* and olives beforehand and anticipation of the cheese, salad, and dessert to follow.

I thought of my mother's table, laden with seconds and thirds for everyone, all the dishes brought to the table at the same time. In the States, I could easily eat triple the amount that was now on my plate without considering whether I was actually hungry. I looked at Nicole, spooning ratatouille, as bright as a summer garden, onto her plate. I made another mental note. If my calculations were correct, this was the main reason why, with no particular effort, I had not gained a single ounce since I moved to Paris. A French portion is half of an American portion, and a French meal takes twice as long to eat. You do the math.

I was conducting myself like a pro. I had succeeded in tuning my body to the French routine; my inner gremlin was no longer screaming "Feed me!" I began to feel the slow fullness that comes from a light meal, lingered over for several hours. It was different from the stuffed turkey feeling I usually had at home.

Then Marie-Chantal brought out the cake. "This was made for me by one of my constituents," she said, "*un vrai gâteau Breton.*"

I didn't know it at the time, but a *gâteau Breton* is essentially salted butter, with just enough flour and sugar to hold the thing together.

"*Elizabeth*," she said, holding out her hand for my plate. "*Une petite part ou une normale*" — a small piece or a normal one?

"*Normale*," I said, without thinking twice. But as the second syllable left my tongue, I felt an awful stillness in the room, and I knew I'd made a mistake. I didn't quite know where the error was, and I waited for someone to throw me a line.

"Are you sure?" said Marie-Chantal, still holding my plate in midair. "It's very rich." Her husband, a family doctor, looked at me intently, like a father trying to prompt his child to the right answer in a spelling bee. I knew without turning my head that Nicole wanted to crawl under the table on my behalf. I'd let down the sisterhood.

"*Oui, petite*," I said, trying to regain lost ground and still wanting my normal piece of cake. I ate in silence.

It took me years to understand exactly what had happened that night. To understand why it wasn't meant to be mean or humiliating, even though it was. Simply put, in France, eating is a social activity, and it is socially unacceptable to be heavy. To them, my American body was already on the verge of being overweight, and naturally, in the French way, I would want to watch myself. I'm sure nobody, not even Marie-Chantal, thought I should deny myself dessert. But surely, I wouldn't want to overdo it. I wouldn't want to be greedy. It was one little step, one small choice among so many others, that would keep things from ever getting out of hand.

That's the real reason why French women don't get fat: every day they make *petites* decisions that keep the larger weight loss struggle from ever having to begin.

Three Slimming Summer Recipes

In the French way, none of the recipes below will remind you of "diet" food, but they will happily be eaten by anyone at your table who is looking to get back into a bikini.

MUSSELS WITH WHITE WINE AND FENNEL
Moules Marinières

1.5 kg mussels
2 tablespoons butter
2 tablespoons extra-virgin olive oil
1 onion, finely chopped
½ bulb fennel, finely chopped
2 cloves garlic, thinly sliced
1 tomato, chopped
½ cup dry white wine
Freshly ground black pepper to taste (no need to add salt; the mussels will release some salt water)

Rinse the mussels, remove their beards, and discard any open or broken shells.

In your largest frying pan (with a cover), melt the butter, along with the oil, sauté the onion, fennel, and garlic till soft, 5 to 10 minutes. Add the tomato and cook for 2 minutes more. Add the white wine. Add the mussels, stir to coat with the sauce, cover and steam for 10 minutes. The mussels are done when they are fully open and the flesh is firm.

Remove the mussels with a slotted spoon, discarding any that have not opened.

Turn up the heat, and simmer the sauce until slightly reduced. Grind in some pepper. Pour the sauce over the mussels.

Serve with toasted slices of country bread, rubbed with a clove of raw garlic.

Yield: Serves 2 as a main course, 4 as an appetizer

WHOLE FISH BAKED IN SEA SALT
Bar en Croûte de Sel

This is an impressive (and very easy) method of cooking a large whole fish. The result is not overly salty, just incredibly tender with a hint of the deep blue sea.

> 1 large sea bass, 1–1.5 kg (do not scrape the scales)
> A handful of mixed fresh herbs (parsley, dill, coriander, fennel)
> 3–3.5 kg coarse sea salt

Preheat the oven to 200°C.

Rinse the fish and pat it dry. Stuff with fresh herbs.

Choose an ovenproof platter (or a baking sheet lined with several layers of heavy-duty foil) large enough to comfortably accommodate the fish. Spread a bottom layer of salt (about 2 cm thick, 1 to 1¼ kg) in the form of an oval 5 cm larger than the fish. Place the fish gently on top.

Completely cover the fish with a good layer of salt, patting lightly to make sure the edges are well sealed. Avoid pushing the salt into the cavity of the fish (it should already be full of herbs).

Bake for 30 minutes. Let the fish rest for 10 minutes outside of the oven.

Be sure to crack it open at the table. You'll need a hammer or an ice pick, plus an extra platter for the crust and the bones. Gently remove all the salt from the top of the fish, then make a shallow lengthwise incision with a sharp knife down the center and carefully peel back the skin. Serve the top fillet, then remove the spine to your *poubelle de table* (garbage plate) and serve the fillet underneath.

Yield: Serves 4 (or 6 Marie-Chantal portions)

SUMMER RATATOUILLE
Ratatouille

I've been blessed with two ratatouille mentors: first Agnès, and now our friend Anne, who also comes from the south of France. Anne cuts her vegetables in good-sized chunks and is careful not to overcook them. The result should feel like a walk in your neighbor's garden, not vegetable hash.

Anne's secret ingredient is a good pinch of saffron at the end, and, "if the vegetables lack sunshine," a cube of sugar. I add the sugar anyway — because who couldn't use a little extra sunshine?

> *⅓ cup olive oil (don't skimp, you can't add more later)*
> *1¼ kg onions (7–8 medium), thickly sliced*
> *750 g aubergine (2 small), cut into vertical chunks about 1 cm by 5 cm*
> *750 g sweet peppers (3 small: 2 yellow, 1 red), seeded and sliced*
> *500 g courgette (4 small), quartered the long way and cut into thirds*
> *1 kg sun-ripened tomatoes (6 medium), coarsely chopped, with their juice*
> *5–6 sprigs fresh thyme*
> *2 good pinches saffron (⅛ teaspoon)*
> *1 cube sugar (a scant teaspoon)*

Warm the oil over medium heat in your largest frying pan. Add the onions. Sauté, stirring occasionally, until they are wilted and just beginning to color (about 25 minutes). Don't skimp on the time here, as the onions need to sweeten; they provide the base for the whole dish.

Add the aubergine. Stir to coat. Sauté 10 minutes.

Add the peppers. You might need to lower the heat to maintain just a bit of sizzle. Sauté 10 minutes. The peppers will release some water, which will start the sauce.

Add the courgette. Sauté 10 minutes.

Add the tomatoes and fresh thyme. Heat until the tomatoes release some juice. Dissolve the saffron and sugar in the sauce. Cover. Cook for 10 minutes. Leave to cool.

Ratatouille tastes even better the next day. You can use it as a side dish, pasta sauce, filling for a quiche or an omelette, or over quinoa for a full vegetarian meal. It freezes beautifully, so make a few batches in the summer, before the tomatoes disappear.

Yield: Serves 8

Tip: Buy 2 smaller courgettes (or aubergines), instead of 1 large one. Smaller veggies have less water and a more concentrated flavor.

CHAPTER 13

THE CIRCLE LINE

Not only does intercultural romance require two languages, two countries, and two bank accounts; it also requires two weddings.

Because there was no religious ceremony in Paris, we decided to have a Jewish ceremony and a small cocktail party back in the United States. In early October, Gwendal and I packed up with Nicole, Yanig, Affif, and Annick for a trip to New York.

True, the New Jersey Turnpike would not have been my chosen introduction to my homeland, but you have to start somewhere. We parked in front of the house in Teaneck. It's a Tudor on a corner, not especially large, but with a little turret and some ivy that made it seem like a castle to me when I returned from school each day. My mother and father bought the house just before I was born. (The then shabby brownstone in Brooklyn Heights they *didn't* buy is still a subject of lament.) My room has slanted walls and shelves filled with all the books I've ever read. It's the only home I've ever known; the place I've come back to, whether dumping my laundry after a trip to India, or just showing up for dinner on the bus from Manhattan.

Nothing makes a new family cozy like sharing a bathroom. Affif and Annick were sleeping downstairs in the den. Everyone else was upstairs: Yanig and Nicole in my room, Gwendal and I on an inflatable mattress in the third bedroom turned walk-in closet. As I pushed aside my mother's silk blouses to make room for my pillow, I was glad we'd already gone on our honeymoon.

It was a little surreal: two people who had been married for three months gearing up for another wedding. I was still settling into my new title. I liked the words: *husband and wife*, so grown-up and serious, like playing house. I repeated them every day, as Gwendal walked in the door after work. *Hello, Husband*, I said, looking for an imaginary briefcase to snatch or a scotch and soda to stir. I turned the word over on my tongue like a hard candy, shiny and formal on the outside, liquid and sentimental in the center. Hus-band. I have a husband. It sounded even weirder in French. The first time I heard Gwendal call me his wife, it took me a second to figure out who he was referring to. *Je vais chercher ma femme.* That's me. Bizarre.

When Nicole and Yanig came down for breakfast the next morning they looked around, wondering, I'm guessing, where the other thirty guests were hiding. The dining room table was set for eight, but there was food for a battalion: Paul had run out to get fresh bagels, and there was a platter the size of a birdbath laden with smoked salmon and whitefish, surrounded by romaine lettuce, sliced tomatoes, and red onion.

My mother had taken out the silver. In our house, any excuse will do. Ever since I can remember, my mother has collected odd serving pieces: art deco grabbers for ice cubes, and a Victorian meat fork that almost got me arrested at

Heathrow. Her favorite is a set of individual silver asparagus tongs, in the shape of asparagus. At the kind of candlelit dinners Edith Wharton or Henry James attended, there would have been one of these at every place setting, so the ladies and gents could elegantly nibble their whole asparagus without cutting (heaven forbid), or sullying their fingers. This love of pomp and circumstance, an affection for the elegance and specificity of bygone days, is part of my mother's inheritance to me, along with the asparagus picker-uppers.

Watching my in-laws construct a bagel sandwich was like watching children play with their first set of Tinkertoys, trying to decide which piece to put where. Yanig followed Paul's lead, spreading a thick layer of cream cheese and draping the salmon in wavelike folds so it didn't hang too far off the edge. Nicole tried my mother's low-carb method, a piece of salmon and a slice of tomato, rolled in a large lettuce leaf.

My mother was determined to reproduce some of the elegance of our Paris wedding back home in New Jersey. She sought out a cheese shop in Ridgewood and took me to a tasting. Because of USDA regulations, raw milk cheeses aged less than sixty days are contraband in the United States, so most of what we sampled was a pale imitation of what I'd been eating in France. She had a local "French" bakery take a stab at our *pièce montée*. Instead of a proud pyramid of caramelized cream puffs, we ended up with the leaning tower of Hackensack.

It was like getting dressed for the encore performance of a play: same dress, different audience. Neither Gwendal nor my in-laws had ever been to a Jewish wedding. Religion in France is a very private matter, rarely shared with those outside the family or community. As I explained the symbols I'd grown up with and took for granted, I found myself coming up with surprisingly poetic and heartfelt answers for someone who had avoided organized religion as a rule. "The chuppah," I said to Nicole the night before, "is the tent that the bride and groom stand under during the ceremony. It represents the Temple, God's house, but also the new home Gwendal and I will build together."

We were using four plain wooden poles, just like they must have done in the desert, topped with a lace tablecloth (a modern addition) and my father's *tallis*. I thought he should be there, even in this small way. The rabbi had chosen a text from the book of Ruth: *Whither thou goest, I will go. Your land shall be my land. Your people shall be my people.*

I'm pretty sure that Nicole was expecting to step off the plane from Paris directly into a Martin Scorsese film. For the French, particularly for Nicole and Gwendal, America is supposed to look like the movies. The first time I brought Gwendal to New York, we walked down the snow-filled streets of Greenwich Village in the middle of the night, the windowsills and even the lampposts heavy with freshly fallen snow. He looked back at the path of his footsteps in the yellow light and swung himself around a tree with boyish glee. I knew he was waiting for Frank Sinatra to emerge from one of the bars, cigar lit and hat pulled low against the wind.

It had been a while since I'd done the tourist thing in New York. There are certain tastes and smells that I associate with the city, that feel right for the towering scale of the buildings and the shine of flattened quarters on the asphalt. If it had been December, I would have taken them on the same pilgrimage my father and I did each Christmas to Bendel's and Rockefeller Center, buying each of them a hot pretzel to warm their frozen fingers. But it was still bright, beautiful, crunchy-leafed autumn, just the right weather for standing outside Joe's Pizza on the corner of Sixth Avenue and Bleecker Street with a pepperoni slice.

You certainly wouldn't call it "cuisine," but along with a piece of carrot cake with cream cheese frosting, it's what I'd been craving since I got off the plane. We stood in line behind two students and watched as they sprinkled oregano and flakes of hot pepper onto their mottled red and white triangles. All this hand-held food was something of a novelty, and eating lunch standing up off an oily paper plate was as exotic to my new French family as a Turkish bath. To this day, I keep a photo on my desk of the eight of us, twisted in various attitudes, like a Delacroix painting of the imaginary East.

We went to the top of the Empire State Building on a rainy Tuesday, just before closing. This is a New York ritual I'd already endured with Gwendal, who is fanatical about views. (I should have known: if you're willing to stand in the three-hour line the day after Christmas, it's love.) I stood near my parents, feeling like I was on a school trip. When we got up to the ticket window, Paul turned to Gwendal. "She's all yours." I had been traded. I was now on somebody else's tab. I felt supremely stupid, almost thirty years old, and still nobody assumed I would be paying my own way.

There were awkward moments like this, when the twentyfirst-century woman in my head was forced to confront the consequences of my deliberately cultivated, poorly paid nineteenth-century interests. It was like I had Charlotte Brontë sitting on one shoulder and Gloria Steinem on the other. Gloria leaned over and whispered into my ear: *Where's your fucking parasol?*

We decided not to go to the Statue of Liberty, but to admire the view from the Ellis Island museum instead. I had a special reason for wanting to take them there: my paternal grandmother's Russian birth certificate was on display. These vaulted halls had been the funnel for millions of immigrants, including my grandparents, who boarded ships from elsewhere to become part of the American dream.

The American dream had become a hot topic of conversation between Gwendal and me over the past few months. He had taken my not so subtle nudge, and decided to expand his professional horizons. He had started looking for a new job. While he was in town, he was doing his first U.S.-style networking.

I had now been living outside the United States for a good portion of my adult life — I could no longer tell you what was on television, or who was playing in the World Series. What I clung to was the *idea* of my country: a can-do optimism and eye for the next big thing, a land full of good-natured opportunists willing to take a chance on the talent in front of them.

"You need a project," I said. "It doesn't matter if that's exactly what you end up doing, as long as it helps you meet the right people." In fact his background had his future project already built in. The next generation of movies would be shown, not on reels of thirty-five-millimeter film, but off of computer files. It was already starting in the United States; what would it take to bring this innovation to Europe? And who better than a cinema nut with a PhD in computer science to do it?

"But I don't have anything to tell them."

"Oh, yes you do."

Gwendal was about to learn the governing principle of the American dream: fake it till you make it.

Auntie Lynn set him up with a friend who was a consultant to the entertainment industry. Paul gave him an American cell phone, and of course she called him back while he was walking up Madison Avenue on his way to the Frick. He put a finger in one ear, trying to block out the traffic noise. We had worked on his "elevator speech" — how to present your idea in the time it takes to get from the lobby to the third floor. This was harder for him than you might imagine. In France, you spend your entire life learning how to bury the lead — the point comes somewhere in the middle of the fourth paragraph, and money can't possibly be discussed until after a five-course meal. But Gwendal is a fast learner, so he took a deep breath and gave her the two-minute pitch. It was like watching a really good pantomime. First his brow went all wrinkly, like he was trying to solve a geometry proof, then his eyes went wide, like a man facing the guillotine over how many jelly beans are in the jar at the county fair, and finally there was an urgent nodding of the head and a bewildered smile.

All she said was this, three little things he had never heard in France:

That sounds really interesting.

How much are you looking for?

Please send me your business plan.

Then she hung up. It was a five-minute conversation. But I could see it. "Ms. Madison Avenue," as we came to call her, had fired the engines of the possible — and the wheels started turning in Gwendal's head.

The late afternoon sun was glinting off the skyscrapers of Wall Street as we exited the Ellis Island pavilion and headed toward the dock for the ride home. Then, my sense of direction being what it is, we got on the wrong boat. We were halfway to Battery Park before I noticed. The captain generously agreed to take us back to the Jersey side — all by ourselves. As we sat on the prow of our own private ferry, chugging toward the Statue of Liberty at full speed, I knew I'd outdone Martin Scorsese *and* Ms. Madison Avenue, delivering my own perfect slice of the American dream.

Recipes That Feel Like Home

MY MOTHER'S NOODLE PUDDING

This dish — egg noodles and ricotta studded with golden raisins and sprinkled with cinnamon — is the very essence of home to me. Serve with a roast chicken or just cut yourself a big piece for dinner, like sweet lasagna.

> 350 g large egg noodles
> 160 g butter, melted
> 5 eggs, separated
> ½ cup sugar
> 500 g ricotta cheese
> 500 ml sour cream
> ¾ cup golden raisins
> Cinnamon

Preheat the oven to 180°C. Butter a 23 by 32 cm casserole dish.

Parboil the noodles for 5 minutes. Drain and rinse them with cool water to stop the cooking process.

Melt the butter in a small frying pan over a low heat.

In a large bowl, whisk the egg yolks and sugar until the mixture is a nice lemon yellow. Add the ricotta, sour cream, and melted butter; whisk to combine.

Add the noodles and raisins, stirring to coat.

Beat the egg whites until stiff. Fold them into the noodle mixture. Transfer to your buttered casserole, sprinkle with cinnamon (my mom makes a lattice pattern, as on a pie), and bake for 45 minutes (up to 1 hour), until golden.

Yield: Serves 8

GRANDMA ELSIE'S SPAGHETTI SAUCE WITH PORK RIBS AND MEATBALLS

My grandma Elsie Kishner's spaghetti sauce would make Martin Scorsese proud. My grandparents lived in Utica, New York, during the Second World War; he designed airplanes and she stood in line at the butcher. She learned to cook from the Italian ladies she met there — thus the great American contradiction of a Jewish grandma's sauce full of juicy pork ribs.

SAUCE

2 kg country-style pork spareribs
Salt and pepper
500 g minced beef (not too lean)
1 tablespoon dried parsley
1–2 tablespoons olive oil
2 medium onions, finely chopped
6 cloves garlic (left whole)
8 × 400 g cans crushed tomatoes with added purée
2 cups tomato water swished around from the empty cans
800 g passata
1 × 375 g can tomato paste
3 bay leaves
2 tablespoons sugar
1 tablespoon Italian seasoning (or 1 teaspoon each parsley, oregano, thyme)
1 tablespoon dried basil
1 tablespoon dried oregano
A pinch of hot pepper (optional)

MEATBALLS

1 kg minced beef (not too lean)
2 eggs
1 tablespoon dried parsley
1 tablespoon dried oregano
1 teaspoon garlic powder
1 teaspoon onion flakes
1 teaspoon Italian seasoning

A good grinding of black pepper
½ cup Italian-style breadcrumbs
⅓ cup ice water

For the sauce: In a large stockpot, brown the spareribs in 2 or 3 batches and sprinkle with a little bit of salt and black pepper. Set aside.

In the same pot, brown the minced beef and sprinkle with black pepper and parsley. Drain the fat and set the mixture aside.

In the same pot, heat the olive oil; sauté the onion and garlic cloves.

Add the beef and spareribs (and any meat juice), tomato liquids, and seasoning. Bring to a boil. Lower the heat and cover the pot, leaving the lid slightly ajar. Simmer over low heat for 2 hours.

While the sauce is simmering away, make the meatballs.

Aunt Joyce insists that the key to fluffy meatballs is to handle the meat as little as possible. That, and the ice water.

Put the beef in a large bowl, breaking it into small pieces with your hands.

In another bowl, whisk together the eggs and seasonings until light and slightly foamy — this just adds a bit of extra air to your meatballs. Pour the egg mixture over the meat. Sprinkle with the breadcrumbs. Mix lightly with your fingers. Sprinkle with ice water and combine. Working gingerly, pat into small balls.

Brown the meatballs in 2 batches — no need to cook them all the way through; they will continue cooking in the sauce.

Add the meatballs to the sauce. Simmer for a further 30 to 45 minutes.

Serve with spaghetti or penne. (When I was little, I insisted on pasta shaped like wagon wheels.) Have a pair of tongs handy to make sure everyone gets a sparerib.

Yield: Serves 8 (with enough for seconds)

CHAPTER 14

AFTER THE FAIRY TALE, THE PARSNIP

I've read enough fairy tales in my time to know that the wedding is supposed to come at the end of the story. But in real life, even in Paris, happily ever after is just the beginning.

Three months after our wedding in New York, my father-in-law, Yanig, was diagnosed with stage IV colon cancer. I wanted to yell at somebody. More specifically, being American, I wanted to sue somebody. But there was no one to blame. His family doctor, who had ignored ten years of stomach pains and diarrhea without so much as suggesting a colonoscopy, was the head of the local medical board. We did not want to spend what little time we had left writing letters.

There was no more "getting to know you"; I was now part of the family. Gwendal and I traded weekends, taking the three-hour train ride to Saint-Malo. We drove home from the station past the winter sea, a dark mirror, calm and matte. While Nicole continued to see patients in her office upstairs, I handled the shopping and the cooking.

Maybe it was the urgency of the situation, but Nicole was surprising graceful in letting me take over her kitchen. In the past year I had tried to be a careful assistant, observing the way she spread a little mustard on the bottom of a quiche crust or pooled a few drops of vinegar into one of Yanig's ceramic bowls to make dressing for a salad.

It was a slow, solitary time. I diced onions, boiled small red potatoes, trimmed leeks, and washed heads of purple-tipped lettuce. Gwendal and I were supposed to be thinking about our future, but my thoughts kept wandering toward the past. And while I was supposed to be thinking about Gwendal's father, I was thinking about my own.

My father and I spent a lot time in the kitchen together; he liked experimenting. He used to volunteer as a teacher of English as a second language; he had a lot of Asian students, and probably more than one Asian girlfriend. Some time in the early eighties, he bought a wok, and the cabinets were often stocked with ingredients I'd never seen before — bags of dehydrated mushrooms and jars of oil with labels in Japanese. He had a sweet tooth; he kept raisins in the refrigerator and mini Milky Way bars in the freezer — very dangerous for my braces. His studio apartment in Chelsea (before it was trendy, or gay) had what was, by Manhattan standards, an eat-in kitchen. There was just enough room for a small round table and two chairs overlooking the black tar roofs and riveted water towers of Eighth Avenue.

On Sunday mornings, before my mother picked me up, he would bring back two croissants from the French bakery around the corner. He heated them briefly in the oven and put them on the plates we'd picked out together upstairs at Zabar's. They had a white rim and featured a village scene in the center like a child's drawing: green grass, tiny women in red aprons standing in front of Monopoly-sized houses whose chimneys puffed curlicues of gray smoke. I have a picture in my mind's eye: when my father finished his croissant, he would press the tip of his thumb into the center of the plate to pick up any last crumbs. When he died I gave away a lot of things, but I kept the plates and the wok, its metal base blackened by years of grease and fire. Six years after his death, what was left of my father were these flashes of memory, often easier to live with than the reality of the man I knew. I wondered what Gwendal would remember when Yanig was gone.

Yanig was sleeping a lot. Bach cantatas played softly on the stereo; he sat on the couch with a book, eyes closed. When I dropped a pot cover on the kitchen floor he would wake up. "*Je dors pas. Je ferme les yeux.*" That's exactly what my father used to say. I would be sprawled out on the rug or on my little chair bed watching *The Love Boat* or *Fantasy Island*. "Daddy," I would say to the couch behind me. And the answer was always the same. "I'm not sleeping. I'm just resting my eyes."

In fact, the food I made most during Yanig's illness wasn't French at all; I made chocolate chip cookies. It felt like the right thing to do. They are warm, lumpy, and imperfect, so different from their more sophisticated cousins in the window of the *boulangeries*. The brown sugar makes them forthrightly sweet in a way that's conspicuously American. My mother sent an extra set of plastic measuring cups and bags of Nestlé Toll House Morsels. When I ran out of chocolate chips, I chopped thick bars of bittersweet chocolate I found at the local supermarket. The weeks when Gwendal went without me, he carried a batch under his arm on the train.

Yanig had them with tea in the afternoon. He became rather possessive about them, tucking them in the back of the cupboard and jokingly refusing to share them with Affif, whose visits became more frequent. Yanig's appetite, along with his massive frame, was shrinking. Physical tasks were wordlessly delegated to others. Yanig used to shuck oysters like he was popping a soda can. Soon Gwendal got up to do it without being asked. A neighbor came by to mow the lawn. To everyone's relief, even during the chemotherapy, Yanig never lost his beard. Neither Nicole nor Gwendal had ever seen him without it; it would have made him unrecognizable.

Hospitals smell the same all over the world. Like death and disinfectant.

When you live in another culture, sometimes even life-and-death decisions are made in a way that you don't understand. Suddenly I was plunged into a world where a second opinion was an insult to your doctor; patient and family received different, often contradictory sets of facts; and a precise diagnosis, never mind a comprehensive list of treatment options, was simply never presented.

The French are often touted as having the best health care in the world. It's universal, it's cheap, and it's technically up to snuff. The system's fine. The part they don't tell you about is the doctors themselves — an entire generation trained on the premise "doctor knows best." They look down from on high, feeling no need to explain themselves or involve you in any way. Like other French figures of authority — teachers, bankers, politicians, priests — it's OK to grumble about their performance over dinner, but not to challenge them.

The doctor said there was something they would "try." I waited for Nicole or Gwendal to come back with a list of questions. I had been to the National Cancer Institute website; it was all there in black and white: stage IV colon cancer. Spread to liver? Yes. Lungs? No. Diagnosis, prognosis, treatment, clinical trials. There was no such website in France. La Ligue Contre le Cancer had a hotline you could call for information from nine to four; it rang and rang into the void.

They never told us he was dying, which of course he was. They never gave him the choice to get up while he still could and go for a last sailing trip around the world. So we just waited, while they "tried things." Time, which should have become so concrete, so precious, was knotted up in their evasive web of words. I waited for Nicole or Gwendal to confront the doctors, to demand to be part of this process. They couldn't, or wouldn't. When Gwendal finally asked for Yanig's records to get a second opinion in Paris, the doctor refused to release them. When we insisted, the doctor tucked his chin into his neck and snorted through his nose like a horse. "You need to *decide* who his doctor is."

There was something else. When Gwendal's father left boat-building to become an artist, his official status, the one that showed up on the hospital admission records, was *chômeur* — unemployed. He had chosen to step outside of France's sacred societal superstructure, and this made him, in some way, expendable. Gwendal and Nicole never lost their conviction that this influenced the quality of his care.

I'm sure everyone feels helpless in these situations, but my helplessness was compounded by the fact that I was working with a cultural handicap. I didn't know how to make an impact. If I had been in New York, I would simply have stood there until someone gave me an answer. I would have called the nurse, the doctor, the head of the hospital, made enough noise so that someone would have to listen to me. We found the French doctors to be experts at avoiding this type of confrontation. Legions of secretaries, phone messages unreturned, endless public holidays, ski vacations. In France, the squeaky wheel doesn't get the oil, it gets the evil eye.

I was frightened and frustrated by Gwendal's behavior. Why wouldn't he fight with these people? Would he fight for me? What if one of our children was sick? Would he stand there mute and bewildered and say that he simply couldn't get anyone on the phone? That the doctor was on vacation?

If I was dying, would he say that there was "something they would try"?

It dawned on me for the first time. In coming to Paris, in marrying Gwendal, I had signed up for more than flaky croissants and shiny mackerel. I had accepted a way of dealing with life and death. If I got sick tomorrow, there would be no Sloan-Kettering, no fourth opinion from a specialist in Minneapolis with a promising new drug. I felt trapped in someone else's system, like I'd bought a one-way ticket to a place I didn't understand.

Back in Paris, Gwendal and I were lying in bed with the dictionary open between us. "It's like a big, fat white carrot," I said, flipping through the pages. I was looking for a parsnip to make matzo ball soup.

We found "parsnip" in the dictionary. *Panais*. "Never heard the word," said Gwendal, "never seen one."

Whenever someone wants to make an unfair substitution in life, it is usually accompanied by the phrase "not bad, just different." But there is no such thing as "different" matzo ball soup. My mother's is a steaming pot of chicken broth, doctored with dill and parsley, slices of carrot bobbing to the surface. The matzo balls — floaters, never sinkers — are pale fluffy dumplings that soak up the broth and fill up the tummy. Never mind that the broth comes out of a can and the matzo balls out of a box. This was my chicken soup for the soul and, as with any magic spell, there could be no changes, no substitutions. My mother's recipe called for a parsnip. Damn if I wasn't going to have a parsnip. I was a woman on a mission.

Clearly this was not just about root vegetables. In the weeks since Yanig's diagnosis, fear and frustration had infected every corner of my life. I fought the little battles because I couldn't fight the big ones.

At the market the next morning, I could see my breath as I inspected the piles of winter vegetables. The *vendeurs* had been there since seven a.m., wearing dark hats, hooded sweatshirts, several layers of woolen sweaters, and knit gloves with the fingertips cut off. Their hands were cracked and dry, like the skin of the onions loosely piled on the wooden stands. I surveyed my choices: there were white radishes and black radishes, both as long and thick as cucumbers. There were turnips — colored like a basket of marbles — deep purple and white, sherbet orange and pale green. There was always my pet celery root. But this particular day I wasn't looking to experiment. What I wanted was an exact match. Where was my dun-colored, slightly hairy, tapering-down-to-a-point parsnip — the same one I could buy in ShopRite for $1.99 a pound?

I decided to table the root vegetable issue and move on to the supermarket. Turns out, there was no point in worrying about the parsnip at all. I had a bigger problem: there was no chicken broth. I don't know why I'd never noticed it before, but the only broth sold in France comes in the form of dehydrated powders or cubes. What did the French do when they wanted honest-to-God bouillon? *Make their own?* I took a deep breath, puffing out my cheeks and exhaling in the middle of the aisle. Soup, justice, and the American way just wasn't happening. I was going to have learn to make soup *à la française*.

I went back to the market, my breath rising like a column of smoke from a fire-breathing dragon, and took home as many onions as I could carry. If I couldn't make my classic, I would make their classic. I would make French Onion Soup. Screw 'em. I would make "Better than French" onion soup.

Onion soup used to be made especially for winter marketgoers like me. It's the kind of soup my parents ate on their first trip to Paris in the narrow cobblestone streets next to Les Halles. (My father, apparently, was tickled pink to be approached by a middle-aged prostitute on the rue Saint-

Denis.) The trucks would converge on Paris's central market at around five a.m., and the *vendeurs* would fill up on a bowl of steaming broth before spending hours in the cold hawking apples, oysters, and recently plucked chickens.

I got home and began peeling with a vengeance. Working with one dullish serrated knife, I sliced a small Kilimanjaro of onions, tears stinging my eyes and fogging up my contact lenses. Surely this was some kind of initiation. French soup required suffering.

That winter, I became a soup machine. Unlike the chunky American ones I'd grown up with, most French soups are smooth vegetable *veloutés*, eaten as a first course or with bread and cheese for a light meal. The idea of making soup out of *fresh* vegetables was new to me. In our house, matzo balls aside, soup was something you made from leftovers — bits and bobs that had been hiding for an indeterminate length of time at the back of the fridge. Naturally, it never turned out the same way twice. This concoction even had a name; we called it Tuesday Soup. Auntie Lynn used to make Sunday Soup, throwing in the week's scraps. When my mother got married, she decided she should have her own day of the week.

The best thing about learning to make French soup was that it required power tools. The hand blender became my new best friend; the deafening bbbrrrizzzzzzzzzzz was a satisfying outlet for my frustrations. I had to be tender with Gwendal, solicitous toward Nicole, jocund with Yanig, but the vegetables received no mercy. Carrots were crushed, potatoes pulverized, leeks boiled to within an inch of their lives. I filled up the freezer with Ziploc bags of liquid solace.

My onion soup was a success. I stopped short of the ugly brown crocks with the single blunt handle, buying myself some thick white ovenproof bowls instead. I bashed apart a *boule* of sourdough bread, so stale the knife barely scratched the surface. I sprinkled a cushy layer of Gruyère on top, putting the whole thing under the grill until the cheese bubbled and the oven threatened to fill with smoke. It was good. In fact, it was excellent. But a warm bowl of soup wasn't quite enough to fill the cold spot that had opened up inside me.

(Other) Winter Soups

I always make soup in big batches; it freezes beautifully, so you'll always have something easy and warm to heat up on a cold day.

"BETTER THAN FRENCH" ONION SOUP
Soupe à l'Oignon Gratinée

I used to brown the onions on the stovetop, but a flip through Aunt Joyce's *Cook's Illustrated* magazine revealed that it's much easier to do this in the oven. A French classic improved by American ingenuity. Ha!

> 2 kg (10–12 medium) onions, halved and sliced
> 4 tablespoons unsalted butter, cut into chunks
> 2 tablespoons extra-virgin olive oil
> Scant ½ teaspoon coarse sea salt
> A few sprigs of fresh thyme
> 1 bay leaf
> ½ cup dry sherry
> 8 cups broth (I use chicken broth; some people prefer a combo of beef and chicken)
> 8 slices stale baguette or sourdough bread (the older the better)
> 500 g Gruyère or Comté cheese, grated

Preheat the oven to 200°C.

In a casserole dish, combine the onions, butter, olive oil, salt, thyme, and bay leaf. Cook, covered, in the oven for 1 hour. Stir and, leaving the lid slightly askew, continue to let the mixture cook in the oven for an additional 1½ hours.

Transfer the dish to the stovetop. Cook the onion mixture over medium-high heat, until the liquid is evaporated and the onions are golden, about 20 minutes.

Add the sherry and cook 5 minutes more.

Add the broth, scraping the bottom of the pot to loosen any

caramelized onions. Bring the soup to a boil and simmer for 30 minutes.

Spoon the soup into eight individual ovenproof crocks and top each with a crouton and a layer of grated cheese.

Place the crocks under the grill for 1 to 2 minutes, until the cheese is brown and bubbly.

Yield: Serves 8

CREAMY CARROT SOUP
Velouté de Carottes

Because this soup is really a one-man show, the quality of the carrots will affect the taste. Try to buy carrots with their greens still attached. Do not, I repeat, *do not* attempt this (or any) recipe with those baby carrots sold in the plastic bag. They are fine for dip but miserable for cooking.

⅓ cup olive oil
2 onions, diced
1 kg carrots, sliced into ½ cm rounds
5–6 cups chicken broth
1 cup milk
½ teaspoon freshly grated ginger (optional)

Heat the oil in a stockpot; add the onions and sauté until translucent and just beginning to caramelize, 7 to 10 minutes.

Add carrots and stir to coat. Cook, partially covered, for 30 minutes, stirring occasionally, until carrots are sweet and tender.

Add 5 to 6 cups chicken broth (if you like your soup extra thick, start with 5), and purée until the mixture is chunky.

Add the milk and ginger and purée until smooth.

Yield: Serves 6–8

Tip: I serve this soup with Camembert, baked in its own wooden box (200°C, 20 minutes) for a cozy winter lunch.

CAULIFLOWER AND TAHINI SOUP
Velouté de Choufleur au Tahini

This soup was inspired by a winter lunch at Scoop, a small American-run restaurant near the Louvre. The owner, Anne Leder, always keeps a stock of long-grain wild rice and animal crackers on hand, and she makes the best yogurt ice cream I've ever tasted. This soup is a traditional French velouté that uses tahini (sesame seed paste) instead of cream to add richness and depth. Subtly flavored and as white as freshly fallen snow, it looks lovely garnished with a few poppy seeds.

3 tablespoons extra-virgin olive oil
1 medium white onion, diced
1 kg (1 medium) cauliflower, cut into 1 cm cubes
5½ cups chicken broth
1½ tablespoons tahini (sesame seed paste)
Poppy seeds

In a stockpot, heat the olive oil; add the onion and sauté until softened but not colored, 5 to 7 minutes.

Add the cauliflower and stir to coat. Add ½ cup chicken broth, cover, and steam for 20 minutes, stirring once at the halfway point.

Add the remaining chicken broth, bring to a boil, lower heat, and simmer for 5 to 10 minutes, until the cauliflower is tender. Cauliflower doesn't like to be overcooked — it gets gray and smelly — so don't just leave the pot on the heat forever.

Get out your trusty hand blender and blend until smooth.

Stir in the tahini. Ladle the soup into bowls and sprinkle with poppy seeds.

Yield: Serves 6

Party time: This soup can be elegant as well as homey. For a winter-white New Year's Eve, serve a small portion of soup in a shallow bowl, topped with poppy seeds, chervil, and a trio of seared scallops.

CHAPTER 15

HOW TO MAKE CHEESECAKE IN A PÂTÉ PAN

On my mother's most recent trip to Paris we stopped into Dehillerin, a famous French kitchenware supplier near Les Halles. My mother was in search of a long rectangular springform pan; Aunt Joyce bought one in Paris twenty years ago and never found another. We browsed the worn wooden aisles filled with miniature tart molds and sieves big enough to drain pasta for the Italian army. We spotted the pan, and my mother, flushed with the thrill of the find, raced up to a gentleman in a white coat, and before I could intervene, blurted out in English, "I'd like to buy this. Please." I saw a half smile emerge, then disappear under his mustache.

"Do you know what this is for?" asked the gentleman, in his best Maurice Chevalier English.

"I'm going to make cheesecake," said my mother innocently.

"*Ah, mais non, madame,*" said the gentleman. "This is for pâté, madame, not for *gâteau.*" And with a perfectly straight face, he added, "Why do you want to buy *somesing* when you do *not* know what it is for?"

Americans take a sense of endless possibility for granted. It makes us optimistic, sometimes insensitive, often a little greedy. In the States, a salesperson would sell you his left foot if you wanted it, and probably gift-wrap it to boot. The idea that an object has an immutable — a *correct* — use is a subtlety lost in our culture of the two-in-one. The idea that someone would prevent you from spending money to prove this point is positively unimaginable.

There is something else at stake here, and that is the personal integrity of your *vendeur.* In France, the customer isn't always right. On the contrary, the customer is often deeply wrong, and the person behind the counter will not hesitate to tell you so. Why would you come into their shop to buy a skirt that doesn't fit or a bottle of wine that doesn't complement your meal? There is still very much a *proper* way to do things, and more often than not, it's the way things have always been done. Change is threatening; innovation is considered downright dangerous. A salesperson in France is not so much there to do your bidding as to impart a morsel of their folkloric knowledge, be it about wine, vanilla beans, or plumbing supplies. Since I moved to Paris I've radically expanded my definition of an expert.

The *vendeur* stared us down, his hand stuffed, Napoleon style, over his heart, under his smock. To prevent a Waterloo-sized diplomatic incident, I shoved my mother out onto the street, quickly paid for the pan, and left.

Back on the curb, I handed my mother the bag. "What was *that* all about?" she said.

I hardly knew where to begin. "You forgot to say *bonjour.*"

I was having some trouble getting my family to understand the parameters of my new life.

Suddenly everything my mother said or did felt like a criticism. Believe it or not, this was a new feeling for me. I'd been lucky. Unlike so many teenagers and young adults, I'd always felt like my mother really "got" me. Now she didn't understand a thing. She just kept piling on the questions. Of course it was natural for her to ask about my life. But the deeper she dug, the more I got the sense that she didn't want to know how my life in Paris functioned. What she wanted to know was why I wasn't doing all the things I would be doing if I still lived in New York.

This wasn't new. Even now, I know we are gearing up for a fight when she starts a sentence with "Why can't you *just...*"

As in: Why can't you *just:*

Get a job

Make some friends

Find a dentist

Buy some mothballs

Get a life

This kind of inquisition began during my first winter in London. On a drizzly evening after dinner my mother and I were upstairs in my bedroom in the narrow brick town house in Islington that I shared with an English lawyer and an American day trader. While I put away laundry, my mother was fingering the curtains.

"I know. They're disgusting," I said, as I arranged my T-shirts in the sagging walnut veneer armoire that served as my closet. She continued to inspect the heavy mustard-colored velour. The curtains were pleated, to trap as much dust as possible, with a dangling plastic pulley I could tug to let in some daylight. They were supposed to keep out the draft. I imagine they'd been doing just that — uninterrupted by a trip to the dry cleaner — since 1963.

"Why can't we *just* go and buy some new curtains?" she said. "We can go now." I looked at my alarm clock; it was nine p.m. on a Sunday.

The comment made me instantly and disproportionately furious. It was as if my mother didn't realize she'd gotten on a plane at all. There are exactly *three* stores in central London that sell curtains, *all* of them are on the other side of the earth, and *none* of them is even *close* to being open at nine p.m. on a Sunday night. Do you see a car? Do you see a shopping mall? Is there a Bed Bath & Beyond between here and the Angel tube station? No, no, and no, we can't *just* go and buy some new curtains.

I knew I was being short. Yes, certain things, lots of things, were easier in the United States. But we *weren't* in the United States. I was still American, and the hideous asthma-inducing curtains frustrated me too. But I had made a choice, and it had nothing to do with convenience. My mother did not share my feeling of awe as I stepped into the hushed rotunda of the British Library with my reader's card for the first time. She didn't linger with me over the glass cases filled with illegible inky scratchings, the handwritten letters and manuscripts of Milton, Shelley, and Auden. She didn't come with me two or three times a week when I popped in to see my favorite painting at the National Gallery, a Rubens portrait of a wealthy merchant in his gossamer ruff, a dab of white paint shining from the corner of his eye like a freshly formed tear. There were reasons, private reasons, why I was here, and — I guess this was the hardest part — none of them had anything to do with her. Europe was all the ways in which I wanted my life to be different from my parents', all the things they couldn't give me. At least in London she could understand the language. Paris was just one step further away, into my own world, one she couldn't fully participate in.

If I was touchy in London, at the moment I was downright electric — positively *third-rail* sensitive — about Paris. This was not a semester aboard, a holiday, a tryout for some future version of my life. This was it. Yes, the story line thus far was very appealing: I was young and in love and had my whole life ahead of me. I was living "every girl's" dream. But I had yet to find my own. I had yet to find my own passion, my personal project, the thing that would help make Paris *mine*. Until I did, I knew that every comment would set me on edge like the scratch of a fingernail against a chalkboard. My mother was right. I did need a job, a dentist, and, in general, a life. But I was doing the best I could, and for the time being at least I couldn't bear criticism of my choice. I was trying so hard to convince myself it was the right one. I didn't need anyone else talking this country down.

But the questions just kept coming, and I had only one exasperating answer. Because I'm *not* in New York, and things just don't work like that here. It's hard enough trying to build a new life in another culture without having to explain the process to everyone back home. The journalism was coming in at a very slow trickle — I seemed to spend eighty percent of my time pitching ideas to editors, twenty percent actually writing. I found that travel articles tended to be written by staffers on vacation rather than freelancers on the ground. I was getting a piece of art criticism here and there, but mostly in London or New York, so I spent my fees going back and forth to do interviews and see exhibitions. My mother decided that to pick up the slack, I should start a museum tour company. Start a company? How could I make her understand that just going to the post office in Paris was sometimes an all-day project? There were days when each step I took was like wading through a room full of cold mashed potatoes. The idea of diverting what little energy I had left into a business that was not my ultimate goal left me wanting to curl up into a little ball and cry.

My mother wasn't the only one asking questions. My friends back home were asking too. When I called Amanda in LA, we talked about Yanig, about Gwendal, about my mom.

She slowly tried to bring the conversation around to me. "So, when do you think you'll be going back to work?"

I didn't know how to say it any other way: *Honey, this is work.*

Nothing presented more opportunities for misunderstandings than dinner.

Anyone who has so much as been on vacation in another country knows that dinner is a loaded concept, full of opportunities for both heartfelt communication and mortal embarrassment. I first realized this the summer my mother, my friend Sarah, and I spent in Israel when Sarah and I were twelve. We were renting a small apartment in Jerusalem, and Auntie Lynn joined us for part of the trip. Auntie Lynn has been my mother's best friend since they first taught together at Ditmas Junior High School in Brooklyn in 1965. Lynn left teaching to get a PhD, eventually becoming a corporate trainer and executive coach. She is a fearless businesswoman, the kind who will promise you a pink private jet out of thin air on Friday afternoon and somehow have it ready by Monday morning. She stepped off the airplane and immediately whipped us into a frenzy of activity. She has a naturally low body temperature, so she wore a knit dress with a carefully knotted silk scarf and pearls on our hike up Mount Masada (I fainted in the Roman baths). One of the items on her busy agenda was an Israeli business contact, Simon, whom we arranged to meet for dinner. The night before, Sarah and I hand-washed our only skirts in the apartment bathtub. Just before seven, my mother opened a can of olives and placed them in a glass bowl on the Formica coffee table.

Simon arrived, wearing a sport jacket and pressed khakis. He sat down on the couch. After an hour, the olives had been exhausted and Sarah and I politely excused ourselves to go to our room. Another hour passed, the adults still sitting on the sofa making polite conversation. My mother waited until Auntie Lynn was gesticulating wildly in front of Simon and rolled a jar of peanut butter and two apples across the tile floor into our bedroom. I don't like peanut butter, but I ate it anyway. Two hours later, Simon finally got up to leave, with a bewildered bow. My mother shut the door and raised her eyebrows at Auntie Lynn. Clearly, we had missed something. We assumed, as two women and two children in a strange land, that surely we would be going *out* for dinner, at a restaurant of Simon's choosing. He assumed that two women and two children in their own apartment would be cooking. As my father used to say: "assume" makes an "a-s-s" out of "u" and "m-e."

Now that we had a real kitchen in Paris and four chairs to sit on, I was eager to impress my parents, show them the part of my Paris routine I liked the best — shopping and cooking. The apartment was coming along nicely. Gwendal had put in a whole wall of bookshelves in the bedroom and one of Yanig's vases, black with a red rim like the mouth of a volcano, was filled with twisty, droopy *renoncules*.

Making dinner in Paris can be an hours-long affair. Normally, I enjoy this, going from one shop to another, picking up my walnuts here, my fish there, my bread somewhere else. But with my mother in tow, this routine required a running commentary and a military schedule. "Just let me finish my coffee," she would say when she finally arrived at the apartment to pick me up. "Mom, the market closes at one. If we don't get there, we're not going to eat."

"OK, just let me go the bathroom." Paul, on the other hand, had discovered the chocolate hazelnut spread Nutella, and was never to be heard criticizing France ever again.

Walking up the rue du Faubourg du Temple took half an hour. My mother is an even more committed window-shopper than I; she stopped to look at the cellulite creams in the window of the pharmacy and the prickly durian fruit outside the Chinese grocer.

My accent in French is good enough that the *vendeurs* at the market think I'm something other than American or English, usually Italian, which I take as an enormous compliment. With my mother at my side, the cat was out of the bag, and they all started speaking in pidgin English. *Hel-lo, hel-lo, lady. Lady. Iz good. Good. No cher. No cher.*

I got in line at my usual vegetable stand behind two grannies and a young African woman with a double stroller. "There are green beans over here," my mother said, inspecting the half-rotten peppers across the way.

"Yes, but the good green beans are over here. There's a line for a reason."

They had only salmon steaks at the market, so we ended up at the local Monoprix supermarket to buy salmon fillets. This was much safer territory for my mother — fluorescent lit with a reassuring number of things under plastic. "You should buy some more," my mother said. "What if someone wants seconds? We can eat it for lunch tomorrow. Or you can freeze it."

"But I don't *want* to eat leftovers." I was on the verge of throwing a temper tantrum worthy of the two-year-old restacking yogurt containers just in front of me. I realized how French my shopping habits had become. Particularly where protein is concerned, I now buy only one serving per person. Have you seen the price? Besides, I don't want lots of little mystery containers hiding in the back of the fridge at the end of the week. There's another wonderful market to go to tomorrow, and, it so happens, I get a lot of pleasure out of it.

Portion size had been a particular source of contention since I started cooking for my parents in France. I come from a long line of New York Jewish cooks — if you don't have leftovers, you didn't make enough. The first time my parents had dinner in Saint-Malo, I could see the look of panic in my mother's eyes when Nicole brought out a single fish to serve six people and a bowl of rice that wouldn't have added up to the leftovers we took home from our local Chinese restaurant. My mother is a very good sport. When she is at Nicole's, it's *do as the Romans do*. But when she's in her own daughter's home, damn it, she wanted something to *eat*.

As I walked up and down the aisles looking for a jar of sun-dried tomatoes, she loaded up the cart. "Mom, we have to carry all this." She suddenly remembered that the car was not out back. She put the six-pack of San Pellegrino back on the shelf.

We were trudging up the stairs with the groceries. "It's a good thing you live on the first floor," she said, huffing up to the landing with her bags. "Actually," I said, "there might be a bigger apartment free just upstairs." Her ears pricked up with interest. We had been in our new apartment less than a year, but I could see the metal cogs turning in her head, the neon sign flashing, *Baby's Room, Baby's Room.* "The owners are ready to sell," I said, "and the price is amazing, but there seems to be a problem with the tenants." I saw her face fall as I explained. I could read her mind: *How is it that my only daughter ended up schlepping her own groceries and living below a Chinese Mafia brothel?*

Setting the table, at least, was not a problem. My mother simply can't stop bringing things. In my two-room Parisian apartment with one closet, I now own an orange plastic egg poacher, a cake timer (shaped like a cake), five plastic spatulas, three sets of tongs, a state-of-the-art lemon zester, and service for twelve in 1950s metallic ice-cream dishes. The Mixmaster is on its way. All this is part of my mother's "stuff is love" theory, which states that if you transfer enough objects from your old home to your new home, you never left. It's her own special form of denial, silver plated.

My mother has a game she plays with Gwendal. She arrives, with her two overstuffed suitcases (checked), two shopping bags (carry-on), and two cardboard cartons (precisely packed and weighed by Paul not to exceed the excess baggage limit). They make sure to arrive on a weekday morning, just after Gwendal leaves for the office. The challenge is this: If she can bring it, unpack it, and hide it before he gets home from work, it stays. If he finds it again before she leaves for the States, he has the right to send it back. Since Gwendal would never go digging in the back of the closet without a very good reason, she's winning, having tucked away the rolling pin, the punch bowl, and Grandma Helen's mother-of-pearl-handled fish knives.

Even the dinner hour was a debate. My parents were used to eating at seven p.m., certainly no later than seven thirty — but often Gwendal and I didn't sit down till nine. They couldn't possibly go to bed on a full stomach, so they were often up till two or three in the morning, permanently jet-lagged by their stomachs. My mother resurrected her old schoolteacher's habit of eating an extra meal at four p.m., usually standing up in front of the refrigerator.

At least she was complimentary about my cooking. "Why do these green beans taste so good?" *Because we waited in line*, I wanted to say, but I stopped myself. "I tossed them with a little walnut oil and some *fleur de sel*. They have less water in them, so they stay crunchy even if you cook them a little longer."

Then came the cheese and salad.

I watched my mother at the table, knife poised above the cheese platter, making calculations in her head. In France, dinner is a ritual, and each food has its own particular little dance to learn. Like the pâté pan, there is a correct way to approach the cheese. Round ones, like *chèvre* or Saint-Felicien, are cut from the center like tiny pieces of pie. A triangular wedge of Brie or *bleu* must be cut from the side, into ever thinning slivers, and a large rectangular slab of

Comté or Cantal should be approached from the inside edge, working toward the hardened *croûte,* until it is roughly the length of your knife blade, in which case it should be sliced from the side. The idea is never to leave any diner with just the moldy crust. And of course, to avoid, if at all possible, taking the last piece.

The salad was a test, not so much of geometry, but of manual dexterity. My mother was already suspicious. The same *vendeur* who weighed out our five-hundred grams of *haricots verts* also wrapped up a large head of red leaf lettuce. "*Attention, il y a de la viande dedans,*" he said, winking at my mother.

"What did he say?"

He said, "Watch out, there's meat in there." As salad from the market comes out of the actual ground, and not prewashed out of a plastic bag, there are often small flies and the occasional slug to be rinsed away before dinner. The lettuce leaves can be as big as linen napkins, and for some reason you are not allowed to cut them. You have to fold instead. It's like making origami with a knife and fork, and it takes some practice. I watched my mother struggle with an unruly leaf, flicking a bit of vinaigrette onto her sweater.

It was an odd role reversal. Suddenly I was the master of etiquette, the holder of the keys to a whole bunch of social cues that my mother hadn't fully mastered. I felt powerful, and surprised at how much I was enjoying her discomfort.

I was reminded of the first time I had ever really been in over my head at a dinner table. The food, of course, was French. My cousin Steven, who I thought walked on water, had just graduated from Princeton, and Auntie Lynn threw a dinner in the private dining room of a Manhattan brownstone. The warm wood of the art nouveau interior enveloped us in flowers and flourishes as we walked in. At fourteen, I was the only teen invited, and I was dressed in a cream raw silk suit, heels, and makeup that made me to look twenty-four. As at a proper grown-up dinner party, the seating was mixed and I was nowhere near my mother. I was sitting next to Tom Tuttle, Steven's best friend, lanky with tiny glasses and a mop of curly brown hair. I smiled shyly, hoping there was no lipstick on my teeth, as he pulled out my overstuffed chair.

The first course was *escargots*, and although I was a pro with the mussels, I'd never quite tackled snails. They arrived in a porcelain dish fitted with circular indentations. Each iridescent shell had its own little hole, like a miniature golf course, filled with a pungent green paste of parsley and garlic butter. I could hear a low sizzle coming from the plate.

I had certainly been taught my forks and knives, but the *escargots* had their own special thingamadoo, a pair of mental tongs with curved pincers at the end, a lot like the eyelash curler my friend Carol tried on me before our last school dance. I smoothed my napkin, stalling for time, but it was no use. I couldn't catch my mother's eye. Without turning my head, I snuck a quick look at Tom's hands and followed suit. I picked up my tongs, trapped a shell, and wiggled out the snail with my itty-bitty fork.

Now what? I felt like I was standing in the middle of an etiquette intersection, ten years of rules and regulations whipping by at warp speed. I decided to go with the cardinal rule "never put too much food in your mouth at once." So I picked up my knife and started sawing away. No love. The knife just bounced back and forth, making not a dent in the slippery surface of the snail. I pressed harder. I was now in danger of doing a Julia Roberts in *Pretty Woman* and sending the thing flying across the room. Tom stepped in just in the nick of time. He leaned over, placed his hand gently on my wrist, and whispered in my ear, "You don't have to do that." Then he popped a whole *escargot* into his mouth. Tom Tuttle, my hero.

I cleared the table and bent to take the dark chocolate ice cream out of the freezer for dessert. Paul has fallen madly in love with Carte d'Or, the standard-issue French supermarket ice cream. He insists it tastes better than the stuff back home. I made the coffee, enough decaf for eight people, to fill my parents' mugs.

Back in the living room, I set four of my imported 1950s metallic ice cream dishes on the table.

My mother looked out our naked window. "I still think you could use some curtains."

Dinner in Paris

SALMON WITH FENNEL COMPOTE IN A PUFF PASTRY CRUST
Saumon en Croûte

Baking anything in a puff pastry crust used to remind me of
Charles Dickens — pork pies and whatnot — but this presentation
is so easy and elegant that I now think of it as quintessentially
French — perfect for mothers (and other people to whom you need
to prove yourself upon occasion). This dish is essentially two
salmon fillets stacked one on top of the other (with fennel compote
in the middle) baked between two sheets of puff pastry. Think of it
as a huge salmon turnover if you like. This particular combination
is adapted from *Restez à table avec vos amis* by Thierry Breton,
Yves Camdeborde, Thierry Faucher, Rodolphe Paquin, and Sylvia
Gabet (Minerva, 2004).

FENNEL COMPOTE

> 2 tablespoons olive oil
> 1 medium bulb fennel, diced (about 2 cups)
> 4 shallots or 1 small onion, diced
> 1 tablespoon chopped fresh dill (packed)
> 1 tablespoon pastis, anisette, or other licorice-flavored
>   liqueur
> 3 sun-dried tomatoes in oil, diced
> 1.25 kg boneless, skinless salmon fillet (see if you can get
>   the center cut, without the narrow end)
> 2 sheets puff pastry
> 1 egg yolk
> Coarse sea salt and freshly ground black pepper

Heat the olive oil in a saucepan; add the fennel and shallots and
sauté for 10 minutes. Add salt and pepper to taste. Stir in the
dill, anise, and sun-dried tomatoes. Set aside. The compote can
be made a day ahead.

Cut the salmon into two parts of equal length.

Line a baking sheet with a large piece of baking paper. Roll out one sheet of puff pastry, roughly in the form of a rectangle 5 cm larger than the fish. Brush with beaten egg yolk. This will be your bottom crust.

Place half the salmon in the center of the puff pastry. Salt and pepper the fillet and spread with the fennel compote. Place the second piece of salmon gently on top.

On a piece of baking paper, roll out the second sheet of puff pastry into a rectangle slightly longer and wider than the first. This will be your top crust.

Leave the pastry on the parchment paper (this makes it easier to handle), flip the top crust, and drape it over the fish. Discard the baking paper and press the edges of the crusts together with a fork to seal, careful not to make any holes. Trim any excess pastry. If you have cookie cutters, you can use the extra dough to make designs for the top. I usually make a little school of fish, Cheesy? Perhaps, but I don't think Dickens would disapprove.

Place the turnover in the fridge, covered in plastic wrap. Bring it to room temperature before baking.

Preheat the oven to 180°C. Bake for 40 minutes, until the pastry is puffed and golden.

Gently slide the finished fish, in all its glory, from the baking sheet onto a serving platter. Cut at the table, serve in slices.

Yield: Serves 6

HARICOTS VERTS IN WALNUT OIL
Haricots Verts à l'Huile de Noix

In my humble opinion, slim French *haricots verts* beat the pants off of regular old green beans, and are worth searching around for. They cook quickly yet retain their snap.

> 750 g haricots verts *(extra-slim French green beans),*
> *topped but not tailed*
> *1 tablespoon extra-virgin olive oil*
> *2 tablespoons walnut oil*
> *Coarse sea salt*
> *Freshly ground black pepper*

In a large frying pan, heat the oil. Add the green beans and stir to coat. Cook at a low sizzle for 3 minutes and keep the beans moving around. Add a good sprinkle of sea salt.

Cover with the lid slightly ajar and cook for 6 more minutes, stirring every 2 minutes or so. Add more salt to taste and a good grinding of pepper.

Serve warm or at room temperature. (If you have leftovers — doubtful — eat them topped with big chunks of tuna or a poached egg for lunch the next day.)

Yield: Serves 4

CHAPTER 16

FOREVER IN FRANCE

I'm a sitting in a bar, wearing my most flattering black trousers and a carefully knotted scarf. My palms are a little sweaty, and I'm fussing with my hair. If only to get my mother off my back, I have a hot date — with a new friend. She's a bit older than I am, went to Brown, then to Germany on a fellowship from the Goethe Institute. She also has a French boyfriend, a freelance job, and an imperfect grasp of irregular verbs. The boyfriend is an old colleague of Gwendal's, so we have been set up. Courtney calls this "friend dating," the hopeful shopping around for kindred spirits of the same sex. If you think about it that way, I've dated a lot more women than men.

Making friends in a new country is a constant negotiation between sympathy and convenience. Like any dating experience, there will be those who say they'll call and never do, those who invite you somewhere only to ignore you — and the worst, those with whom you share a passionate moment of laughter who literally flee the country the next day.

Katherine suggested we meet at an Irish pub near the Louvre. Irish pubs are better at brand management than Starbucks. They look and smell exactly the same all over the world: dark booths, sticky tables, and smoky carpet in hunting green. If Katherine was a man, she wouldn't have gained any points for site selection. I had brought along a French magazine (I'm trying to improve my vocabulary on breakup tips and beauty quizzes), my feeble attempt to look busy while I was waiting. It was just getting dark as she came through the door. The place instantly got a little less ugly. She is, it's true, a perfect 10: five foot eleven, with long brown hair, the shoulders of a rower, and the legs of a supermodel.

She kissed me on both cheeks and sat down. "Have you been to the *préfecture* yet?" Asking whether you've been to the police station to deal with your carte *de séjour* is the most basic form of expat small talk, like commenting on the weather.

"No, I have an appointment for July."

"Go early, and make sure you bring the photocopy *and* the original." For all that she could be frolicking on the beach in a Bain de Soleil ad, I have a feeling that Katherine is, like me, comfortingly pragmatic, bordering on anal.

She ordered a *blanche* and I ordered a glass of Muscat. The conversation was easy, fluid, without halts for translation or searching for words. I love Gwendal, but sometimes I just need to wake up in the morning and talk to an American. I discovered that Katherine is from Pennsylvania, and that she went to college with her identical twin sister. There was a brief pause as I imagined the two of them tag-teaming at a Friday-night party, holding a beer by the neck of the bottle, trailed by scores of baggy-jeaned boys determined to have sex in a Doublemint commercial. I also discovered that her French boyfriend is actually her French husband, though she doesn't wear a ring and introduces him as her *copain*.

"I didn't even tell my parents we were getting married. I mean, we decided to do it, for the papers, but Syl doesn't believe in marriage."

This wasn't the first time I'd heard this. Several of Gwendal's friends had been living together for years, were having children even, with no intention of getting married. "It was a really simple ceremony, just the two of us and two witnesses at the *mairie*. I told my parents afterward."

"Wow," I said, "that must have been hard." I imagined my mother, chin held up at an impossible angle, refusing to speak to me ever again, tearing her clothes like the guy in *The Jazz Singer*. I couldn't wait to get home and call her. At least I didn't do that.

Katherine and I left with a promise to get together for dinner in the coming weeks. A second date. Very promising. Very promising indeed.

One pragmatic perfect 10 does not a social circle make, so I finally agreed to do what I'd been dreading and began exploring the more formalized American expat community.

Why doesn't she try to make some French friends? you say. She is, after all, living in Paris. If only it were that simple. Americans are used to meeting people. It's how we expand our horizons, create opportunities — personal, professional, romantic. I found that, for whatever reason, people in Europe don't need more friends. They have their families, the people they grew up with, the people they went to university with, colleagues to talk to on a cigarette break. Their social world is made up of tiny circles, closed but overlapping like those Chinese ring toys you can never untangle from one another. In Paris, it is not unusual to walk into a room of thirty-five-year-olds and find out everyone has known each other since high school. A new sexual partner — *le mec* of the moment — seems to be the only revolving door.

I had already banged my head against this wall in London. Thank God I went to school there, or I might have spent several years of Saturday nights alone with a spoon in a jar of lemon curd, watching *EastEnders*. I would go to a party, spend the evening talking to someone, and, naturally for me anyway, before I left I would look for a way to follow up. My mistake was impatience. An English acquaintance was once drunk enough to explain it to me. We would have to meet at at least *three* events, he said, before I could even *consider* suggesting that we see each other outside a group context. His assumption was, if I was at *this* party, then surely we knew someone in common, and therefore I would be at the *next* party (or dinner or play or rugby match) in six months' time. After a couple of these mutual-friend events, all spaced at appropriate intervals, maybe, *maybe* there would be an exchange of salient contact details or a vague plan to meet at the pub after work. Call me crazy, but life is short, and I just don't have that kind of time. I come from a city of eight million people. If you meet someone you like at a party, you'd better get something down on paper, or chances are you'll never see them again. "But what if there was no other group context?" I said. He shrugged. "Well, then we don't come from the same world and there is no reason for us to be friends anyway."

There is no way to make European friends overnight (unless you sleep with them). But Americans, particularly abroad, travel in packs, and they will talk to anyone. I had to start somewhere.

I found a group called Forever in France, a club for American women married to Frenchmen or other species of European. Gwendal calls it my Stuck Here meeting, where women with multiple graduate degrees who cannot find gainful employment complain about their underpaid husbands and swap the phone numbers of ob-gyns. We are the ladies who can't afford to lunch.

That's where I picked up Kelda.

This month's meeting was at the home of a woman named Nancy from South Carolina. When I exited the metro with my map I did a double take to make sure I hadn't gotten off in Versailles by mistake. I was surrounded by huge Haussmannian buildings of pale limestone, punctuated with stately wrought-iron balconies. Way up top, against the starless sky, were rows of tiny round dormer windows, lit like unblinking eyes. At the corner, overlooking a small park, was a particularly curvy specimen, the portico draped with reclining nudes and topped with a marshmallow dome. It was seven p.m. and there was not a soul in sight. I walked up to a set of varnished doors and tapped in the entry code I'd been given.

Forever in France was a renegade operation. It had recently broken away from one of the larger women's groups at the American Church — Wives of American Oil Executives with Expense Accounts etc. Nancy was a little bit of a cheat — she was married to another American, a lawyer — but they were here for the long haul and she wanted to make some friends who weren't leaving next week for a posting in Abu Dhabi. When she opened the door, blonde hair tucked behind her ears, I smiled sweetly and immediately asked for the powder room. She pointed me to a hallway that looked as if it went on for miles. There was a choice of doors, four or five of them. I didn't know anyone in Paris with a choice of doors.

I fixed my hair and tried to psych myself up to walk out into a room of perfect strangers. It was the same feeling of dread that used to come over me when I was dragged to Jewish singles events in New York. Why would anyone assume I had something in common with these people just because they're American?

I spotted her as soon as I walked into the living room. She was talking with a group of women in cashmere twin sets the color of tree bark. She was wearing a turquoise tunic and carrying a boxy black vintage handbag — a tropical parrot among the sparrows. She was pale and platinum blonde, with the perfectly outlined red lips of a forties starlet. If Kelda looked like Veronica Lake, she sounded more like Andrew Dice Clay. Were I to put our meeting in a movie (and Kelda deserves to be in movies) she would be at the center of an expectant crowd. You wouldn't see her face, you would simply hear her voice, hard like rock candy, and see the glass of white wine raised above her head. She was — she always is — in the middle of a good story. In her best homegirl jive, and at a volume significantly louder than the polite hum of conversation around us, she burst out: "I *told* my husband. I said: 'Listen *up,* mother*fucker.* I left my *home,* I left my *family* for you. I want a PUPPY.' When I saw little Starsky in the window — *man,* it was like a fucking *meeting of the minds.*" She flicked her hands back and forth between our foreheads like a hypnotist. Then her face went all soft and her voice went all Barbra Streisand. "We had a moment," she said, as she pinched two imaginary cheeks in front of her. "'Who's your mommy?'" she cooed, puckering up her lips like someone's dangerous great-aunt Shirley who spits. "Whoosoomommy. Whoosoomommy." Suddenly the homegirl reappeared. "'I *get* you baby. You mine. You *mine.*'"

In fact, the truth was considerably more embarrassing. I followed her into the elevator. I knew it was a bold move, but we'd had a nice conversation, she was a singer, married to a French jazz musician, and I saw her roll her eyes when the hostess clinked a teaspoon against her glass to make an announcement. It wasn't much, but I'd encouraged guys in bars for less.

"Hold the door," I said, slipping in after her. It was one of those old-fashioned elevators, shiny hardwood with gumdrop-sized green buttons and a brass accordion grille instead of a door. Parisian elevators are famously cramped, made for trysts rather than transportation.

I let out a sigh of relief as I wedged myself in beside her. She smiled. "Hey, you weren't here last month. You missed the PowerPoint presentation: *Scrapbooking: This Is Not a Joke*. I thought I was going to put a bullet through my skull."

I wanted to kiss her. Instead I said, "Do you want to have coffee sometime?"

Outside on the deserted street, I tapped her number into my cell phone and descended into the metro.

When I got home, Gwendal was reading a book on the couch, waiting up for me.

"So?"

God, this really is like dating.

Apparently, Kelda went home flapping her wings. She whooshed in the door and announced to Nico: "I have a new friend. And she's so *normal*."

I've had a breakthrough. I think there is a French woman in my life. Gwendal's friend Axelle wants to meet me for a coffee this afternoon — without Gwendal. I've been courting her slowly. Like approaching a deer in the woods, I make no sudden movements. I'm afraid to scare her away.

Gwendal met Axelle at tap class. When he first introduced us, she seemed smiley, so I tried to do a little reconnaissance. Gwendal was no help at all.

"What does she do?" I said, while popping the laundry in one night.

"I don't know exactly."

"You don't *know*?" I said, looking at him in bewildered astonishment. "You've known her for over a year. She was at our wedding. How is it that you don't know what she does for a living?"

"I don't think it is very important to her." I was no closer to understanding this very French answer. "She is involved in many other things. I think she is the elected official for culture in her hometown. She organizes a music festival."

Despite this blank in the job department, I was drawn to her. She seemed open and curious. She also loves to travel. I don't know where she gets the money, but she is always away: Jordan, Burma, Benin — and she brings back weird stuff.

She loves animals, but not cute and cuddly animals: big, meat-bearing, transportation-providing animals, particularly cows and camels. She came back from her most recent vacation, a hiking trip in the desert, with a present for us: red sand from the Sahara. Her own prize was a dried camel turd, supposedly laid by the mount of a famous explorer.

I knew I was getting somewhere when she offered to take me to some of her favorite boutiques during the January sales. It's not nothing when a French woman asks you to go shopping with her. She is choosing to let you in on some of her secret chic spots. And there are no two women in the world who can't bond over a beautiful pair of shoes.

Axelle is about my height, though smaller on top, with short brown hair. She is *chic* in a very original way. She wears more color than most French women; instead of a fitted jacket in gray or black, she'll have one in stoplight red or canary yellow. She often wears asymmetrical cuts; one side of a skirt will be shorter than the other, or there might be a strap or a buckle leading over her shoulder to nowhere.

This afternoon's coffee seemed urgent, and she clearly didn't want Gwendal around. I soon learned the source of the hullabaloo. Among Axelle's many enthusiasms is a love of Radio France — French public radio. She had met an older radio producer. He was in Saint-Malo for the weekend and suggested she join him.

"His latest text said" — she scrolled through her messages — "'Do you like sex on the beach?'" She bit her lip shyly. "Should I go?"

"*Je ne sais pas*, " I said. "Where I come from, Sex on the Beach is a drink. Is it capitalized?" I said, leaning over the phone to take a look. "Or in quotes?"

But no, in France, sex on the beach is apparently just that: sex on the beach.

Was I imagining it? Or was a French girl asking me for dating advice? I felt giddy. Weightless. Like the guy I'd had a crush on since junior high just asked me to the senior prom. I'd been invited into the private world of a French person. We each ordered a second *café noisette* and commiserated until the sun went down.

Dinner Among Friends

For dinner with the girls, I tend to go for light and creative: bright, fresh tastes and, of course, a little booze to keep the gossip going strong.

AUBERGINE STUFFED WITH QUINOA
Aubergines Farcies au Quinoa

4 medium aubergines, 300 g each
1 tablespoon plus 2 tablespoons olive oil
1 small red onion, diced
3 cloves garlic, thinly sliced
5 ripe tomatoes, coarsely chopped
½ teaspoon sugar
⅓ cup white wine
1⅓ cups chicken broth
1 cup quinoa (available at health food stores and many
   large supermarkets)
Coarse sea salt
Freshly ground black pepper
A pinch of cinnamon
A small handful of coriander, coarsely chopped, plus more
   for garnish
250 g soft goat cheese, sliced into 8 rounds

Choose aubergines that are firm, shiny, and without blemishes — the smaller and heavier, the better. Preheat the oven to 180°C. Rinse the aubergines and pat them dry. Line a baking sheet with aluminium foil. Prick five or six holes in each aubergine with a fork to allow steam to escape. Rub the surface of the aubergines with 1 tablespoon olive oil. Bake for 1 hour, until the flesh is tender.

Meanwhile, in a medium frying pan, heat the remaining 2 tablespoons olive oil. Add the onion and garlic and sauté over medium heat for 3 to 4 minutes. Add the tomatoes and sugar, and cook for 10 minutes. Add the white wine, lower the heat to medium-low, and cook for a further 10 minutes. Remove ¾ cup tomato sauce from the pan and set aside.

In a small saucepan, bring the chicken broth to a boil. Add the quinoa and bring back to a boil. Cover tightly, lower the heat, and simmer for 15 minutes, until water is absorbed. The quinoa should have the consistency of couscous. Fluff with a fork and leave to cool.

When the aubergines are done, drain any liquid from the baking sheet and let the aubergines cool slightly. Make a 10 cm cut in the top of each aubergine and carefully scoop out most of the flesh without piercing the skin. Put the aubergine shells in a shallow casserole dish (you will stuff them later). Put the flesh in a colander, pressing firmly with the back of a fork (or your hand) to drain any excess liquid. Season the flesh with salt, pepper, and cinnamon.

Chop the seasoned aubergine flesh into small chunks and add to the tomato sauce in the frying pan, along with a small handful of coriander. Heat through. Add the quinoa, stir to combine.

Stuff the aubergine shells with the quinoa mixture; they should be heaping. Top each aubergine with a spoonful or two of your reserved tomato sauce. (You can refrigerate the aubergines at this point. Reheat at 180°C, tightly covered with foil, for 30 minutes. Proceed as below.)

Set the oven to grill.

Top each aubergine with 2 slices of goat cheese. Cook on the middle rack of the oven for 3 to 4 minutes, until the cheese is softened and beginning to color.

Sprinkle with fresh coriander. Serve with a large green salad.

Yield: Serves 4

LEMON SORBET WITH VODKA
Coupe Colonel

1 litre lemon sorbet
A good bottle of vodka or eau-de-vie

Serve 3 small scoops of lemon sorbet in each of four glass *coupes*. Pour a shot of vodka over each one.

Yield: Serves 4

CHAPTER 17

LADIES WHO LUNCH

I know I'm not a tourist anymore, because I have started to play mean games with Americans on the metro. When you live abroad for a certain amount of time, you develop a special brand of disdain for the bumblings of your fellow countrymen. You despise them for all the things they don't know and can't say, which are the same things you didn't know and couldn't say only a few months ago. Why must they consistently block the escalators on both sides? Are they really making a dinner reservation for six thirty p.m.? You're sure you want that steak *well done*?

The cultural short circuit that amazes me the most is that Americans in Paris still think no one can understand them when they speak. Packed like sardines on the metro they will talk as if they are in an empty room — the man next to them smells terrible, the flush mechanism on the hotel toilet is *completely inadequate* to deal with their recent bout of diarrhea. Yet they're not speaking Finnish, or Swahili. They are standing toe to toe with a generation of Parisians brought up on MTV. So my new game is to sit down next to some Americans, chat with Gwendal in French until they say something truly *gauche,* then switch to English and watch them turn purple with shame.

Sometimes it gets downright kinky. The seats on the metro are arranged in snug blocks of four, so it's no work at all to hear the nuances of other people's conversations. One Saturday afternoon Gwendal and I sat down across from an older American couple. They were your classic conspicuous tourists: sixty-somethings with fanny packs, white sneakers, pleated khaki pants and elastic-waist jeans. At the beginning it was sweet. They were in town for their fortieth wedding anniversary. "Just wait till I get you back to the hotel," said the husband, putting his hand on his wife's knee, centimeters from my own. This, *à la limite,* was normal; I'm used to couples groping each other on the metro. Suddenly things took a turn toward the cringe-worthy. In the tone he might have used to ask for extra peanuts on the airplane, he looked over at her: "Did you pack the K-Y?"

Gwendal and I stood up at the next stop. "Let go," I said, louder than necessary, catching the husband's eye as I inched my pelvis past his wire-rimmed glasses toward the door. He looked stricken, like he'd watched his pension fund plummet or lost a very important round of golf.

I'm on the metro more often these days, because I'm on my way to work. I hate to prove my mother right so much of the time, but I recently started giving private tours at the Louvre.

One of my editors at an art magazine in New York had a friend who was finishing up a PhD in Paris and had starting giving high-end art tours. With *Da Vinci Code* mania in full swing, she was suddenly overwhelmed and looking for help. I knew myself well enough to anticipate the upcoming identity crisis about being an Ivy League tour guide, but I pushed it aside. My mother was right; if I didn't get away from my computer soon, I was going to turn into a space bar.

It was perfect. Back in the world of museums, I felt like a caged animal released into my natural habitat. Walking under the limestone arcades, past the spray of the fountains, and down into the cool marble atrium beneath I. M. Pei's glass pyramid, I was my old self again. Speaking English, I was once again smiling and articulate, capable of transmitting something that was deeply important to me. How I'd missed that, being able to grab hold of language, mold it, and use it to put myself into the world.

Taking people around the Louvre is a seduction. Every object has a tale to tell — and once people get past the overwhelming size of the place, they just look at you like kids expecting a bedtime story.

Of course I didn't do all the talking. If you can get them started, almost everyone has a strong opinion on the works of art they see, and they approach them in light of their own expertise. The doctors in particular have a lot to say. There was an orthopedic surgeon who had his wife, two daughters, and me in front of the sculpture of the Venus de Milo for ten minutes, trying to imitate her pose. Apparently her hip rotation is physically impossible without breaking something that he would then have to fix.

Even the *Mona Lisa* is not immune to diagnosis. A makeup artist once told me she looks much more feminine from the left side because of the way her hair is parted. Who knew? Then there was the chiropractor. "She has a ganglion cyst. See that lump, on her thumb." And for the first time, I did. "We should write a paper together," I said. "I bet no one has ever published that before."

The greatest days are when I convert someone. Particularly to a work as overexposed and bastardized as the *Mona Lisa*. It's difficult to get someone to look past the reproduction they've seen a thousand times to the woman that Leonardo brought to life.

My most recent visit was with a couple from Berlin, a French girl and her German boyfriend. She had booked it as a surprise. He had never been to the Louvre, and she hadn't been since she was a child.

There's always a moment when you walk in to see her. She is in a room the size of a basketball court, filled at any given moment with three hundred people, and just as many cameras snapping away. She remains serene, unperturbed by her celebrity.

The boyfriend started to walk up to her and promptly turned around. He had decided he was more interested in the colorful fifty-foot painting of the *Marriage at Cana* on the wall behind us.

I knew I had to get us a little closer. "This is where it pays to have played a little college football," I said. "Just follow my elbows." We snuck up around the side, not more than four or five feet from the glass. He stared for a moment, pursed his lips, and shook his head, like a man sizing up a girl at a party. He didn't say it out loud, but I could hear his thoughts: *She's not all that.* "Personally," I began, "I think they should hang the *Mona Lisa* in a different spot in the Louvre every day." He smiled (he looked like the scavenger-hunt type). "If you just came upon her in an empty room, next to that painting — I pointed to a pouting Venus on the wall next to us — "or that one" — a dull-eyed courtier — "I think you would turn around as if you had met *someone* you knew. Not a painting of someone, but an actual person. She's so *present*."

I nudged them closer to the rope, so there was as little distraction as possible between them and the painting. I leaned in to speak quietly so only they could hear: "Vasari, an Italian historian who was writing in the generation after Leonardo's death, said that if you look carefully at her neck, you can see the beating of her pulse." The boyfriend leaned so far forward, he almost fell over. That was it. He abandoned me and his date, like so many before him, for the irresistible woman behind the glass.

While he was taking pictures, I stood to one side with the French girlfriend. "So, do you like living in Germany?" I asked. "*Ja,*" she said thoughtfully, not noticing her use of the German affirmative. "There was a time a few years ago when I thought about coming home. I had this ideal vision of France. You know. Perfect and beautiful. But I'm not really French anymore. I'm different now."

"I know exactly what you mean."

Sometimes people come to the Louvre with expectations that no oratorical gift will fulfill. Because the Louvre is a large and famous museum, visitors sometimes assume that all the famous paintings in the world are here. One afternoon, I was taking around four college students from California. After seeing the *Mona Lisa*, one young woman turned to me and said, "Is that painting of the people in the sky here?"

That painting of the people in the sky. I waited for her to elaborate.

"You know, the one with the fingers touching?"

It took me a second. "Ah, um, well, no," I said, with what I hope was infinite politeness. *That would be the Sistine Chapel. In the Vatican. In Rome.*

My favorite part about going back to work is that now I have an excuse to go out for lunch. When I was working all day at the computer at home, no one knew if I ate muesli out of the box. Lunch is my gift to myself, a pat on the back for rejoining the land of the living. The visits are three hours of walking and talking, so by the time I head across the street from the Louvre toward the Palais Royal, I'm ready to let someone else do the entertaining. The area around the Louvre is a *mélange* of chic boutiques, government offices, and tourists, so it makes for some of the best street theater in Paris.

I never sat down for lunch alone in a restaurant in the United States. In fact, I barely sat for lunch at all. In New York, lunch was essentially a chance to stretch my legs, all the way from the office to the salad bar, the noodle bar, or the sandwich bar, where I'd grab something to take back to my desk. From the very first day, lunch alone in Paris became *dining*. It felt luxurious.

The French are beginning to work longer hours, but *le déjeuner* remains sacred. I know what you're thinking: where in God's name do they find the time to take an hour, maybe more, in the middle of a workday for something as gracious, as old-fashioned, as a sit-down lunch?

Let me ask you something. Are you reading this on the way to your spin class? Are you late for your acupuncturist? Your life coach? Your shrink? That's four hours already out of *your* week, which the French replace with the relaxing and replenishing ritual of lunch. It's not that lunch solves everything, but it goes a long way.

If I am lucky, I will get a table outside at the Café Palais Royal. There, perched on my woven plastic chair, wedged behind a small round table, I have an excellent view not only of the foot traffic coming and going along the rue Saint-Honoré, but also of the rollerbladers in the square in front of the Conseil d'Etat and the facade of the Louvre, with its exhibition banners unfurled outside. But the main event usually turns out to be my fellow diners, particularly the women.

Certainly Nicole and Marie-Chantal taught me that French eating habits are about tiny acts of discipline, but these solitary lunches are the meals that taught me that they are also about pleasure and, above all, performance. You see, it's not just the lacy negligees and designer handbags that are on display along the rue Saint-Honoré — it's the women themselves. Being a French woman, especially a woman dining alone, means being contemplated, lingered over, like the dark chocolate stiletto in the window of the famous chocolatier Jean-Paul Hévin.

The French have always known what I've long suspected; there is nothing sexier than watching a woman eat. Men love this. I'm positive that I owe many a second date in New York to a chocolate cannoli or a late-night coupe of rice pudding with whipped cream. It's simple: Women who pick at their food hate sex. Women who suck the meat off of lobster claws, order (and finish) dessert — these are the women who are going to rip your clothes off and come back for seconds. I have a friend in the States who never considered herself a very good flirt, but I never worried for her, because she is a fabulous cook and an adventurous eater. I never doubted that when the right guy came along she would devour him like a hot fudge sundae, and I was right.

Maybe it's the way the French hold the knife and fork. They never put them down, making it impossible to read a magazine or talk on the phone while you eat. You must concentrate, smile to yourself, or you can cry. I've seen that too. Either way, you are the spectacle.

Today I am sitting next to a regular Sarah Bernhardt: a petite brunette with shoulder-length hair clipped up into a careless twist at the back of her neck. She is wearing a black and white flowered skirt, slightly flared at the bottom, showing just a hint of knee. Her white blouse, of some sort of silky material, has three buttons and tiny pleats, like a tuxedo. The deep V of her short black jacket sits smoothly over her waist and bust. The shoes have a low kitten heel and a T-strap that flatters her slender ankles. Expensive sunglasses are perched on top of her head and a cell phone is resting beside her hand on the small round table. I have no idea what she had for lunch, but for the moment she is sipping her *café* and smoking. She holds the cigarette behind her, her wrist arched like the neck of a swan with a twig caught in its beak. There is a gold foil wrapper crumpled on the table — all that remains of the single square of dark chocolate that came nestled in the saucer of her espresso. It's as postcoital a scene as I've ever witnessed in public.

I ordered a salad with smoked salmon. I know that doesn't sound like a particularly decadent repast, but it is. That's because the French long ago mastered the art of serving salad so it doesn't feel like a punishment for something. There are always a few caramel-crusted potatoes on your *salade niçoise*, or a plump chicken liver or two bedded down in a nest of lamb's lettuce. Or your salad might be topped with what is called a *tartine* — a large thin slice of country bread (*Poilâne* if you're lucky) topped with anything from melted goat cheese to shrimp and avocado.

My lunch arrived, a well-worn wooden *planche* heaped with pillowy green lettuce, folded in a creamy, cloudy, mustardy vinaigrette. Balanced on top were three half slices of *pain Poilâne*, spread with the merest millimeter of butter, topped with coral folds of salmon. I put away my phone, and asked for the pepper mill and a Perrier. Lowering my sunglasses against the noontime glare, I felt, in the middle of a workday, very much like a lady who lunches.

If I want the Louvre to myself, I come on Wednesday in late afternoon. Walking past the windows of the Cour Napoléon, I can see the sun setting over the Tuileries. The last light catches the golden tip of the obelisk in the Place de la Concorde, and the cars twinkle like a strand of Christmas lights on the Champs-Elysées. The Louvre at night looks much more as it must have when kings lived here. The low lights don't quite reach the dark corners of the soaring ceilings, and there are fewer people climbing the sweeping marble staircases.

Just as in every other museum I've ever been in, I've started visiting my favorite painting, the one I would take home with me under my trench coat if I had the chance. I believe most art historians are just poor collectors, traveling the world making a secret inventory. I'll take that, and that, and *that*.

Raphael's portrait of Castiglione is far enough down the Grande Galerie so as not to be surrounded by tourists. It's next to a pillar on the left and, famous as it is, I imagine a lot of people miss it on their way to other things. Castiglione was a Renaissance diplomat and writer, known for his book *The Courtier*, a gentleman's guide to leading a civilized and noble life. The portrait is painted entirely in a subdued palette of grays and browns; it's clear that Raphael tried to conserve some of the modesty and erudition dictated by the text. But pride and luxury also have their place. I love the way his silk foulard puffs out just a bit more than necessary, and the quiet sheen of the squirrel fur on his doublet. Like my old merchant friend at the National Gallery in London, he too has a touch of white paint in the corner of his eye. I guess I have a thing for teary old men.

One evening in May, I walked out of the Louvre just as they switched on the exterior lights. The statues of scientists and philosophers that line the balconies were lit from below like children telling a ghost story with a flashlight to their chin.

I. M. Pei's glass pyramid glowed like a spaceship just touched down in the central courtyard. Tonight I noticed something else — the little machine that washes the windows. It's like a robotic poodle, with four rotating brushes for paws. It clings to the side of the pyramid at a vertiginous angle, slowly crawling up and down, side to side, its rubber hose of a tail dangling behind. I suddenly felt an immense rush of gratitude. What luck to be standing where I am, when I am.

How many people get to go to the Louvre often enough to catch them washing the windows?

Something else happened to me on the metro recently: I learned to read.

I know it didn't happen all at once, but today it felt like someone flicked a switch. Suddenly the lights went on inside my head and the words passed through, like one of those healings you read about at a tent revival, where blind men see and mute children speak. I was midway through a novel I'd bought a few weeks ago, the one that won this year's Prix Goncourt. It wasn't good, but for once that was entirely beside the point. I felt tears well up in my eyes. Reading, the pleasure I most took for granted, finally restored. I looked around me, wondering if anyone had noticed. No one did. I was part of the urban wallpaper.

A dark-haired boy got on at the next stop; he couldn't have been more than eight, wearing navy track pants and an oversized T-shirt. He had a big set of keys around his neck that hung almost to his knees. He had to fight to hoist himself up onto the flipdown booster seat next to the door. I watched as he held it steady with both hands and, looking over his shoulder, inched his bottom toward the back. Then he took out a comic book and stated reading. He nibbled on a fingernail and turned the page. We were fellow passengers now. Just a couple of Parisians passing the time on our daily commute.

I got off the train hugging the book to my chest.

I can really do this, I can make this work.

Three Fabulous Solo Lunches

OMELETTE WITH GOAT CHEESE AND ARTICHOKE HEARTS
Omelette au Fromage de Chèvre et aux Coeurs d'Artichaut

The omelette is ubiquitous French luncheon fare, and almost as easy to make at home as it is to order in a restaurant. There are as many omelette methods as there are omelette makers. This is mine.

> *3 eggs*
> *Coarse sea salt*
> *2 artichoke hearts packed in oil*
> *2 slices soft goat cheese*
> *Black pepper to taste*

In a small bowl, lightly whisk the eggs and a good pinch of salt. Drain the artichoke hearts and cut them into quarters.

Heat a 20 cm nonstick omelette pan over medium-high heat, add the artichoke hearts, and wait until you hear a sizzle.

Add the eggs. Gently top with the goat cheese and a good grind of pepper. Reduce the heat to low, cover, and cook for 5 minutes.

Take off the cover and lift the edge of the omelette with a fork. Tilt the pan slightly to let the uncooked egg run underneath the already cooked portion of the omelette.

Cover and leave in the pan for 3 to 4 minutes more. Fold in half and serve.

Yield: Serves 1

ASPARAGUS WITH PISTOU, CURED HAM, AND A POACHED EGG

Asperges au Pistou, Jambon Cru, et Oeuf Poché

There's a moment in May when everything's coming up asparagus. It's a short window, so I feel like I want to eat them at every meal. France's asparagus come from Provence, so it's natural to dress them with *pistou*, a mix of basil, garlic, and olive oil. Topped with a poached egg and transparent ribbons of cured ham, it's springtime on a plate.

> *300 g asparagus (the thinner, the better)*
> *1 heaping tablespoon pistou (a quality brand of Italian*
> *pesto is a good substitute)*
> *1 extra-fresh egg*
> *2–3 paper-thin slices cured ham*
> *Freshly ground black pepper*

Trim the asparagus, discarding the tough white ends. Blanch them in a pot of salted water for 3 to 5 minutes, depending on their thickness. (It is a mortal sin to overcook asparagus, so taste as you go.) Drain, pat dry, and toss with the *pistou*.

Bring a small saucepan of water to a steady simmer. Crack open the egg and gently slide it into the water. Cook for 3 minutes, remove with a slotted spoon, and drain completely.

Arrange the asparagus on your plate, top with ribbons of ham, the poached egg, and a grind of fresh pepper. Split the egg to release the runny yolk and enjoy.

Yield: Serves 1

OVEN-GRILLED SARDINES
Sardines Grillées Au Four

When summer vacation just won't come soon enough, I resort to sardines. They remind me of portside cafés with shady awnings and crisp white wine. Sardines cook almost instantly. Gwendal used to panfry them; I've taken to grilling them in the oven so they don't smell up the whole apartment.

> 4–5 whole sardines or sardine fillets
> 1 tomato, chopped
> A small handful of flat-leaf parsley, chopped
> Juice of ½ lemon
> A drizzle of extra-virgin olive oil
> Coarse sea salt and freshly ground black pepper

Preheat your grill. Line a baking sheet or shallow roasting pan with foil. Rinse the sardines, removing all the clear scales. Top the sardines with the tomato, parsley, lemon juice, and a generous drizzle of olive oil. Sprinkle with salt and pepper. Grill for 6 to 8 minutes, depending on size. Serve with a green salad; use the pan juices as your dressing.

Yield: Serves 1

CHAPTER 18

COMFORT FOOD

Pastry aside, I hate this country and everything it stands for. One sunny day in June, on impulse, I bought two pairs of sandals. They weren't perfect, but black is always useful and silver is in, so I figured, What the heck. Later that week I went to the doctor for a backache; she said I shouldn't be wearing flat shoes, so I decided to return them.

Clearly this was hubris. Folly. I unleashed the floodgates, and now the deluge was upon me.

I passed by the store on my way home the next day. I didn't know the word for "refund." I didn't want an exchange. The salesman asked me what was wrong with the shoes. "Nothing is wrong with them," I said. "I just don't want them anymore." *Free markets, free will, goddamn it.*

"We don't just take things back, *comme ça*," he said, snapping his fingers in the air. His disdain was so complete, his tone so withering, that I stepped back as if I'd been struck. I opened my mouth to explain, but he stared me down like a six-headed Hydra, like I had worn the shoes to a muddy rave and was now trying to put one over on him, like I was a criminal: a wasteful, horrid, annoying creature, a shoe hound, a shrill and irresponsible taker of his time. The story about the doctor evaporated like the dog that ate my homework. My French grammar retreated to the farthest corner of my brain. My vocabulary dwindled to a series of helpless shrugs. By the time I left the shop, trailing my shopping bag behind me, I was almost in tears. I was too weak for indignation and too disgusted with myself to go back in. That was the moment things hit rock bottom. The girl who was going to set the world on fire couldn't even return a pair of shoes.

There is only one antidote for a day like that: chocolate. I needed comfort food and I needed it fast. For me, comfort food is the kind of thing you can make in your sleep — you've memorized the recipe, and you usually have all the ingredients lying around the house. You can do it with one hand, or one ear cocked to the phone. It's not going to fall apart if a few tears or a trail of snot end up in the batter. My new comfort food of choice, now that I've left the land of Pillsbury ready-made cookie dough, is Gwendal's quick and dirty chocolate soufflé.

I know it sounds terribly ambitious — making chocolate soufflé with snot coming out of my nose. That's the beautiful thing: at the time I didn't know I was making soufflé, I thought I was making the world's easiest chocolate cake. It was one of Gwendal's standard recipes. He knew it by heart, but at my request he'd printed a version off the Internet. In a tart pan, it puffed up in the oven and immediately fell back down again (I knew exactly how it felt). But poured into small buttered soufflé dishes, it immediately took on a more elegant guise (this gave me hope).

While I was melting the chocolate, I dialed my mother. Despite recent evidence to the contrary, she is pretty good in a crisis. I've been away from home since I was fifteen, so this was hardly the first long-distance phone call she'd received from her daughter in hysterical tears.

My first year in London, I went out on a date with a Norwegian banker. He had come to interview for my spot in a shared apartment, and before he left we agreed to meet for a drink. "A" drink in London is a radical misnomer. My favorite pub was having its five-year anniversary bash, and by ten p.m. I had seen the bottom of more glasses of wine than I have toenails and it seemed like a good idea to get up and dance on our pedestal table. The evening ended in a crescendo of shattered glass and blood dripping from my arm onto my white silk blouse. The bartender whisked us into the kitchen, washed us off, and shoved us out the door.

Mr. Norway took me back to his flat, and instead of stripping off my bloody clothes, taking me in his arms, and licking my wounds like an adoring panther, he sent me home. On the bus. Bastard didn't even put me in a cab. As soon as I found my keys (after the miracle of finding my apartment), I called my mother, drunk and hyperventilating. With the five-hour time difference, I no doubt interrupted her in the middle of dinner.

"Elizabeth?"

"Mom," I gasped. I was crying so hard I could barely breathe. "How'd you get blood out of a white silk shirt?" I paused to suck in some air. "He sent (gulp). He sent. He sent me. Home. On on on. On the *buuuus*." By this point I was lying on the kitchen floor, the ceiling tiles spinning above my head.

My mother, on the other side of the world, not knowing if I'd been raped or drugged or had recently escaped from the trunk of somebody's car, summoned all her wisdom and Zen-like composure and said: "Put the blouse in a big pot of cold water and call me in the morning."

That, my friends, is the definition of a good parent.

Needless to say, she was not surprised to hear that the world was ending yet again, this time over a pair of shoes.

I was spitting into the phone as I shouted over the eggbeater. "How could anyone choose to live in this pathetic excuse for a country? Is individual liberty really such a dangerous thing? What about a little professionalism, service? How about basic human kindness?" I looked at the puddle of chocolate in the top of the double boiler. I wanted to dive in and swim away. "I feel like I've been here forever, and I can't even take on a snotty salesclerk. I just don't know if this is ever going to get any easier."

I stopped short, as I always did, of saying "I want to come home." I was at my classic impasse. I had one foot on either side of the ocean, and my knees were beginning to wobble.

The cake takes only twenty minutes to bake, which is as close to instant gratification as homemade gets. In deference to my mother-in-law, I tried cutting a small piece, which I ate off an actual plate. But by the end of the afternoon I was just standing at the counter, licking the knife. By the time Gwendal got home from work the worst had passed. I didn't feel like telling the story twice, so he listened while I called Kelda and reiterated the whole thing over the phone.

"FWA, baby." I could see her shaking her head on the other end of the line. "FWA."

France wins again.

I wouldn't have thought it was possible, but the summer went downhill from there.

In February, Gwendal had quit his job at the cinema archive to become the technical director of a digital cinema start-up. In May, his salary was two weeks late, and his boss refused to give him his promised shares in the company. In June, his salary failed to appear at all. Gwendal wrote a letter citing breach of contract and left. His boss accused him of quitting and refused to give him the papers necessary for his unemployment benefits. We were going to have to take them to court.

Once again, I was stranded without my network. In the United States, everyone I know is a lawyer. I feel like I took torts by osmosis. Gwendal didn't know anyone. When we finally did find a lawyer, her office had a lot of dusty molding, and when she appeared for our court date three months later, she was wearing a black polyester robe like the one I wore to my high school graduation. The event itself was a farce. We showed up in the morning, not knowing in what order we would be called. There was a list taped to the door, but as the day wore on it became clear that the list was purely decorative. It was like Monty Python court: a guy came out (he might as well have been dressed as a court jester) and called number 5, then number 14, then number 9.

It was five thirty by the time we made our way into the wood-paneled chamber. In France this kind of workplace arbitration is overseen by one representative of the labor unions and one representative of the management lobby. When Mr. Management heard the level of Gwendal's salary (relatively elevated for France), he cut our lawyer off midsentence and turned to Gwendal's boss. "I'm sure you had noble reasons for not paying your employee."

Excuse me?

Fortunately, Ms. Union didn't agree. There would be no verdict that day. The appeal was set for November. Meanwhile Gwendal would go another four months without the papers for his benefits. The lawyer said we had no choice, we had to wait. That old feeling of helplessness welled up again. I felt like I was pushing against the ocean. If one more person told me to wait, to sit still and grit my teeth while my family's rights and health and financial well-being were being trampled on, I was going to go loony tunes. My head was ready to start spinning on my neck like the little girl in *The Exorcist*. How could anyone live like this? — and in the meantime we had nothing to live on.

My rage I could express, but my fear I had to keep inside. I knew Gwendal was at a turning point. He could either see this leap into the private sector as a disastrous aberration — or an opportunity.

I was pretty sure what the French answer would be: *See what happens when you go out on a limb — the lawyers, the trouble, the stress. You had a nice safe job. Why did you change?* It was up to me to represent the other side. I didn't want Gwendal to think that taking a chance meant failure. Despite working for a feckless criminal, Gwendal enjoyed the business and was clearly doing well. We were at a crossroads. I wanted to see him try. I wanted to be the safety net he never had so he could spread his wings and give it a shot. I wanted France to be wrong.

So I put on my brave face, the cultural equivalent of a very short cheerleader skirt, got out the pom-poms, and went to work. He and two colleagues decided to start a consulting company. I wrote press releases and thank-you notes and copy for the English website. I cooked and cleaned, gave tours, and generally swept my own ambitions and enormous fear of financial insecurity under the table. *Yeah, team.*

It was a brilliant piece of bait and switch. Instead of figuring out what I wanted to do with the rest of *my* life, we would figure out what to do with his. Instead of worrying about my own lack of direction, I directed him. I threw myself 150 percent into the business. We talked through every decision, every move. Everything he did right I cheered on, every stumble I cheered anyway — shutting myself in the bathroom while he went to "the office" (his partner's dining room table), trying not to show my rage and insecurity that he didn't know *everything already*. In another tour de force of Bard Economics, Paul borrowed some money for us to live on, and I started paying at the supermarket with my American Visa card.

I would love to say home was a solace — but it wasn't. The Chinese Mafia was still firmly ensconced in the apartment upstairs, with no end in sight. As soon as the lawyers got involved, the bunk beds and the brothel girls disappeared, leaving the "official" renter, Mr. Dong, his wife, and their two young children. The room with the moldering mattresses on the floor was magically transformed into a playroom full of Fisher-Price toys.

French real-estate law favors the tenant, and even if they have no lease and don't pay a *centime* of rent, it is impossible to evict so much as a family of dormice between the first of November and the first of March. Meanwhile, the kids were making such a racket we thought that maybe we would be the ones who had to move. We awoke one Sunday morning at around eight thirty, thinking someone had opened a bowling alley on our bedroom ceiling. Gwendal finally pulled on some pants and knocked on the door upstairs. When Mr. Dong opened the door, behind him was a *tableau vivant* worthy of Molière — the Dongs' four-year-old daughter was riding her tricycle in a circle around the apartment, followed closely by her little brother, who was dragging the vacuum cleaner. Mr. Dong shrugged as if to say, "Kids, what can you do?"

The sudden prominence of small children in the apartment had other unforeseen consequences. Social service got involved, and they found lead paint in the apartment. There's lead paint in many old buildings in Paris, and when the occupants — legal or not — have young children, the owners are responsible for its removal. The owners started doing cartwheels. If the squatters had to move out so they could fix the lead paint, why couldn't they simply change the locks and refuse to let them back in? Too simple. The city, it seems, gets a kickback from the painters, and didn't want to lose the job. So we ended up with a surreal solution to a surreal problem.

The owners put the Chinese Mafia squatters up in a hotel, did a 15,000-euro paint job, and moved them back in, just before the November deadline, when regardless of the eviction notice they would be allowed to stay another winter. I was considering setting fire to the building with a copy of the Napoleonic Code.

All the while, adorable bistros and photography galleries began to spring up along the canal, and prices in the neighborhood continued to rise about 10,000 euros a month. One sticky Saturday morning, Gwendal and I were on our way out to the market when we saw a gay couple with Rollerblades descend from the fourth floor. I looked at Gwendal with panic in my eyes.

"Gotta buy. Now."

In late July, Gwendal's dad came to Paris for the last time. He was on a break between rounds of chemotherapy and seemed to be feeling up to it. He wanted to go to La Coupole, an art deco brasserie on the boulevard du Montparnasse, for a very unseasonal meal of *choucroute*, a Alsatian specialty that involves a mound of sauerkraut and as many kinds of pork as you can reasonably fit onto one plate.

La Coupole is an institution; Josephine Baker danced in the basement and Hemingway drank on the terrace (where didn't he?). Now it's owned by a chain. The cavernous dining room makes for abominable acoustics, and the din of clattering forks and knives quickly drowned out any meaningful attempt at conversation.

After lunch, we slowly walked the few blocks to the Luxembourg Gardens. We sat on a bench near the puppet theater, giving Yanig time to catch his breath. It was only an hour before he and Nicole needed to catch their train. We should have accompanied them to the station, but I felt how much Gwendal wanted to stay out in the sunshine; he was suffocating from the panic and dread. As soon as we shut the door to the taxi we knew it was the wrong decision. I looked at Gwendal and we began walking at a clip down the boulevard du Montparnasse. The platform was crowded and there was nowhere to sit. We found Yanig leaning on a short barrier pole next to a vending machine. He looked so weak I thought he might collapse. I had never seen Nicole look so utterly helpless. We ran up to them. We stood there, huddled together, Gwendal supporting Yanig under one arm. Everyone was crying and apologizing at the same time.

By August, I was so exhausted I could barely stand up. France had beaten me into submission. I was crippled. Literally. I had herniated a disk dragging a suitcase home from the airport, a suitcase full of shoes. Oh, the cruel irony of the gods.

Desperate times call for desperate measures. Saturday night I convinced Gwendal to stay in and try comfort food American style. There's nothing like physical pain and mental distress to send you running back into the arms of your childhood. I found myself longing for a can of Pillsbury vanilla frosting and a spoon. I settled for Chinese food out of the container and a DVD of *Grease*.

Chinese food quickly turned into Thai-Laotian. Takeout here comes in aluminium containers with cardboard tops, so it doesn't quite match those white paper boxes with the red Chinese characters on the side; there is no satisfying scrape as you hunt with your chopsticks for the last lo mein noodle at the bottom. We opened the sofa bed in the living room, and I changed into my mother's genuine 1973 blue velveteen lounge pajamas with the satin ties.

Gwendal was thrilled with the film, and even watched the bonus features. (Did you know that they had to *sew* Olivia

Newton John into those black pants for the finale?) But he couldn't get into the idea of eating out of a box. He just looked awkward, perched on the edge of the bed, balancing a pad thai on his knee. He kept looking around with a forced smile, eager to humor me, to participate in my little game, but clearly wishing for a plate, a table, and a napkin. For the French, food is a meal, and a meal is meant to be consumed in a civilized manner — not walking, not standing, not driving, and not hunched over a plastic container on the sofa.

We would have to agree to disagree. I felt better than I had in months. Greased out and sated, I threw my feet over the arm of the couch, ready to doze off. It was almost perfect.

My kingdom for a Twizzler.

Comfort Food à la Française

GWENDAL'S QUICK AND DIRTY CHOCOLATE SOUFFLÉ CAKE
Gâteau au Chocolat

Call it cake, soufflé, baked chocolate mousse — call it a chocolate omelette if you want — all I know is that it always does the trick. Along with the *Gâteau au Yaourt*, this is the cake I bake most often, both for my own personal satisfaction and for guests. Made with no butter and minimal flour, it is intensely chocolaty without being heavy. Rich but not deadly.

> *Butter and sugar for the mould(s)*
> *225 g ounces bittersweet chocolate (65 percent cocoa is*
> *   ideal)*
> *2 tablespoons espresso or strong filter coffee*
> *5 eggs, separated*
> *½ cup sugar*
> *A pinch of salt*
> *1 tablespoon flour (omit if you are making mini soufflés)*

Preheat the oven to 180°C. Lightly butter and sugar a 25 cm ceramic tart mold. (Or, to make individual soufflés, follow the instructions in the variation below.)

In the top of a double boiler or in the microwave, melt the chocolate with the coffee. Let cool.

Separate the eggs — whites into a large mixing bowl, yolks into a medium mixing bowl.

Whisk together the egg yolks and ½ cup sugar until the mixture is a light lemon yellow.

Pour the melted chocolate into the egg yolks and quickly whisk to combine; it will be quite thick. Add flour (if you are making the mini soufflés, omit the flour altogether).

In the large bowl, beat egg whites with a pinch of salt until they hold a stiff peak.

Gently fold a third of the beaten egg whites into the chocolate mixture to lighten it. Then add the chocolate mixture back into the remaining egg whites; fold gently to combine. I know this seems like a lot of transferring back and forth, but the best way to keep the air in the mix is to add the heavier substance to the lighter one.

Pour the batter into the prepared dish and bake for 20 minutes. It will have puffed up quite a bit. Touch the center; if it feels reasonably firm, remove the cake from the oven. If not, give it an extra minute or two, but no more. The cake will fall and wrinkle a tiny bit after you take it out of the oven — don't despair. I think this gives it a homemade charm.

Yield: Serves 6–8

Variation: To make individual chocolate soufflés; butter and sugar six ramekins (mine are 200 ml each) and divide the batter evenly among them. Make sure to wipe the rims so that your soufflés rise evenly. Bake at 200°C for approximately 14 minutes. The cakes should still be a little jiggly, but not raw, on top. If you wait until they are stiff and springy on top, they will likely be overcooked underneath. Serve straight from the oven.

Tip: Everyone wants her soufflés to reach towering heights. Our friend Virginie has an interesting trick. When you butter the sides of the ramekins, use vertical strokes, going from bottom to top. It helps the soufflé "crawl" up the sides as it bakes.

CHAPTER 19

CONQUERING THE WORLD

That's not going to work.

Yes it is.

No. It's not. They are not just going to *give* me an appointment.

Why not?

Because. -

This was a circular conversation Gwendal and I had been having for weeks. He didn't believe that if we wrote a great letter, he could get five minutes with almost anyone.

"It's not out of the kindness of their hearts," I said. "You could be useful. Europe is like a giant black hole to these people, a mystery. You are giving them as much information as they're giving you."

These discussions end, as often as not, with a fake boxing match in our kitchen. As the forces of optimism and pessimism collide, Gwendal and I, in the style of a Three Stooges self-help seminar, duck our heads, jog back and forth, and pretend to punch each other. I'm Rocky, wearing the U.S. of A. silk shorts, doing battle for the American dream.

"Pow!" I shout, putting up my dukes for a mean left jab. "Right in the kisser."

We were trying to get out more, meet some new people, people with ideas. Still thinking like an American, I encouraged Gwendal to get involved with the alumni association of his engineering school. Hearing that he worked in the world of cinema, and not designing parts for cars, they invited him to speak at an event on "changing direction in your career." He put on a suit and tie and talked about the importance of networking, speaking English, and reaching out to European partners. He was met with a lot of blank stares. During the Q and A one young woman raised her hand: "How can I work less and earn more?"

The evening did yield one interesting encounter. Gwendal got back in touch with Michaël. Even when they were students, Michaël had been something of a character. He paid someone else to do his six-month graduate internship while he started a film business, traveled around the world writing articles, chaperoning vital organs, and doing God knows what for the French intelligence services. He had just returned from a trip to the mountains of Bhutan. We were digging into a *tagine* of lamb and pears at L'Homme Bleu, our favorite Moroccan restaurant, as he explained his newest idea.

"I want to start a chain of restaurants to give McDonald's a run for their money. It will be called Papillote. Each combination of ingredients will be steamed in its own package, cooked to order."

I love this guy. *En papillote* is the French term for cooking in sealed foil or parchment. Since we now have an oven, this has become my favorite method for cooking fish and veggies. The fish makes its own sauce, and the package releases a fragrant burst of steam when you slice it open. I tried to imagine a whole trout, covered with chopped tomatoes, fresh garden peas, and coriander — maybe a sprinkle of *lardons* for extra flavor — doing battle with a Filet-O-Fish. Clearly there were at least two people in France willing to think big and sound a little crazy. Gwendal and I both left feeling a little better.

Unfortunately, not all Gwendal's friends were so encouraging. The next week we saw Nadine and Jean-Paul, friends from Orléans. While I made some tea, Gwendal talked them through the consulting company — the funding, the frustration, the new contacts in Los Angeles. They looked bemused. He was planning more in the next six months than they imagined for a lifetime.

"You get back to us when you're finished conquering the world," said Jean-Paul. "We'll have a drink."

It was the last time we ever saw them.

Gwendal's parents watched his progress with caution. Nicole did her silent best to cover the panic about him being without a fixed salary. As a family who always worried about money, they had a residual fear that any risk would leave Gwendal to dissolve, like a character in a Paul Auster novel, from respectable citizen to lunatic street wanderer.

Curiously, for Yanig, Gwendal's new business turned out to be the best medicine. As the weather turned chilly, he wasn't getting out of the house much anymore. We bought a paperback edition of *The Count of Monte Cristo* to help pass the time, but it was Gwendal's story that was the greatest adventure that fall. He called his father every morning on the way to work to report his latest exploits.

Suddenly the man whose own fears had cut off so many of Gwendal's hopes became his biggest fan. He watched his son slay opponents and pull off feats of derring-do. Setting up a business in France had more twists than Dumas, more petty villains than Dickens. There was a new cloak and dagger every day.

Gwendal's grandparents were less enthusiastic. It's not that the French don't believe in social mobility, but it is supposed to happen incrementally, across generations. Jumping several rungs on the ladder at once is considered arrogant and opportunistic. It's just plain impolite — and people were as shocked as they were wary.

Gwendal's grandfather reads the Communist newspaper. Refused mandatory work service in Germany in 1943, and *walked* back from a camp in Poland after the war. He spent his life in a factory, making fiberglass insulation. He rose from the factory floor to foreman, grew his own vegetables, and built two homes with his own hands. As far as he was concerned, Gwendal's PhD already made him a bit of an alien—too much unnecessary book stuff, a bourgeois luxury. But at least it was harmless, unsullied by the search for cash and power.

Once Gwendal entered the business world, everything changed. Money is an awkward subject in France — in Europe in general. Working at a cinema archive is *culture*; turning a profit by transforming the entire industry is cold, calculating, and *arriviste*. By starting his own business Gwendal was committing two cardinal sins against French society: he was running after money (never mind that there is an electric bill to pay), which challenges the aristocratic origins of the elite, and he was catapulting himself to the head of something — potentially bossing other people around — which goes against the egalitarian ideals of the French Revolution and anti-establishment rhetoric of the 1968 hippies. As if he didn't have enough to do, Gwendal was fighting a battle with history.

When Gwendal told his grandfather he'd started a company, he nodded knowingly. "So, you're one of them now. *Management.*"

It's the same response Nicole's mother gave her when they finally stopped renting and built the house: "*Tu pètes plus haut de ton cul.*" You're farting above your ass.

It was the middle of the night in Paris when Gwendal called my parents from the top of Mulholland Drive. "You'll never guess where I am," he said. "I'm looking at the Hollywood sign."

"He sounded elated," my mother reported to me later that day. "Like a man with wings."

It happened like this: a journalist in New York listened to Gwendal's questions and, like everyone else, said, "That's very interesting. But the man you should really talk to about digital cinema is George Lucas." Gwendal's heart sank into his shoes. *Sure, I'll just go and have a chat with George Lucas. About* Star Wars. *No problem.* "George is a bit aloof," continued the journalist, "but his producer is a really great guy. Let me give him a call." There was no time to blink, never mind pass out. Gwendal was experiencing his first episode of what I call *paradigm vertigo.* For him, such professional generosity seemed upside down and backwards. In France, people often show their power by saying no — by their ability to block things, to show that nothing happens without them. To close the store, if you like, whenever they please. In the United States, people show their power by their ability to say yes — to get things done in a hurry. To keep the store open an extra hour, just for you.

The journalist took out his cell phone, checked the time difference, and dialed. "Listen, I've got this guy in my office... has a D-cinema project in Europe... got a model he wants to discuss. Coming to California. Uh-huh. Uh-huh. Uh-huh."

From there the dominoes began to fall. Lucas got him a meeting with Fox, Fox got him a meeting with Disney. Disney got him a meeting with Sony. And so on, all the way up Mulholland Drive to the Hollywood sign.

It was fascinating to watch Gwendal navigate between our two cultures. At times, he had a very fine needle to thread. He now had a wealth of information on exactly what the studios wanted to make digital cinema happen in Europe, but when he brought what he had learned back to his fellow Frenchmen, he had trouble convincing them that he was legit. At the age of thirty-three, in France he was too young to be credible, an arrogant upstart who should wait his turn. In the States, he was almost too old: *If you're so smart, how come you're just getting to the big leagues now?*

The frustration reached peak levels during a meeting with the head of a major cinema chain in Paris. The man had been listening for an hour, trying to digest the wealth of numbers Gwendal was throwing at him.

"How do you know all this?"

"I was just in LA last week."

"Yes, but how do you know all this?"

The idea that he busted his ass, flew back and forth to LA, spoke English, wrote letters, took meetings, crunched numbers — none of this made the slightest bit of sense to the people in front of him. The cinema industry, like many professions in France, is filled with *fils de*, literally "sons of," people who got where they are with family connections and family money. Gwendal knew what they were thinking: *Who the hell is this kid? If he were really of interest, we would know him already.*

The man shook his head and said it again, "But how do you know all this?"

"Because I asked."

"But why do they talk to you?"

Because I asked.

Finally Gwendal just gave up and did it the French way. "You know, my wife is American. She's actually Jack Warner's granddaughter." (I'm not.)

"*Ahhh, bien oui.*" There was a huge exhalation and nods of comprehension around the table.

They simply couldn't conceive of the fact that he'd gotten there any other way. Turns out, France has its own version of "fake it till you make it."

As Gwendal's confidence grew, mine disintegrated. His American dreamer, with all her big plans, was stalled like a rusty Dodge on the side of I-95. As Gwendal continued to refine his plans, mine became more vague, even nonexistent. I started to disappear.

Here it was, right on schedule: my mini existential crisis. Yes, the writing was still coming in dribs and drabs. But it was so slow. Yup, the tours were great. I felt like I was doing something really valuable — sharing the love of museums my father had given me. But it wasn't *mine*. Once again, I was a charming cog in someone else's wheel. I was once again forced to confront (with the accompanying self-loathing) the fact that I had the goods, but not the discipline or perseverance to create something for myself. How could anyone so ambitious be so inert?

While Gwendal was mining the American dream for all it was worth, I was forced to come to terms with the flip side of my American optimism. Implicit in the American dream is the idea of self-determination. The result of our just-do-it attitude is that anything you *don't* do is your fault. This ethic of personal responsibility informs American attitudes on everything from obesity to college admissions to welfare reform. In the end, our level of expectation — and the accompanying fear of failure — can be just as paralyzing as the French notion that nothing is possible in the first place.

Take, for example, my weekly rants to Amanda in California. Most Sundays, we sit on the phone for an hour, hooting with laughter at the depth of our collective failure. It helps if there is some timely comparison. A classmate of hers from Yale Law School just published a Pulitzer-nominated book of short stories. Amanda just turned thirty, and still no contract with HBO. What were all those $15 martinis at the Four Seasons for, anyway? We were supposed to be famous, or at least rich by now. What the fuck have we been doing with our time?

Part of me knows it's perverse, but I find this kind of self-flagellation comforting. Somehow these conversations leave me refreshed, buoyant, ready for another week of precisely phrased e-mails, unreturned phone calls, and unpaid invoices. Gwendal finds them ridiculous, a waste of useful time and energy.

It is clear that I have created a monster.

Now that Gwendal has doubled his salary and seen the deer at Skywalker Ranch, he's the one counseling me on my career. He asks me questions straight off the Harvard MBA application. "What is your passion?" he says, as if this should be enough to get me out of bed in the morning. "Where do you see yourself in five years? What do you really *want*?" It's psychological torture, having my own weapons used against me.

The fact is, I don't have an answer for him anymore. What I *want* is to go to lots of cocktail parties with famous writers — peers, mind you — sign books, and eat tuna carpaccio on wasabi flat bread, all while never having to sit down at my computer ever again. Bless him, he just doesn't get it.

All of a sudden, my French husband is better at the American dream than I am. He has latched on to endless possibility, and all the hard work it entails — without the arrogance or impatience that can cause us native Yanks to think we have it coming to us. Strangely enough, any time we start to talk about where my life is going, I've always got an excuse — and for every suggestion he makes, I start to throw out the standard French answer: *pas possible*.

While Gwendal was driving through the lot at Warner Brothers, parking his rented car next to the set where James Dean met Natalie Wood, I was at the butcher. A hotel room with a view of the Hollywood sign may have been his idea of arriving; these days mine was successfully ordering a leg of lamb. It may not sound like much, but of all the rites of passage I've experienced in France, none has given me greater satisfaction than flying solo at our local butcher. These outings were part of an ongoing battle between my French and American selves. The *Parisienne* in me said I was making progress — it felt good to be a habitué of the neighborhood, integrated into the French rhythm. The American in me was scared that I was turning into a 1950s housewife.

I found a book recently, called *The Goodman of Paris: A Treatise on Moral and Domestic Economy by a Citizen of Paris, c. 1393*. It was written by a husband for his young wife, to instruct her on all she would need to know to run a harmonious household. There are chapters on God and gardening, on hiring servants and curing a toothache. There are also extensive instructions for the butcher:

"The fourth article is that you, as sovereign mistress of your house, know how to order dinners, suppers, dishes, and courses, and must be wise in that which concerns the butcher and the poulterer, and have knowledge of spices."

I've only been on this earth since 1974, and in France since 2002. You see my dilemma. I had centuries of catching up to do.

The Boucherie Saint-Jacques on the corner of the avenue Parmentier and the rue du Faubourg-du-Temple is not for wimps. These butchers are serious men. They wear white coats and ties and, like a team of surgeons, wield knives with a casual precision, never looking down as cleavers descend millimeters from their fingers. There is something of the operating theater about the place: bright white light, spotless metal, and exposed flesh. The opening hours alone require enough extra planning to scare away the casual customer: closed on Mondays, open Tuesday through Saturday but closed for lunch from one to three thirty, open Sunday mornings but closed Thursday afternoons.

Plus, one of them looks like Matt Dillon.

It's normal for a *Parisienne* to develop a little crush on her butcher. It's the equivalent of an American developing a crush on her handsome young doctor. There's something macho and authoritative about tearing apart hunks of raw meat. It requires good hands.

Naturally, he doesn't know I'm alive. In fact, a trip to the butcher is a lot like high school — a Darwinian feeding frenzy. Instead of blonde girls with lip gloss, the alpha females are blue-haired grannies with plaid shopping caddies, clicking their tongues with contempt as you dither over cuts of veal or forget the French word for "deboned." You'd better know which line you're in. There's one to order, another to pay. Once you've picked out your whole rabbit, skinned from the tip of his head to what was once his fluffy tail, and given the appropriate instructions for boning, chopping, or grinding, you can pass over to the other queue. The cashier stamps your ticket with a red inky PAYÉ, and you sidle back to the counter to pick up your bag. Matt Dillon has already served three people in the time it takes you to fish out the twenty centimes from the bottom of your purse (exact change is appreciated), but somehow you always end up with your *côte de porc* and not your neighbor's *côte de veau*. Once (very early on) I found myself in the cashier's line by mistake and was suddenly at the register with no ticket to pay. The woman's face was like a stone tablet, as if the president of the chess club had wandered over to the Goth corner of the schoolyard and asked to touch a tongue piercing.

Sometimes there will be a Matt Dillon sighting in the neighborhood. The kind of encounter that would have produced hours of intense analysis between my fourteen-year-old self and whatever friend was on the other end of my new cordless phone. I was at the café next to the metro one day, finishing an article. I looked up from my typing and there he was, with his perfectly spiked black hair, leaning against the doorway, smoking a cigarette. There was a slash of blood across his white smock, and a baguette tucked under his arm. I felt a flurry of butterflies in my stomach, and just barely stopped myself from running my fingers through my hair. I looked up again, not *at* him, but, *you know,* in his general direction. He nodded. *Ohmigod.* You couldn't call it a smile exactly, just some acknowledgment that he recognized me. I instantly dipped my gaze back down to the computer screen, my fingers tingling as they touched the keys.

Sometimes life really is just like high school.

In early October, we went to San Francisco for Afra's wedding. I caught something on the plane, and by the time the rehearsal dinner rolled around I was worried that I'd have barely enough voice to croak out my toast the next day.

While Gwendal slept in, I was being lectured. The morning of the wedding, Afra and Amanda staged an intervention over coffee and carrot muffins at a local café. Afra is the big sister of our troika, a status accorded by her years and years of unwavering devotion to her life plan. "We're worried about you," she said, wiping a coffee ring from our recently vacated table. "How come every time we ask how you are, all you talk about is Gwendal's business? What about you?"

I stared into my tissue. I just wasn't in the mood. Over the past several months I had taken on the role of full-time woman behind the throne. The helpmeet, the cheerleader.

There was only so much *rah-rah* to go around. I took a sip from my mug of cappuccino; it was a bathtub full of coffee, at least five times what I'd be served in Paris. I was so proud of Gwendal, but at the same time I felt hollow inside. I knew my friends hardly recognized me. I hardly recognized myself.

I was between two worlds, and what made perfect sense for one, didn't make any sense for the other. I could still talk a good game — cover my empty agenda with fancy-sounding smoke and mirrors — Louvre, new media editor, *International Herald Tribune*. But alone at my desk in Paris, without anyone to perform for, I was lost. Removed from the straight and narrow path of what I was supposed to do, far from the great expectations of my childhood and the constant striving of my New York set, I had very little idea what I wanted. I had made and discarded so many five year plans, all some version of who I was supposed to be — a fantasy me.

Paris presented different questions. If no one asked me for the rest of my life what I did for a living, how much money I made, who I knew, where I went to school — what would I want to do with my time? What if I stopped to ask myself what would make me happy, instead of what would make me successful, respectable, worthy? If that answer had to come from the inside, rather than the outside, what would it be?

Afra added a sweetener to her latte and took a sip. "You can't spend the rest of your life at the market."

I blew my nose into a paper napkin. I didn't have the courage to say it out loud just yet, but a tiny voice popped up inside me: *why not?*

Michaël's Papillotes and Matt Dillon's Bunny Rabbit

TROUT WITH CHERRY TOMATOES BAKED IN FOIL
Truite en Papillote

This is one of the easiest and most satisfying meals I know. Cooking *en papillote* changed my whole approach to fish — no worries about burning, drying, or dressing. The fish makes its own sauce and, if you like, its own side dish. Feel free to vary the spices and the veggies. You can make it as simple as lemon, olive oil, and courgettes or you can zing it with freshly grated ginger, spring onions, and soy. This recipe is simply a place to start.

> *2 whole trout, 250 g each, gutted and rinsed*
> *Coarse sea salt*
> *Freshly ground mixed peppercorns*
> *250 g cherry tomatoes, halved*
> *A drizzle of best-quality extra-virgin olive oil*
> *1 tablespoon fresh chopped dill*
> *Lemon wedges to serve*

Preheat the oven to 200°C.

Rinse the fish and lay each one on a separate piece of aluminium foil (you'll need to seal the edges later, so leave a good 10 cm of foil on each end of the fish). Sprinkle a bit of sea salt and a grind of mixed peppercorns into the cavity.

Scatter the tomatoes around the fish. Season with more salt and pepper, a good drizzle of olive oil, and the dill. Cover each fish with a second length of foil and carefully fold the edges together to seal them into a neat little pouch. Transfer to a baking sheet and bake for 20 minutes. Your *papillotes* should puff with steam.

Carefully pierce each *papillote* with a knife to release the steam. Serve each with a lemon wedge. Wild rice or quinoa is a nice side.

Yield: Serves 2

Tip: Cooking en papillote *is also great for thick fillets. You can cook several salmon or cod fillets in the same pouch (leave a couple of centimetres of space between them for the steam to circulate). You'll need to reduce the cooking time a bit: 10 to 12 minutes for rare salmon, 14 to 15 minutes for cooked through.*

RABBIT WITH CIDER AND HONEY
Lapin au Cidre et au Miel

If you've never made rabbit (and I know how Americans cherish anything with a cottontail), this is a wonderful place to start. This recipe is adapted from *Le miel au menu* by Lily Ambroisie (Edisud, 1998). The spike of the cider and mellow sweetness of the honey are perfect complements to the slight gaminess of the meat. This is a festive preparation; I made it instead of turkey for my first Parisian Thanksgiving.

> 3 tablespoons olive oil
> 1½ tablespoons butter
> 1 rabbit, cut into 6 pieces, with the liver
> Coarse sea salt
> Freshly ground black pepper
> 2 carrots, roughly chopped
> 125 g fresh pearl onions, whole (or 4 shallots, coarsely
>   chopped)
> 1 stalk celery, roughly chopped
> 1 clove garlic, whole
> 1 tablespoon Calvados (apple brandy)
> 1 cup hard cider (the dryer, the better)
> 1 bouquet garni (fresh thyme, parsley, bay leaf, tied with
>   a string)
> ½ cup heavy cream
> 3 tablespoons honey
> ½ teaspoon cornflour, or a bit more if necessary
> Fresh chervil to garnish

In a large frying pan, heat the oil and butter. Brown the rabbit, sprinkling as you go with salt and pepper. Remove the meat from the pan and set it aside.

Lower the heat, add the vegetables and garlic, and sauté for 5 minutes. Return the rabbit to the pan, add the Calvados, and let sizzle for a minute. Add the cider and the bouquet garni. Bring to a boil, lower the heat, cover, and simmer for 40 minutes, turning the rabbit once at the halfway mark.

Remove the rabbit from the pan; keep it warm under aluminium foil. Add the cream and the honey to the pan, bring the sauce to a boil, then reduce for 5 to 10 minutes. Meanwhile, transfer a few tablespoons of the sauce to a small bowl and mix with the cornflour. Add this mixture back to the sauce. Simmer until slightly thickened. Return the rabbit to the pot and heat through. Discard the bouquet garni.

Serve sprinkled with fresh chervil. Long-grain wild rice, polenta, or sweet potatoes will happily share a plate.

Yield: Serves 4

CHAPTER 20

WHEN NEW YORKERS COME TO VISIT

If *Sex and the City* taught us anything, it's that Paris is the only city in the world that New Yorkers actually fantasize about. Mayur and Kate arrived for a week in October, and the apartment turned into an obstacle course of shopping bags. I love it when my friends from New York come to visit me in Paris. It's a thrill to see that Kiss My Face organic toothpaste on the sink, to trip over the beribboned Ladurée bags in the hall. They don't care that the chocolate and rosewater macaroons will be stale by the time they hit JFK or that the Longchamp totes are probably cheaper in duty free. New Yorkers never want to visit the Eiffel Tower (they've had their own near-death experience waiting in line to go to the top of the Empire State Building the day after Christmas). They want you to take them to your "little gem," your "local," the twin of the bistro one of their racquetball partners just fronted in deepest, darkest Brooklyn. *Do you think those art deco chandeliers are for sale?*

Mayur is a friend from college days, a(nother) lawyer who works in new energy. Like Gwendal, he has a right brain and left brain that function at the same time, and can discuss with equal passion physics, poetry, and how to make a good vermouth. His girlfriend Kate is a favorite of mine, a willowy brunette with a few scattered freckles and a huge Irish smile. She is political and spiritual — one of the only people with whom I can talk about my interest in religion without getting into an argument about God. After college, she taught public school in East Harlem. Last January, on her way to the entrance exam for the Columbia School of Journalism, she got a headache that almost killed her. A small aneurysm was followed by a big one; she received her acceptance letters to Yale and Harvard Divinity Schools in the ICU. Nine months later, she is walking with a cane, slowly learning to speak and read again through the gaps in her memory. She is twenty-five. I admire her, as much as I admire Mayur, whom I might previously have described as the Playboy of the Western World. In addition to being Kate's boyfriend, he has become an expert logistician and caregiver. Here are two people thrust into a much darker unknown than I'd ever experienced, and they seem to be handling it with grace and as much good humor as humanly possible.

Mayur is also an excellent cook. When he is around, I tend to play *sous-chef*: chopping, cleaning, and practicing my proper folding technique.

Taking Mayur to the market is a little bit like taking a foot fetishist shoe shopping. He gets this look in his eyes, and he likes to pet the vegetables. I had discovered a new market, open Wednesdays and Saturdays, just on the other side of the boulevard de Belleville. This one was more expensive than my regular market — there were smaller producers, more wicker baskets and baby courgettes.

Like most American foodies when they come to France, Mayur was in ecstasy over the variety of mushrooms, the comparatively low cost of oysters, foie gras, and, of course, champagne. I thought he was going to cheer when he saw the scallops. "They sell them *live*," he said, loading us up with three kilos. They offered to shell them for us. "*Non, non,*" he insisted with a defiant wave. "We'll do it ourselves."

I let Mayur do the menu planning for the week. He wanted to make wild boar. I was just relieved that he didn't want to go out to the forest at Fontainebleau, Henri IV style, and kill it himself. Instead, we got in line behind the grannies at the butcher; Matt Dillon barely looked up as I placed my order and took my ticket over to the cashier. Like a pro. Like I'd been doing it all my life.

By six p.m. the kitchen looked like a bomb had exploded. Mayur was over the sink, wresting open scallop shells with one of my many dull knifes. He carefully poured the juice into a bowl and rinsed the scallops to remove any sand caught between the tender white meat and the firmer coral-colored roe, wrapped around it like a socialite's fur stole.

Mayur is the kind of cook (my kind), who thinks the chef should always have a drink in hand. He was making the scallops with champagne custard, so naturally the rest of the bottle would have to disappear before dinner. He poured a cup of champagne into a small pot and set it to reduce on the stove. Then he put a sugar cube in the bottom of a wide champagne *coupe* (Lalique, service for sixteen, direct from the attic on my mother's last visit). After a bit of a search, he found the *crème de violette* in one of his shopping bags and poured in just a dash. He topped it up with champagne and gave it a swift stir.

"To dinner in Paris," he said, glass aloft.

"To the chef," I answered, dodging swiftly out of the way as he poured the reduced champagne over some egg yolks and began whisking like his life depended on it.

"Do you have fish stock?"

"Nope."

"Chicken?"

"Just cubes. Are you sure that will work?"

"Sure. This is the Mr. Potato Head School of Cooking," he said. "Interchangeable parts. If you don't have something, think of what that ingredient does, and attach another one."

I counted, in addition to the champagne, three other bottles of alcohol open in the kitchen. The boar, rubbed lovingly with a paste of cider vinegar, garlic, thyme, and rosemary, was marinating in olive oil and red wine. It was then to be seared, deglazed with hard cider, roasted with whole apples, and finished with Calvados and a bit of cream. Mayur had his nose in a small glass of the apple liqueur, inhaling like a fugitive breathing the air of the open road.

As soon as we were all assembled at the table, Mayur put the raw scallops back in their shells, spooned over some custard, and put them ever so briefly under the grill — no more than a minute or two. The custard formed a very thin skin with one or two peaks of caramel. It was, quite simply, heaven.

The pork was presented neatly sliced, restaurant style, surrounded with the whole apples, baked to juicy, sagging perfection.

Mayur and I were sitting on the couch, drinking tea and catching up on the news about mutual friends. Kate called from the bathroom. He came out looking bewildered. Could I go in? They had a reservation at a Michelin-starred restaurant that night, and she was having trouble with her mascara. The facade of the expert caregiver cracked for just a second. He looked frustrated, exhausted, worn out from a collective effort spent on the smallest things. More than my mother, more than Afra and Amanda, more than the self-admonishing voice inside my head, this was the moment that made me feel like a spoiled brat. I had everything, so maybe it was time to stop feeling like nothing at all.

For whatever reason, I couldn't stop doing the math, the comparison shopping. The news from New York was the usual — promotions, partnerships, and pension plans — or the lack thereof. Sometimes meteoric success, sometimes burning out, or selling out. Always something to do with money. I knew where they were going for dinner; it would cost half of what Gwendal earned in a month. I was starting to notice what the French would call a *décalage*, a kind of cultural jet lag in these conversations. Part of me still thought these things were very important, and was scared not to have them. But part of me knew my life couldn't be judged or summed up in quite that way. At some point I was going to have to stop comparing apples and oranges. If I wanted to be happy here, I was going to have to evaluate my life in Paris on its own terms.

The next day, Kate and I went to vespers at Notre Dame. Kate was raised Catholic, and I'm convinced I would have made a very good Catholic, particularly in the sixteenth century, on account of the music. I respond to churches in much the same way that I respond to museums, as buildings whose search for beauty and meaning take us outside ourselves for a moment. Mayur had rented a car, because Kate wasn't up to walking long distances yet. The boys went to look for a parking spot, have a drink, and talk about comic books, leaving the religion to us.

It was getting dark as we made our way over the cobblestone square toward the cathedral. It is difficult to imagine that the same imposing towers and jutting gargoyles have been presiding over Paris since before the printing press, or the bubonic plague. Kate is still missing a lot of the connectors in her sentences; they tend to come out in short bursts — subject, verb, object. "God, testing, me," she said, with a little rise in her voice that was both a question and an answer. I grabbed her hand. I didn't have anything useful to say. I thought about the road that lay in front of her. Everything she took for granted that was gone, everything she used to know that she would have to relearn.

The thing I like best about churches is that they are thinking spaces. Sitting on the austere straight-back chairs in the crowded nave, I felt the chill of the stone under my feet. My gaze was drawn upward to the points of the graceful arches. It's one of the tricks of Gothic architecture; there is so much air above your head that you can't help but raise your eyes toward the heavens.

The vibrations of the organ hit us from behind, prickling the hair on the back of my neck. I needed a plan, and not the old kind — not a checklist, not someone else's hardened wisdom about the nature of success. Success means different things here. Time, as well as money; family life, not just public recognition. I was still searching for a project. Something I really wanted, instead of something I was supposed to want. I needed a feeling, as well as a five-year plan. And the courage to do something about it.

Since God isn't usually who I consult on such matters, I started thinking about a different kind of teacher.

I had an English professor at Northfield named Anthony Chastain-Chapman; his students called him Cha-Cha. He had wrinkles and big glasses and terrible prewar English teeth. He was a specialist in Elizabethan theater. He never tired of reminding us that Shakespeare probably wrote his prologues to summarize the story, so that the guy feeling up his girlfriend in the front row didn't miss anything.

When we finished reading *Hamlet* he put down his yellowed copy and looked at us. "Do you know why Fortinbras comes back at the end of the play?" There was a blank as he looked around the classroom. "To drag the dead bodies off the stage. There was no curtain in Shakespeare's theater, and actors who had just been killed in a duel couldn't simply get back up again and take a bow."

I think of Cha-Cha every time I need to stop my existential dithering and just get something done. Life is not always poetry. Sometimes it's about the heavy lifting, the reality check. Sometimes it's about dragging the dead bodies off the stage.

Gwendal recently came back from LA with an article he'd ripped out of the Air France magazine. It was about country music. He'd been collecting odd song titles since he came back from a conference in Atlantic City, where the hotel played "She Thinks My Tractor's Sexy" on a continuous loop. There were a few born classics — a breakup tune called "Shove This in Your Pipe and Smoke It, You Harpy," followed closely by "Do You Have a Sister?"

"This one's my favorite," said Gwendal, pointing to the bottom of the page:

"Cause the Ass Ain't Gonna Kick Itself."

Cooking Dinner with New Yorkers in Paris

MAYUR'S CHAMPAGNE COCKTAIL

1 sugar cube
A dash (½ teaspoon) of crème de violette *(violet liqueur)*
1 glass champagne

Place a sugar cube in the bottom of a champagne glass; add the *crème de violette*. Top up with champagne and give it a quick stir.

Yield: Serves 1, cook or helper

SCALLOPS WITH
CHAMPAGNE CUSTARD
Coquilles Saint-Jacques au Champagne

12 scallops, in their shells
¾ cup champagne
¾ cup fish (or chicken) stock
¾ cup whipping cream
3 egg yolks

Shell and rinse the scallops to remove any sand or impurities; set them aside on the counter (you don't want them to be chilled when you put them in the oven). Line 2 baking sheets with aluminium foil. Rinse the top half of each shell and set aside for baking and serving.

In a small saucepan over medium heat, reduce the champagne by half, then set it aside to cool.

Meanwhile, in a second small saucepan, combine the fish stock and any scallop juice collected at the bottom of the bowl; reduce by half. Lower the heat and add the cream. Bring just to a boil and then take off the heat.

Transfer the cooled champagne to a medium mixing bowl, add the egg yolks, and whisk until foamy. Slowly add the hot cream mixture, whisking continuously. This is the beginning of your custard. Transfer it back to the saucepan.

Over low heat, whisk the custard until it coats the back of a wooden spoon. This will take a good 10 to 15 minutes. Don't attempt to rush it by turning up the heat, or your custard will separate.

Preheat the grill.

Cut each scallop in half horizontally, so you have two even coins. If they are especially thick, you might want to cut them into thirds.

Arrange 6 scallop shells per baking sheet. Arrange the scallop slices in each shell. Top with a tablespoon or two of custard.

Put one pan under the grill for 1 to 2 minutes. Serve straight from the oven. Repeat with remaining pan of scallops.

Prepared this way, the scallops will remain almost raw, like a lightly poached carpaccio. I love them, but if you prefer you can sear the scallops in a small frying pan and spoon over the warm custard just before serving. The custard also makes a superb sauce for pasta.

Yield: Serves 3–4 as an appetizer

PORK TENDERLOIN WITH FOUR KINDS OF APPLES

Filet Mignon de Porc aux Quatre Pommes

The combination of cider vinegar, hard cider, tart apples, and Calvados gives this roast an intensely layered flavor. I usually make it with pork tenderloin, but if you have a hankering (like Mayur) for wild boar, by all means, search it out.

1 pork tenderloin, 750 g

MARINADE

3 cloves garlic, grated
1 teaspoon thyme leaves, dried or fresh
½ teaspoon fresh rosemary, chopped
1 teaspoon apple cider vinegar
½ cup red wine
¼ cup olive oil

PORK ROAST

1 tablespoon olive oil
Coarse sea salt and freshly ground pepper
1 tablespoon butter
3 cooking apples or Granny Smiths, cored and quartered
6 shallots, halved
1 cup hard cider
1 tablespoon Calvados (apple brandy)

Make small cuts in the surface of the pork tenderloin.

For the marinade: Make a paste of the garlic, thyme, and rosemary and moisten it with the cider vinegar. Rub the paste all over the meat.

Place the pork in a resealable plastic bag; add the red wine and olive oil. Marinate for 12 hours (or overnight) in the fridge. I've marinated for as little as an hour — and it still tastes great. Bring the pork to room temperature before cooking.

Preheat the oven to 180°C.

Remove the pork from the marinade and pat it dry. In a roasting pan or casserole dish, brown the meat well on all sides, sprinkling generously with sea salt and pepper.

Remove the meat from the pan, set it aside. Add the olive oil and butter to the pot, along with the apples and shallots. Cook for 5 minutes, until lightly colored.

Return the pork to the pot, add the hard cider, and put it in the oven. Cook until the internal temperature reaches 65°C (the meat will continue to cook while it rests). Tenderloin can overcook quickly; I start checking at 15 minutes.

Remove the pork, apples, and shallots to a platter and cover tightly with aluminium foil. Let rest for 10 minutes. Meanwhile, add the Calvados to the pan juices and reduce slightly.

Slice the tenderloin on the diagonal, surrounded by apples and shallots. Spoon the sauce over or pass separately in a small gravy boat.

Yield: Serves 4

CHAPTER 21

SPRING THINKING

Yanig passed away in early April. My parents arrived just in time to squeeze his hand; Affif and Annick drove up after midnight, and he waited for them. That last night, Nicole slept on a mattress on the floor beside his bed. The next morning our small group left Nicole and Gwendal to say good-bye while we went for a walk by the sea. When we returned, he was gone.

It was four days before we could get an appointment at the crematorium. In the meantime, Yanig would stay with us. The embalmer came to the house and we went for another walk. This time when we returned, the door to the garden was open and the living room smelled faintly of formaldehyde. Yanig was laid out on his hospital bed, fully dressed in jeans and a wool vest, his beard neatly combed. Actually, he looked better than he had in months.

I didn't know quite what to do with this picture. I'd never seen a dead body before. My own father died suddenly, from one day to the next. On Sunday afternoon we went to an exhibition on diamonds at the Museum of Natural History. On Tuesday evening the police called me at my office. In one way or another, I had been waiting for this call since I was a little girl. When my father hadn't shown up for work, his colleagues had become suspicious. I asked if there was gas, or pills. "No, nothing like that, ma'am," said the sergeant. In fact, my father had died of a heart attack, sitting at home eating a turkey sandwich. After that I felt little but relief. After so many years of struggle, no one could begrudge my father a bit of peace and quiet. My mother was caught in traffic. In the end it was Auntie Lynn who went in to identify the body while I sat outside on the floor in the hall.

We moved the dining room table upstairs to Nicole's bedroom, to give Yanig a little privacy, and for the next three days we did what almost every culture and religion in the world does after a death in the family: we ate and we reminisced.

Affif and Annick drove home and came back two days later with a trunk full of pots and pans. Affif had made a vegetable couscous, the kind of spicy tomato-based stew that can be endlessly extended with extra carrots and turnips to feed whoever happens to show up for dinner. The *pièce de résistance*, in honor of Yanig, was a pastilla: layer upon layer of flaky, buttery filo, stuffed with painstakingly deboned pigeon, crushed almonds, cinnamon, and sugar.

A revolving cast of friends and relatives arrived, and cases of wine made their way from the garage to our improvised dining room. We stayed up late, me with a book, Gwendal with his computer, writing the eulogy. In the morning, Affif used the leftover couscous to make us a kind of sweet porridge, drizzling hot milk and honey over the grains and dotting the casserole with small nuggets of butter.

The days surrounding my own father's death centered around food as well, but in an entirely different way. More than his body, which I hadn't seen, or his absence, which I could not yet feel, I couldn't stop thinking about the sandwich, untouched on a folding snack table in front of the television. Because he died alone, the police had placed a seal on the door, so his heirs (there was only me) would not steal anything before the probate hearing.

The sandwich haunted my dreams over the next few days. I dreamed of it rotting on the table, roaches swarming between the layers of turkey and tomato and stale rye. I imagined the apartment infested, crawling with life. The police told me it would be days before I could collect his wallet, his bankbook, his cuff links.

The local police precinct was next to a vintage clothing shop on a quiet block in the East Twenties. There was a turquoise dress in the window, a sixties micromini, the kind that makes my mother feel like a relic.

I told the sergeant on duty my predicament. I did not cry, though I was nearing hysteria; I merely mentioned the rotting sandwich. I would have to clean out the apartment after probate court, I explained. I was afraid to find a stinking mess. It was sure to draw bugs and vermin to the neighboring apartments.

"I'm sorry, ma'am." Like all public servants, this man took pleasure in the letter of the law.

When I got up to leave, a young cop followed me outside. "Wait," he said. "Sergeant's off duty at five. Come back then and tell the night sergeant you need clothes for the funeral."

The funeral had taken place the day before, in a chapel on Riverside Drive, but I did exactly as he said. So I ended up with a police escort for the only illegal act I've ever committed. Before that day, I'd never stolen so much as a stick of gum.

The young officer and his partner drove me to the apartment. I had never been in the back of a police car before. It smelled like smoke, artificial vanilla, and vomit.

I went in; the cops stood in the doorway, respectfully looking elsewhere. I took a white shirt, a pair of gray trousers, an undershirt.

I am almost sure I forgot the undershorts. The sandwich was as he had left it; the turkey was hard and brown around the edges, the bread gone limp, and the tomato dry. On the way out I tipped it into the kitchen garbage can, which shut with a thud of the aluminium lid.

I'd somehow gotten used to having Yanig in the living room. I would say a tentative hello as I descended the spiral staircase to get something from the fridge.

"They are talking about you up there," I said, staring into the darkened living room. "You wouldn't like it one bit. They are showing your boy scout pictures and making fun of your knobbly knees."

Yanig wanted his ashes thrown out to sea, but Nicole wanted a place to visit. In a final show of marital compromise, they had agreed that half the ashes would be buried in a small cemetery in Saint-Malo and half released into the bay. We set out on a friend's boat one sunny Saturday in June. The jar sank slowly, with a trail of roses floating behind it. I tried to avoid thinking about how he was going to swim out to eternity with only one arm and one leg.

Spring had come to Paris, and everyone was coming up for air. I could finally pick my head up from family responsibilities and start thinking ahead. It was time for me to find some direction, build something for myself separate from my role as supportive spouse.

Spring had come to the market as well. Everywhere there were young green things, the tips of asparagus, young leeks no bigger than scallions. There was crisp rocket, curled and tangled, and fresh green peas, plump in their pods. I had no idea what I wanted to make for dinner. This didn't pose a problem; on the contrary, it was an opportunity, a mini adventure. The season's new ingredients brought new ideas. The first baby tomatoes were coming in from Sicily. I bought a box of small red globes still on the vine and a red onion in my favorite childhood shade of royal purple. Maybe I would make a salsa for the *dorade* I'd picked up at the fishmonger. I imagined a bright confetti, the tomatoes mixed with freshly chopped coriander, maybe a sunny mango. I thought about Gwendal and his non-recipes — throwing this and that into the pan. This no longer seemed like a totally foreign idea to me. I'd become so experimental in the kitchen, embracing unknown ingredients and making things up as I went along. Could I learn to do that for other parts of my life? In France, composing a well-balanced meal is easy; a well-balanced life is another story. How could I keep my American just-do-it attitude without the accompanying fear of failure? How could I keep the French pleasure of savoring the moment while still building for the future?

My bag was fairly bursting as I placed a head of spiky *frisée* salad on top. Even as I hoisted the sack over my shoulder for the walk down the hill, I was thinking about next week's creations, what new berry would appear, when would the apricots be ripe? More than the museums, more than the ancient streets, these stalls of fruits and vegetables and spices were the Paris that inspired me. What if the market, instead of being part of the problem, as Afra had suggested, was part of the solution?

The Chinese still refused to budge. It was July, and a formal eviction notice had been issued by the courts, but the police, in an election year, had decided not to enforce it. Still clinging to the American hope that a good lawyer can solve anything, we finally got one of our own. In addition to his private practice, he was a professor of real-estate law at the Sorbonne. His secretary showed us into a high-ceilinged office with two polished wooden chairs. The size of the room and the ornate flowering of the moldings inspired confidence. Monsieur Baston leaned forward, the lapels of his gray pin-striped suit touching the leather surface of the desk. "If this were a normal situation I'd recommend a *huissier un peu musclé* — that's lawyer talk for a little local muscle — but since there are children involved, we can't go that way. You could always pay them to leave."

"Pay them?"

"Yes, this is sometimes done."

"How much?"

"How much is the apartment worth to you? I would start with forty thousand and see if they accept."

He saw that we were waiting for a better solution, but he had none to offer. "If you play by the rules and your opponents do not, *monsieur*, you lose. *C'est aussi simple que ça.* It's as simple as that."

I was done. The apartment was simply not meant to be. I could not spend the rest of life keeping up with the Joneses, clawing my way to bigger and better. My mother was right; a baby could sleep in a dresser drawer for at least a year. We paid Monsieur Baston his enormous fee and left.

Then something extraordinary happened. As soon as I gave up control, relaxed the grip of my whitened knuckles, as soon as I admitted that I could not right a tilted universe with my bare hands — the squatters up and left.

It was late August when I headed down the stairs with my suitcase on the way to the airport for a trip back to the United States. At eight thirty on a Wednesday morning the foyer was full of mattresses, boxes, tricycles, and frying pans. We called the owners, who weren't aware of anything. It seems that the Chinese Mafia had stretched the State's patience as far as they cared to, and the Dong family (Gwendal followed the trail of boxes) was moving up the block. On the corner of avenue Parmentier there was a brand-new Chinese furniture store selling velvet-covered barstools and white lacquered vanity tables.

I kissed Gwendal and reluctantly closed the door of the taxi, my palms pressed up against the glass. Bigger and better was back.

I rolled down the window and kissed him again. How long would it take to change the locks? "Sleep in front of the door if you have to."

A Well-Balanced Meal

This meal makes full use of the bounties of the summer market — fruits bursting with natural sweetness and that most thrilling of yearly culinary events, the return of the tomato!

MELON WITH PORT
Melon au Porto

I can't think of a better start to an outdoor meal on a balmy summer evening.

>   2 *small ripe cantaloupe melons*
>   1 *cup port wine, chilled*

Cut the melons in half, scoop out the seeds. Fill the cavity with chilled port.

Yield: Serves 4

GRILLED SEA BASS WITH
TOMATO MANGO SALSA
Bar Grillé avec Salade de Mangues
et de Tomates

This is a remarkably quick dinner, but festive enough for guests. The confetti-colored summer salad works well with any firm, meaty fish. Sea bass, sea bream, salmon, and even tilapia come to mind. A side of raw baby spinach completes the plate.

500 g cherry tomatoes, halved
1 small red onion, diced
1 firm but ripe mango, peeled and cut into 1 cm cubes
1 tablespoon best-quality olive oil
1½ teaspoons red wine vinegar
Sea salt and pepper to taste
4 whole sea bass (250–300 g each), gutted and rinsed
Coarse sea salt
Extra-virgin olive oil
A handful of coriander, chopped

Preheat the grill.

In a large bowl, combine the tomatoes, onion, and mango. Add the oil and vinegar, plus salt and pepper to taste, and toss to coat.

Rinse the sea bass. Line a large baking sheet with aluminium foil; lay out the fish and put a pinch of salt inside each cavity. Drizzle the tops with olive oil and sprinkle with more sea salt. Put under the grill for 5 minutes. Flip the fish and cook for 5 to 6 minutes more, until the flesh is firm and the skin slightly bubbled and charred.

Stir the chopped coriander into the salsa and spoon some over each piece of fish.

Yield: Serves 4

INSTANT YOGURT AND
SUMMER BERRY PARFAITS

Parfaits au Yaourt et aux Fruits Rouges

*500 g summer berries (strawberries, blueberries,
   blackberries, or a mix)*
2 tablespoons honey
1⅓ cups Greek yogurt
*1 cup cookie crumbs, made with spice cookies or
   gingersnaps*

In a medium mixing bowl, quarter the strawberries. Combine
them with the honey and other berries.

In each of 4 tall glasses: Add a layer of fruit, a layer of yogurt
(⅓ cup per glass), and a layer of cookie crumbs (¼ cup per
glass). Top with a second layer of fruit. Serve chilled.

Yield: Serves 4

CHAPTER 22

A NEW YEAR'S FEAST

The cookbook was Affif 's idea. Or rather the idea for a cookbook came to me while I was standing in Affif 's kitchen, nose in a pot, inhaling the cinnamon-scented air.

The whole family had been invited to Affif and Annick's farmhouse in the south of Brittany for New Year's Eve. Mom, Paul, Nicole, Gwendal, and I were already well stuffed from Christmas in Saint-Malo: foie gras, Breton lobsters, and a not entirely successful holiday experiment with sea bass and chocolate sauce.

My mother stepped out of the car in the middle of the dun-colored fields. The grass was crisp with frost. Telephone poles, standing as straight and tall as girls in their last year of finishing school, were the only sign of civilization. The dip of their wires stretched out into the hazy winter morning. I saw one of the cats, with one blue eye and one brown, run for cover as we rolled our suitcases across the clearing next to the barn. "Wow," said my mother, with affectionate bewilderment. "Life leads you to amazing places."

Annick, in a bright shawl and a chunky beaded necklace, met us at the door. "*Bon-JOUR*, Karen," she said to my mother, in an exaggerated professorial tone, kissing her on both cheeks. Annick teaches French as a second language, and over the years my mother has become a favorite, if insubordinate, pupil.

The imposing stone house has been in Annick's family for generations; they have the deeds going back to the eighteenth century. It's the *maison de maître*, the master's house, the seat of a family who would have owned the surrounding land and paid tenant farmers to work it for them. Annick has dozens of stories, most as foggy as the mist that covers the fields at dawn. My favorite involves a daughter of the local gentry, who some time before the First World War was married off to a peasant — punishment for a clandestine love affair and an illegitimate child.

There was a *boulangerie* with a brick oven attached to the house, where the family once baked their bread. Awaiting repairs to the chimney, it now served as a giant pantry. Along one side of the house, Affif keeps a *potager*, a vegetable garden, growing his own beans, lettuce, carrots, and, of course, leeks. The first time I'd visited, not long after my arrival in France, Affif had me on my knees in the dirt, digging potatoes. The photo of me with the bucket made the rounds in New York, much to the amusement of my family and friends. Now I was an old hand, clad in woolen layers and sensible shoes.

My parents had been given a bedroom with a sloped ceiling under the eaves and thick wooden beams you had to remember not to smack your head on in the middle of the night. The house was heated, in a manner of speaking. Even so, I knew my mother would be sleeping fully clothed.

While everyone else went upstairs to rest, I went to spy in the kitchen. Varnished wooden beams and blue and white tiles lined one long wall and the counter, and a huge bouquet of coriander sat in a glass on the windowsill. Mismatched pots and conical ceramic *tagines* were stacked on the shelves and, higher, on the beams themselves. There were ribbons of garlic and dried peppers in a hanging basket and a bin of onions in the corner. The kitchen opened directly into the dining room with its long wooden hunting table and benches on either side. You could easily hibernate all winter long in a room like this.

Affif had been cooking for several days. He was preparing an ambitious North African New Year's feast, sixteen dishes for sixteen honored guests. When I arrived, he was adding a handful of raisins to a simmering pot. Inside were eight tiny quail, nestled together like newborn chicks. The sauce was as thick and dark as molasses; it smelled as if it might rain cinnamon. I inhaled deeply. I wanted my kitchen to smell like this.

I grabbed whatever scrap of paper was handy and tried to take some notes, but Affif is an artist; he doles out information in snippets, as it comes to him, more philosophy than fact. How long he cooks things is a sideways bob of the head, indicating maybe more, maybe less. I managed to pick up some general rules: "You need white onions for a sweet *tagine*, yellow for a *salé*." "You can use ground cinnamon for the quail, but for the *poulet au citron* I use sticks. Otherwise the color gets a little muddy."

While I was in the kitchen with Affif, my mother was outside trying to pet a chicken. Affif keeps several hens and a cock in a wire pen with a corrugated iron roof, attached to the barn.

The chickens were scattered around the yard having a wander, and my mother, in her gray cashmere coat, approached them the way you might solicit a friendly poodle, crouched low to the ground, making cooing noises and holding out her hand. Every time she got within three feet, the hens bolted forward, leaving my mother running, hunched over like Quasimodo, in hot pursuit.

Affif observed the scene from the kitchen window, shaking his head with a smile.

Gwendal was asleep on the couch with a book on his chest. I'm pretty sure he's more tired since he met me. But he still smiles, even in his sleep.

Nicole was writing in a canvas notebook. It was our first holiday without Yanig, and though I occasionally caught her looking lost and lonely, mostly she seemed as she always had, quietly determined. Even as she stared at the blank page in front of her, I felt she was making plans.

Friends arrived throughout the afternoon. Affif 's cousin and his wife were laden with clementines and lychees and tiny tropical pineapples for dessert. Old friends from Normandy brought the cheese, oozing and ripening in the backseat despite the cold. Anne-Laure and her husband arrived from Paris. She is an economist with short blonde hair and substantial but discreet gold jewelry. "*Ah, mais vous êtes américaine?*" she said, shaking my hand with a formality I now found unusual. "But you speak French so well." By now I've learned to enjoy the compliment and ignore the subtle note of surprise.

Before dinner, Paul and Affif went out to inspect the grounds. Over the years, Affif had done almost all the work on the house himself. He was in the process of converting the barn into a makeshift theater, where local performers could be invited. There was no more common language between these two men than there had been at the wedding. But as I watched Affif point and measure with his hands, Paul was enthusiastically nodding along, always a willing participant in a technical conversation, even one he didn't fully understand.

By seven, we were assembled in the *salon*. Gwendal and I had brought the oysters from Saint-Malo. We all sipped crisp white wine and slurped the briny mollusks, clinking glasses and speculating about the wonderful smells coming from the kitchen.

The table was decorated with Annick's brightest linens; a yellow tablecloth was covered with a striped one in sienna, deep purple, and green. A swath of sheer gold fabric covered the center of the table, scattered with small votive candles.

We sat down at eight p.m. and didn't get up from the table until four thirty in the morning, except for a brief pause at midnight for champagne. It was the most spectacular meal I've ever eaten. Like the triumphal procession in Act II of *Aida*, after the spear carriers come the chariots, after the chariots the cavalry, after the cavalry the dancing girls. And just when you think the stage can't hold another thing, they bring out the elephants.

To start, there were small salads — the thinnest slivers of red and yellow pepper, slow roasted and glistening with olive oil, and the simplest blend of carrots and golden onions, heady with the smell of cumin.

Then came the fish, its sauce simmered with saffron and tomatoes, thickened with ground almonds. I served myself the merest spoonful or two. "*Elle est stratégique.*" Affif winked with approval. "She knows what's coming." I wanted to savor every bite, even if it was a small one, nothing blurred by the rebellion of a tired palate. I plucked a toothpick out of the end of an oblong white calamari. It was stuffed with rice and peppers, a curly violet-tipped tentacle poking out here and there.

I looked around the table. Affif and his cousin were engaged in a mock argument about colonialism. Nicole guessed at the herbs — cumin and dill — in the baked squid. Gwendal got up to serve more wine. We had finally succeeded in buying the apartment upstairs. Anne-Laure suggested a store in Paris where we might buy bathroom tiles. I had been working so hard these past few years to figure out what France was about — how it operates, what makes it tick. In fact, most of what was important to the French was around this table: close family, old friends, and fabulous food. I knew I would never entirely leave my New York self behind — never stop wanting, never stop striving — but I also had my place here, among these people, and this endless parade of dishes.

By the time we got to the quail with cinnamon and raisins, everyone else was groaning with the beginnings of a genuine food coma. I was still going strong. I picked up the delicate leg with my fingers, the bone no thicker than a matchstick. The meat melted on my tongue almost before I had a chance to sink my teeth in.

The next dish was a tart contrast to the smoldering sweetness of the quail. Chicken legs and thighs lolling in an unctuous yellow sauce, thick with melted onions, flecks of coriander, and a julienne of fresh ginger. There were two distinct layers of taste, the savory tang of pickled lemons and the sweeter acid pucker of fresh lemon juice, pressed over at the very last minute.

My parents were living it up. Annick had done a judicious job with the seating plan; my mother and Paul were wedged between two English-speaking family friends. After the quail my mother stood up, with Jean-Luc coaching her from one side, and raised her glass toward Affif, reciting carefully, "*C'est* trop *bon*." It's *too* good. Everyone applauded.

It was suddenly ten minutes to midnight, and we stood up to stretch our legs. Affif peeled away the foil of the champagne with Yanig's pocketknife, which Nicole had given him. I sidled up to Gwendal, running my hand over his chest and clinking my glass to his. "*Dans les yeux*," I said, leaning in to give him a kiss. We wedged ourselves in on either side of Nicole, squeezing her shoulders, my parents just beside us. As we counted down toward the new year, it felt more to me like Thanksgiving. I was making a new kind of checklist in my head, all the things I was grateful for.

It seemed impossible that there could be more food, but we sat down again. The main event, we were told, was still to come. Neat little parcels of stuffed cabbage made their way around the table, bubbling under a Frenchified layer of melted cheese. Lamb with artichokes followed, each pale green heart slick with meaty juices.

The final dish was a *tagine* of meatballs stewed with dried apricots, cloves, and cinnamon. Affif brought it to the table in the traditional conical ceramic dish, lifting the cover with a flourish, releasing a fruity steam.

By the time we had finished, there was not an inch of interior space for the cheese, fruit, and fluffy meringue torte, but everyone made a heroic effort. As the guests finally dispersed, I helped Annick with the first round of dishes.

"*Ça va?*" said Gwendal, sneaking up behind me as I rinsed some glasses. He still loves to grab me in the kitchen when my hands are busy. "*Ça va,*" I answered, smiling to myself. I was better than OK, I was happy.

It was five a.m. by the time we settled into bed. I knew this meal would go down in the family annals, a memory we would savor for years to come.

A mere four hours later, we were all gathered around the table again for breakfast. My mother padded downstairs, her hair only slightly tamed from its short rest on the pillow. She was wearing two of her own sweaters and one of Paul's. "*BON-jour,*" mouthed Annick with an exaggerated wave. "*BIEN dormi?*"

"*BON-jour!*" answered my mother crisply, raising her arm in a military-style salute. It was very early for French lessons.

Anne-Laure, already dressed in a camel-colored skirt, tweed blazer, scarf, full jewelry, and high-heeled boots, hung back from the table. When a slice of brioche was offered from the wicker basket, she waved it away with her hand. "*Un café, c'est tout. J'ai trop mangé hier.*" Just a coffee, she said. I ate too much last night.

I squeezed Gwendal's knee under the table and continued to spread my brioche with a sticky layer of blackberry jam.

Maybe I would never be quite that French. I was perfectly ready to sit down and enjoy my next meal.

Recipes from Affif's
New Year's Feast

Affif didn't give me recipes so much as shopping lists, which I've honed and perfected over time. *Tagines* never turn out exactly the same way twice, but they are always delicious.

CHICKEN TAGINE WITH TWO KINDS OF LEMON
Tagine Poulet Citron

¼ cup olive oil
500 g yellow onions, chopped
1 cinnamon stick
6 chicken legs and 6 chicken thighs (preferably organic)
Coarse sea salt and freshly ground black pepper
1 cup white wine
1 cup water
¼ cup fresh ginger, peeled and julienned
1 bunch fresh coriander, washed and tied with kitchen
      string
2 small preserved lemons, cut into eighths
Slivered almonds
Juice of 1 fresh lemon
Chopped coriander

In your largest frying pan, heat the oil. Add the onions and cinnamon; stir to coat. Push the onions to one side of the pan and brown the chicken in two batches, sprinkling with salt and pepper. Mix the onions from time to time.

When all the chicken is browned, return the first batch to the pot. By this time the onions should be caramelized and beginning to melt. Add the wine and water. Bring to a boil. Turn the heat down to low. Add the ginger and tied coriander. Cook gently, covered, for 45 minutes to 1 hour.

Add the preserved lemons. Cook another 20 minutes. In a

small frying pan, toast the slivered almonds until nicely browned. Set aside.

Ten minutes before serving, discard the coriander stems and squeeze the juice of a fresh lemon over the chicken. Serve this dish sprinkled with chopped coriander and toasted almonds.

Yield: Serves 4–6

Tip: Affif cooks this tagine *till the chicken is falling off the bone — ideal for reheating.*

TAGINE WITH MEATBALLS
AND SPICED APRICOTS
Tagine Boulettes Apricots

This is food for a happy crowd; it never seems to pay to make less. Please take my advice and make the *tagine* in a single layer in two separate frying pans. If you move this dish around too much as it cooks, you end up with ground beef and apricot marmalade.

MEATBALLS

1½ kg minced beef (not too lean)
2 medium white onions, grated
¾ cup ground almonds
3 tablespoons fresh coriander, chopped and packed
¼ teaspoon cinnamon
A good grinding of black pepper
2 eggs
1 teaspoon coarse sea salt
¼ cup ice water
Olive oil

TAGINE

1 tablespoon butter
4 medium white onions, finely chopped
Coarse sea salt
10 cloves
6 cinnamon sticks
2 cups white wine
1 cup water
2 tablespoons honey
500 g dried whole apricots

Into a large shallow casserole dish, crumble the meat with your fingers. Top with the grated onions, almonds, coriander, cinnamon, and black pepper. Do not mix.

In a small bowl, lightly beat the eggs and salt until light and foamy, pour over the meat mixture, and, working gently, combine with your hands.

Sprinkle the meat with ice water and gently combine with your hands. Gently pat and roll the mixture into small meatballs. You should have about 45.

Get out your 2 largest frying pans. Heat a bit of olive oil in each. Brown the meatballs in a single layer. Remove from the pans and set aside.

Place ½ tablespoon butter in each frying pan. Divide the chopped onions evenly between the pans, sprinkle with sea salt, and sauté for 7 to 10 minutes, until highly colored.

Divide the meatballs evenly between the pans. Arrange in a single layer.

Into each frying pan, add: 5 cloves, 3 cinnamon sticks, 1 cup white wine, ½ cup water.

Cover and simmer over the lowest heat for 45 minutes.

Add to each frying pan: 1 tablespoon honey and 250 g dried apricots (tuck them in between the meatballs so they soak up the sauce).

Cover and simmer for an additional 20 minutes.

This dish can be cooled and reheated with an extra dribble of white wine. Serve with a mound of fluffy couscous to which you have added a pinch of cinnamon, a pat of butter, and a handful of golden raisins.

Yield: Serves 8

EPILOGUE

NEXT YEAR IN PARIS

Two years had passed, and we still hadn't bought much for the new apartment upstairs. After the plumbing, there wasn't a lot of money left over for furniture. The one thing I really wanted was an enormous table. We chose a long rectangular farm table, the blonde wood darkened by age and use. It seated twelve without touching elbows, sixteen in a pinch. So much of what I'd learned about France I'd discovered *autour de la table* — around the table. Finally I had one of my own.

It had been eight years since that first lunch in Paris, six since I'd dragged my overstuffed suitcases up the spiral stairs to Gwendal's student flat to stay. We still live on the same street, though now there are ornate plaster moldings, a bathtub — and heat.

The kitchen is the first thing you see when you enter our new home. At the moment, it was in chaos; we were preparing for our annual Passover seder. Passover, the holiday commemorating the Jewish people's liberation from slavery in Egypt, was always an important (if not terribly reverent) tradition in my family, one I had decided to import to Paris.

The menu, like the guest list, was a mixture of new friends and old favorites — the tastes I'd grown up with adapted to my market discoveries. Freed from the tyranny of Manischewitz gefilte fish, I had replaced the beige lumps of carp with wild salmon, roasted rare with just a drizzle of good olive oil and some fresh dill. For the main course I decided on a lamb *tagine* with prunes and sweet potatoes; I was looking to make a livelier version of my grandmother's *tzimmes*, a mush of brisket, prunes, and sweet potatoes that she cooked to disintegrating Eastern European death. With a few adjustments, I was sure a slow-cooked *tagine* would yield similar, but prettier, results. I hoped I had absorbed enough of Affif 's technique by now to pull it off.

Though I was anxious to give the meal that special French touch, I had to have at least one old standby, so my mother brought the cans of College Inn chicken broth from New York to make the matzo ball soup. In New York, the cans were an open secret, recognized by all to be better than hours of boiling, skimming, and salting. But in France, food is a labor of love, not a convenience, and I was afraid my French family would be insulted that I had not made it myself. We charted a middle course, cleverly disposing of the cans before everyone's arrival. As a precaution, I considered asking my mother to bring the parsnip as well, but I didn't think they would make it through customs.

I needn't have worried about the parsnip. All things come to those who wait. In fact, gentrification had given me back my humble root. The neighborhood markets had begun to cater to a younger, hipper clientele, nostalgic for comfort food. Heirloom vegetables began to appear — ridged and heart-shaped beefsteak tomatoes, as big as a boxer's fist and as red as your first valentine. Knobbly roots like the *topinambour*, the Jerusalem artichokes that the older generation was forced to survive on during the war, were now being shaved and braised and mashed in the trendiest bistros. On this wave of newly fashionable grub, I finally recovered my parsnip.

Courtney came in from London, and on Saturday morning we got up early to go to the market for last-minute supplies. We picked up the wild salmon from the fishmonger (Courtney is still fascinated by the glassy-eyed stares of whole fish) and garden roses in pale butter yellow, peach, and lavender from the flower stall. The vegetable man wrapped up an equally large bouquet of parsley, coriander, and dill. When we got home, my mother was vigorously wiping wineglasses and Paul was elbow-deep in silver polish. I still needed to go to the butcher to pick up the lamb shank I'd forgotten for the seder plate. This year I would roast it myself.

The nicest thing about Passover — about any family tradition, really — is that it is never one event, but many years of memories rolled into one. Every recipe, every piece of silver, brought up a story from years past. As I placed my paternal grandmother's thimble-sized silver kiddush cup down next to one of Yanig's gold-flecked vases on the long table, I felt my past and present coming together.

My mother's goal when entertaining is to be seated in the living room with a glass of wine one half hour before the guests arrive. Clearly this requires some practice. An hour before our guests were due I had a mini meltdown, hissing at Gwendal, accusing him of hiding the black sweater I *needed* to wear. I shut the door of our new bedroom behind me and took a few deep breaths. The control freak of yore still reared her ugly head from time to time, but she was a less frequent visitor.

Unlike most carefully planned dinner parties, surprise guests are always welcome at the Passover table. Kelda brought Dave, a friend who was in town for the week from California; two more strong voices would help with the songs. Katherine, my friend-date, arrived with her French husband in tow. Gwendal handed her a glass of Vouvray, which she immediately passed on to Sylvestre.

"I'll have water," she said, doing her best to sound casual. I raised my eyebrows in her direction as I stirred the soup. She put her finger to her lips. "It's early days. We're not saying anything yet."

Fernanda, my friend the Argentinean beauty queen, walked in with a perfectly round bouquet of lilacs and roses, formally trussed and tied as only a French florist can do. She had just started dating our *osteopath* — only in Paris does your date get to see you naked *before* he asks you out. Ludovic was from a German Jewish family, and he was thrilled to have a place to go for the holiday. Axelle arrived with a snow-white orchid for our new mantelpiece. "*C'est nouveau?*" I said, admiring her soft gray tights, woven through with a pattern of silver threads. Oscar had called on Friday afternoon — he was in Paris for a trade show, what were we doing for dinner? — and brought the number up to lucky eighteen.

Passover is a symbolic meal; we eat parsley dipped in salt water to remember the tears of our ancestors, and charoset, a mixture of apples, nuts, and dried fruits, to remind us of the mortar that the slaves used to build Pharaoh's cities. Meals can, and do, tell stories.

As I sat down at the head of the table on Saturday evening, I felt the beginning of a new chapter. An idea for a book was taking shape in my head — the tale of an American who discovers Paris, one meal at a time. Gwendal's small consulting company had merged with a larger firm; a few months earlier, he'd signed a deal for the first European cinema chain to go fully digital. At the far end of the table, my mother and Nicole had their heads bent together, inspecting the silver asparagus tongs, a cherished family heirloom brought over for the occasion. It had been three years since Yanig's death; Nicole was looking to move her practice to Paris and start a new life. I'd recently thrown away my last packet of birth control pills; Gwendal and I felt ready to embark on our next adventure, a family of our own.

The Haggadah, the book used to lead the seder service during the meal, is the same one my family has used for twenty years. I held my grandfather's leader's book, following his neatly penciled notes in the margins (he liked to skip pages) and surprising myself as I translated easily into French as I went along. Each year my mother asked her guests to sign the inside cover. I followed her example. The names were different, but the feeling was the same: warmth, community, and a sense of home.

Everyone loved the soup (no questions were asked about its origins), and my *tagine-tzimmes*, with cinnamon sticks poking out between the prunes and slices of bright orange sweet potato, received a deep nod of approval from Affif. Fernanda's finely honed sweet tooth led her to a spot on the couch right next to Aunt Joyce's chewy coconut macaroons.

When my mother walked into the kitchen with the empty coffeepot, she caught Gwendal and me smooching as I loaded the dishwasher. She smiled even as her eyes watered over. With central heating and closet space to spare, a project to keep me busy, and a family and circle of friends to keep me sane, maybe, just maybe, it would finally be OK for her to leave me here.

Every Passover, after we tell the biblical story of where we came from, we say where we are going. The seder meal ends with the words "Next year in Jerusalem." It expresses our hopes for the year ahead, that we may move forward, toward freedom, but also toward home.

When Gwendal and I think about the "promised land," our perfect life, we sometimes imagine an island in the middle of the Atlantic Ocean, halfway between Paris and New York. It's a place where people take professional risks but also have time for personal pleasures. A place with an outdoor market that stretches as far as the eye can see, and one skyscraper, as tall as the market is long, for ambition and effect. There's a café, with chipped art deco mirrors and sugar cube wrappers on the floor. It serves scalding hot *café crème* with buttery, flaky croissants, and, on the first Sunday of the month, an everything bagel with spring-onion cream cheese. There is a museum to preserve the stories of the past, and a movie studio to create the dreams of the future. We imagine a school for our children that teaches philosophy and physics — but also inspiration. It's a place where just-do-it and *joie de vivre* live side by side, hand in hand.

The promised land doesn't quite exist, but we are getting there.

I met Gwendal's gaze down the other end of the table, raised my wineglass, and we recited together: "Next year in Jerusalem."

Next year in Paris sounds good to me.

WILD SALMON WITH DILL
AND CUCUMBER SALAD
Saumon à l'Aneth et Salade de Concombre

I don't have any food allergies, but if I had to invent one, gefilte fish would be it. This salmon starter is a simple and elegant replacement. I cook the fish in foil so it stays moist. It can be served hot or at room temperature, which is convenient when juggling the timing of a large holiday meal.

SALMON

1 wild salmon fillet (1 kg)
Best-quality extra-virgin olive oil
Coarse sea salt
Freshly ground black pepper
A good handful of fresh dill, chopped
Half a lemon
Watercress, to serve

YOGURT SAUCE

2 cups Greek yogurt
2 tablespoons Dijon mustard
½ teaspoon coarse sea salt
1 tablespoon fresh dill, finely chopped

CUCUMBER SALAD

1 kg pickling cucumbers
Best-quality extra-virgin olive oil
Coarse sea salt
Freshly ground black pepper
A small handful of fresh dill, chopped

Preheat the oven to 200°C.

Fish: Wash the salmon and pat dry. On a large baking sheet, lay out an extra-long piece of aluminium foil. Place the salmon on top. Drizzle it with olive oil and season with salt, pepper, and fresh dill. Place a second large piece of foil on top and seal as you would a *papillote*. Cook for 30 to 35 minutes in the oven (I like my salmon a bit rare, and it will continue to cook a bit out of the oven; if you snip open the foil and find that it's too rare for your taste, just remove the top sheet of foil and return to the oven for a few minutes more). Serve on a bed of watercress. Squeeze over half a lemon just before you bring the fish to the table.

Sauce: Combine the ingredients and leave to rest in the fridge. Pass with the salmon.

Salad: Cut the cucumbers into 1 cm slices. If you are using regular cucumbers, be sure to remove the seeds first. The cucumbers can be sliced a few hours in advance, but they must be dressed at the last minute.

Just before you want to serve, drizzle the cucumbers with olive oil and sprinkle them with sea salt, pepper, and dill to taste.

Yield: Serves 8 as a first course

LAMB TAGINE WITH PRUNES AND ROASTED SWEET POTATOES

Tagine d'Agneau aux Pruneaux
et aux Patates Douces

This recipe is inspired by my grandmother's *tzimmes* and executed in the style of one of Affif 's sublime *tagines*.

> 5 tablespoons extra-virgin olive oil
> 1½ kg lamb shoulder, deboned and cut into large chunks
> Sea salt and freshly ground black pepper
> 2 medium white onions, sliced
> ¼ cup freshly grated ginger (slightly less if you are not
>   going to let this sit for a few hours or overnight)
> 3 whole cinnamon sticks
> 1½ cups white wine
> 1 cup water
> 300 g dried prunes
> 3 large sweet potatoes, peeled and cut into 2 cm slices

Preheat the oven to 160°C.

In a large casserole dish, heat 1 tablespoon of the olive oil. Brown the lamb, seasoning generously with salt and pepper.

Remove the lamb from the pot and add 2 tablespoons olive oil along with the onions, ginger, and cinnamon sticks. Sauté until the onions are soft and golden, about 10 minutes.

Return the meat to the pot, add the wine and water, and bring to a boil. Cover tightly and cook in the oven for 1 hour.

Turn the meat, add the prunes, and cook for 1 to 1½ hours more, until the meat is fork-tender. Leave in the refrigerator for a few hours, preferably overnight, so the sweetness of the prunes has time to mellow the ginger in the sauce.

On the day you want to serve, toss the sweet potatoes with the remaining 2 tablespoons olive oil. Arrange in single layer on a baking sheet and roast until tender. Layer the sweet potatoes with the lamb and the prunes at the last minute. Add a dribble of white wine and reheat, tightly wrapped in aluminium foil, in a medium oven.

Serve with wild rice, or couscous dotted with golden raisins and sprinkled with cinnamon.

Yield: Serves 8 (if you want to double the recipe, make two separate batches)

AUNT JOYCE'S COCONUT MACAROONS

These coconut snowballs look like they should be in a glass jar on the counter of an old-fashioned sweetshop. I usually make half in white and half in pink (add a drop of red food coloring) and stack them in a pyramid on a footed dish.

> *2²/₃ cups grated coconut (the fluffier the better!)*
> *395 g can sweetened condensed milk*
> *1 teaspoon vanilla extract*
> *½ teaspoon almond extract*
> *Extra grated coconut to finish*

Preheat the oven to 160°C. Line a baking sheet with aluminium foil.

In a medium mixing bowl, gently combine 2²/₃ cups of the coconut, the condensed milk, and the extracts. Using two teaspoons (or, even better, a melon baller), form into 3 cm balls. Work gently, as you would making meatballs; you don't want the macaroons to be too dense.

Bake in a slow oven for 15 minutes. Depending on the absorbency of your coconut, the macaroons may ooze a bit; pat them gently back into shape and roll them in additional grated coconut.

Cool on a wire rack. Store in an airtight container. These are more like candy than cookies, so serve them sparingly, with good strong coffee.

Yield: Makes 20 macaroons

ELIZABETH BARD'S SUGGESTIONS FOR A WELL-STOCKED BOOKSHELF

Even before I discovered the joys of the kitchen, books nourished my soul. Taste in books is as individual as taste in food. Some like a creamy chocolate creation, lush and overflowing; some like the snap of a crisp green bean. Here are a few of my favorites.

Two cookbooks I read in bed:
  The Joy of Cooking by Irma S. Rombauer,
  Marion Rombauer Becker, and Ethan Becker
  Cooking for Mr. Latte by Amanda Hesser

Two books that made me snort coffee through my nose:
  Me Talk Pretty One Day by David Sedaris
  Bridget Jones's Diary by Helen Fielding

A book so pitch-perfect it made we weep:
   Home by Marilynne Robinson

Two books that made me say, "Dear God, I wish I'd
written that":
   Fugitive Pieces by Anne Michaels
   For Kings and Planets by Ethan Canin

Three books I wish I'd never read so I could read them again
for the first time:
   East of Eden by John Steinbeck
   Possession by A. S. Byatt
   The Known World by Edward P. Jones

Four books I stayed up all night reading:
   The Woman in White by Wilkie Collins
   In Cold Blood by Truman Capote
   The Amazing Adventures of Kavalier & Clay by Michael
   Chabon
   War and Peace by Leo Tolstoy

The only book I ever left on a train (on purpose):
   Enduring Love by Ian McEwan

The one book I wish I had the time to memorize, unabridged:
   Paradise Lost by John Milton

Two memoirs that made me want to have lunch with the author:
   Eat, Pray, Love by Elizabeth Gilbert
   When a Crocodile Eats the Sun: A Memoir of Africa
   by Peter Godwin

Two books I can't wait to share with my son:
   Dr. Seuss's Sleep Book by Dr. Seuss
   Great Expectations by Charles Dickens

A LETTER FROM PROVENCE

Dear Reader,

Time flies when you're making ratatouille.

The time since the initial publication of *Lunch in Paris* has been as wild and wonderful as any I could have imagined. Gwendal and I now have a son, Augustin, who was born exactly one week after I finished editing the manuscript. He's a beautiful, curious, clever blond boy who loves his hunk of fresh baguette in the morning – in other words, a true Frenchman!

In addition to leaping into parenthood, our family has recently made another big move – to Provence, to be exact. Our house, a turny, twisty (and for the moment, rather drafty) affair, was the wartime home of the famous French poet and Resistance leader René Char. He buried his most famous manuscript in the wine cellar, next to the preserved pork cutlets and the bottles of Bordeaux. You might say the house is haunted, in the best possible way.

My passion for Paris remains undiminished; it's been my home for nearly a decade – the first real adult home I've ever had. But Gwendal and I had been looking to make some changes – refresh our personal and professional lives – and give Augustin a world of green to conquer.

We found the house by happy accident. My husband is a great admirer of René Char's poetry, and in April 2009, when I was six months pregnant and unable to fly, we decided to take our Easter holidays in the south of France to explore the region where Char lived during the war, the landscapes and events described in his most famous poems.

When we arrived in Céreste, our English hosts were curious. They were accustomed to guests passing through for a day or two on a tour of the hilltop villages nearby – but here we were, a round and waddling woman and a frankly tired-looking man, staying for ten days. We know now, it was a date with destiny.

When our hostess learned about our special interest in René Char, she got very excited. Turns out, history was living just up the road. During the war, Char had a passionate relationship with a young woman from the village whose own husband was a prisoner of war of Germany. Char's companion had a daughter, Mireille, who was eight years old in 1940. Now seventy-six, she had just written a book about her childhood with René Char. Would we care to meet her?

The next afternoon, we found ourselves invited for coffee in the meticulously renovated coaching inn that Mireille shared with her husband – and her mother. We looked at letters in Char's hand, his pencil box, and his clandestine radio equipment, and we listened to Mireille's tales of the Resistance, the Gestapo, and Char helping her with her homework by the fire. In true Provençal style, we lingered on through the afternoon: one coffee, a second, one cognac, and another. Before we left, Mireille asked Gwendal if he had any other questions. He did. Char adamantly refused to publish under the German occupation; instead, he buried his manuscripts in the cellar of Mireille's family home. After the liberation in 1945, Char dug up the notebooks and sent them to his close friend, the author Albert Camus, in Paris. Published as *Les Feuillets d'Hypnos,* these poems remain Char's masterpiece. "Where," Gwendal asked, "was this famous hole in the floor?"

"That's easy, said Mireille. "We still own the house."

The next morning, we found ourselves in the vaulted stone cellar of La Maison Pons, which had been Mireille's family home for five generations. Gwendal and I ducked as we followed Mireille down the impossibly narrow steps at the far end of the room. She cleared away some empty wine bottles and pointed to a low wooden shelf, about a foot from the earthen floor. "That's where Char buried his manuscript," she said. "He came back for it after the war."

Gwendal looked down. This is the man I love, I thought. A man who can be so visibly moved by a dent in the dirt.

"We used to store pigs down here," continued Mireille. "In those days we ate everything. We sealed the cutlets in a layer of fat, and when you wanted one, you would dig it out." As we were turning to leave, she stamped her foot on the packed earth floor. "My uncle René – he was Char's driver during the war – before he died he said there might still be guns buried under here. But we never looked."

Before we left, we went out to the garden, two large stone terraces overlooking the surrounding fields. "You can feel that your family was happy here," I said. "We were." She smiled briefly. "But I am sad now. I gave this house to my daughter, thinking that she would come back to the village, but instead she wants to sell it."

And there it was. Our date with destiny. We both felt something of our future in these walls. We went back to the B and B, spent a sleepless night in front of an Excel spreadsheet, and the next morning went back to ask if we could buy the house.

It took a year to get ourselves sorted. One of the oddest things about writing and launching *Lunch in Paris* has been reflecting about the past while simultaneously trying to construct our future.

We've only just arrived in Provence, and already we are seduced by the constant blue skies, tomatoes that taste like candy, and peaches that glow like solid sunshine. I know I'll have some wonderful culinary mentors here. Our next-door neighbor keeps coming over with baskets of vegetables for the baby, and he just let slip that his grandmother was once the *chef de cuisine* for the American consulate in Nice.

So here we go. We are off on a new adventure. There's so much to discover; I hope you'll join us.

Perhaps René Char said it best: *Impose ta chance, serre ton bonheur et va vers ton risque. A te regarder, ils s'habitueront.* – *Les Matinaux* (1950)

"Impose your chance, hold tight to your happiness, and go toward your risk. Looking your way, they'll follow." (The translation is mine, and rather liberal.)

You can follow along on the blog, Facebook, and Twitter.
Look forward to seeing you there,
Elizabeth Bard
Provence, September 2010

www.elizabethbard.com

www.facebook.com/LunchinParis

www.twitter.com/ElizabethBard

INDEX TO RECIPES

Page numbers in bold type refer to recipes.

Have you enjoyed this book?
If so, why not write a review on your favourite website?

Thanks very much for buying this Summersdale book.

www.summersdale.com